THE
MIDDLE
OF
INFINITY

A DOCTOR'S JOURNEY THROUGH ILLNESS

BY

KEVIN R. ANDERSON, M.D.

"The Middle of Infinity *is more than a triumphant autobiography of a surgeon overcoming a potentially devastating illness. It is a work of love and introspection about who we are and why we are here, how we can give to others, and the path that good will, often unmeasured and unrecognized, finds its way to help those in need. "*

—John L. Phillips, M.D.
Author of "The Bends"

"How does a prominent surgeon whose happiness is rooted in his strength and ability to serve others respond when he becomes a helpless patient facing his own death? A self described man of faith and science, Kevin Anderson shares his terrifying story of free falling from the high perch of a charmed life into a dark place where he was stripped of all he held dear - only to find hope and healing in a loving God and the kindness and compassion of strangers. This is a must read for all of us who waste our suffering by responding to it with self-pity, anger, and blame rather than seeing our trials as the source of our greatest lessons in hope, healing, and wellness. "

—John Chuck, M.D.

"The Middle of Infinity *is a book unlike any you will read this year, or possibly many years. It is the story of a physician plucked in his prime from a life of prosperity and professional success who is forced to face his own mortality. The descriptions of complex medical events are fascinating, but the intensely personal journey to overcome a debilitating illness where death is certain is even more inspiring."*

— Stephen E. Lamb, M.D.
Author of "Between Husband & Wife"

DEDICATION

For
Barbie, my eternal companion
my children
and for my grandchildren

In memory of
Shane
Your gift gave me my life

Contents

PREFACE

While writing this book I often struggled in determining who was my unseen audience. It was easiest to imagine my as yet unborn grandchildren reading this to perhaps know me better, since I knew it was quite possible that I would not be around to tell them the story myself. On the other hand, I imagined that a book about a doctor who becomes ill might also be of some benefit to others who have been touched by illness, whether in themselves or in a loved one. Illness is, of course, one of our most common shared experiences as humans.

Since both Barbie and I kept a blog which we began early in our journey, I have availed myself of the opportunity to tell this story prospectively, as it is unfolds, with no knowledge of the future. So I have included within the narrative many excerpts from our blog reflecting our condition at the time, with emotions raw and hopes alive as we took each new step into the unknown together.

I have kept the blog posts unchanged, in that I have added nothing. In some cases, however, I have deleted a few lines that would become overly redundant to the reader. The blogs are in italics and finish with author's name.

At times, while writing the book, my personal reflections gave way to an expansion of self analysis that produced *stream of consciousness* writing. The resultant sporadic essays, however, may offer a glimpse in how the nature of who I am struggled to understand the nature of the world around me.

I am a man of science and a man of faith. To separate the one from the other would be akin to removing all of the bones from my body. This story, therefore, reflects the union of both of these aspects of my life.

I often make references to terminology unique to "The Church of Jesus Christ of Latter-day Saints" of which I am a member. As such, I include a simple glossary of terms to assist those unfamiliar with the "Mormon" church:

Ward: The basic congregation or unit of the church containing approximately 500 members.

Bishop: The man ordained to preside over the ward.

Stake: An ecclesiastical and geographical entity containing between 8-12 wards.

Stake President: The man set apart to preside over all of the stake and wards. He is assisted by two counselors, also called presidents.

Priesthood: The power given by God to man to perform ordinances, lead the church and bless others.

Home Teachers: Two priesthood holders assigned to each family in the church to assist in temporal and spiritual matters.

PROLOGUE

Mortality awareness event #2

The first step into danger follows the last step of safety and is often unannounced. Suddenly I found myself completely engulfed in the rapids of the river. Straining, I could look back upstream and see my family playing along the banks. They seemed to be moving away from me at a great speed, whereas the water around me did not seem to be moving at all. It was the illusion you get when two things are moving at the same speed; somehow, relative to each other, they seem motionless. The current and I were one. I tried to cry out, but the rushing waters muted the sound of my small voice.

Moments before, I had been playing along the banks of the Eel River in Northern California. I had strayed downriver perhaps 50 yards. I was still in plain sight of my parents, so I thought that I was safe. The soft sand and mud squishing between my toes gave the illusion of a shallow river and I ventured further when suddenly, there was no more bank, or sand or mud or anything solid, only water. The cold gray water convulsed around me as I frantically tried to get back to shore. Soon, the current increased and I felt as if an unseen force were pulling me down. It was like there was a weight tied to my feet. Over and over, I kicked and paddled with all of my might to get my head above water. At the very moment that I would attempt to breathe in, the current would shift and my lungs were met with water.

Soon, my ability to judge my own position became confused. Water and sky flashed before my eyes in a strobe-like fashion, a kaleidoscope of black, blue, green and mostly gray. It seemed like an eternity. I do not remember being afraid. My only thought was to breathe. If only I could get my head above water long enough to draw one deep breath, then I would be fine. Unfortunately I had only learned how to swim the year prior, and I was still not a very strong swimmer.

I have no idea how long I was in the water. Suddenly, something touched my outstretched right hand. Instinctively, I closed my grip onto this unknown solid object. Immediately, the current that was carrying me now became a rushing force moving past me at great speed. I held on for my life. Slowly, I recognized that I was holding onto the submerged root of a tree growing along the bank of the river. With all of my remaining strength I pulled myself out of the river and onto a grassy space between the water and the trunk of a large oak tree. I lay there, on my back, gasping for breath. Finally, my breathing slowed and a sense of my surroundings returned as I found myself gazing through a beautiful green canopy of leaves, wafting in the breeze, revealing glimpses of a cloudless azure sky.

I was seven; I was *still* seven.

Part 1

THE DESCENT INTO ILLNESS

CHAPTER 1

"No news is good news"; where did that pithy phrase come from? Why should no news be good news? There are times when bad news, even a revelation of awful truth, is far more liberating than being lost in the unknown.

I was sick and I did not know why. The fact that I am a physician and surgeon did not help; it actually made it worse. It was much easier for me to fake health than to admit that something might be wrong. I could convince the world and even myself that I was not as badly off as I was. Some call this denial. Maybe it was, but for me it was psychological and emotional survival. Yet even as I outwardly denied that there was a problem, I was silently frantic to figure it out. As with everything else in my life up to that point, I felt that if I could only find the pattern and apply it to a previously acquired fund of knowledge, the solution would appear. It did not. I was left to wonder and wander through every day, confused about why my body was failing me. "No news" was killing me; yet I had no clue as to the literality of my proximate mortality.

No news; but finally there would be an endpoint. I knew that when I got to the point of developing shortness of breath while walking on level ground, I was in trouble. I knew that upon reaching that milestone of physical limitation, hiding my condition would no longer be possible. I was losing control.

June 7, 2008 became that moment. The scene was my son Jeremy's wedding reception in Moscow, Idaho. That Saturday morning, my wife, Barbie, and I began to walk about five blocks to a family friend's house for a brunch honoring Jeremy and his new bride, Alexandria. Alexandria's father, Randy, met us at the house where neighbors had graciously offered us lodging. Their driveway was a very slight incline leading to the main road. Randy took off walking and Barbie and I followed. Generally, after walking up an incline I had to slow down and rest, but this time I was already a block behind Randy. I did my best to keep up but could not. This was level ground. My immediate family knew that I was limited; however up to this time I had been able to keep it from others (or so I had been deluded to believe). My endpoint had arrived. I could not sustain a short walk on level ground. I knew that this was really bad and I could no longer deny it.

Finally we reached the brunch. After sitting for ten minutes, I regained my strength and carried on as if nothing had occurred. We later shared a wonderful evening at their reception. When it was over, I carried many heavy items to the cars, again not wanting to appear weak or useless. Silently, in the dark, I would lean against anything solid to keep from falling down. I had employed this particular practice for the past six months, even in the operating room, to assist me in stabilizing myself. But I knew that something had to be done. I had reached my limit. I could no longer fake normality. I decided to go see my cardiologist once again when I returned home. I hoped that maybe something else could be done to help me.

The next day we drove back to Spokane via Couer d'Alene, Idaho. In Couer d'Alene we took a short walk along the beach. I was careful to walk about half as far as my limit so I could make it back. Barbie had wanted to continue, but lately she had been adapting to my condition and normally did not push me further than I usually pushed myself. At that point I did not yet understand how silently tortured she had been in slowly watching my demise. She, like me, had learned to suffer in silence.

The following day I dropped in to see my Cardiologist, Dr. Anu Khurana. She had been following my condition for over a year and had performed many tests, but the root cause for my weakness was still elusive. A week and a half prior I had undergone my third echocardiogram in the last year. The first had been done in the summer of 2007 and showed some mild heart thickening with some right heart dysfunction. Right heart dysfunction was the term used by Dr. Khurana, but ironically, even as a physician I did not fully understand the diagnosis. I am a Urologist. Basically I am a plumber. I unclog pipes. I do understand the heart as a pump, but I was not sure what right heart dysfunction was and why I would have it. Was it permanent? Was it progressive? Could it be reversed? To this point, I seemed to be managing. I was still doing surgery. I was the chief of the department of urology at Kaiser in the greater Sacramento area and fulfilled my administrative duties. I wondered how long I would be able to continue.

That day I had a break in my clinic, since a patient had cancelled, so I took the elevator up one floor to Dr. Khurana's office. I found her in the work room where all of the monitors were located for reviewing echocardiograms. I asked her if she had seen mine from the week before. She had not, but she loaded it on the spot and began to analyze it. I stood quietly, leaning against the door jam. Minutes passed and she finally turned around with that concerned look that doctors are very poor at hiding, at least from other doctors. "I see some thickening here," she said. She showed the monitor pointing to a shadow that represented the intraventricular septum of my heart. The intraventricular septum is the wall that separates the right and left ventricles of the heart. Since she really had not had the opportunity to fully evaluate the study, she asked if I could return later in the week to go over the results with her.

Finally, on Friday the 13th of June, I sat in her office and she gave me the first two words that would define what I had (but not why I had it): *Restrictive Cardiomyopathy*. People think that doctors speak in really big words. Actually, medical jargon is made up of smaller words, or roots, strung together. We enjoy the polysyllabic shorthand which actually conveys a lot of information in just a few words. *Restrictive cardiomyopathy* breaks down as follows: *Cardio* refers to heart, *myo* stands for muscle and *path* indicates disease. *Cardiomyopathy*, is then defined as a diseased heart muscle. The word *restrictive* further defines the type of diseased heart as one that is stiff or cannot relax well. All muscle function in the body is accomplished through contraction and relaxation. A heart that cannot relax cannot fill up with blood. Less filling per beat means less blood pumped per beat. This would begin to explain my fatigue; my heart just could not keep up with the demands that my body put on it. But why did my heart get stiff? That answer would not come for another week. In the meantime, though, my outside life continued as normal. And today was no ordinary day. My daughter was going to get engaged, and she did not know it yet.

CHAPTER 2

Barbie and I have four children. Samuel and Jeremy are identical twins. They were born during my fourth year of medical school in March of 1986. I went to medical school at the University of California, San Diego located in beautiful La Jolla, California. If there ever was a place to get married and take off to, it was La Jolla. Medical school was like a four year honeymoon for us. During my first two years I would attend class every day. Barbie worked on campus so that we could meet for lunch between my morning and afternoon lectures. It was a wonderful beginning to a marriage. After work, when the weather was good, (and it was always good) we would go to Torrey Pines State Beach to relax. We would often pick up a carne asada burrito at Roberto's and Barbie would lie on the beach with a good book and I would catch waves with my Boogie Board. We had tried to have kids, once I got through the course on reproductive biology and figured out how to do it, but things did not happen right away. Finally, Barbie got pregnant and we were so excited. A miscarriage at eight weeks ended the pregnancy and left my wife deeply saddened.

However, a few months later, she was again pregnant. At 8 weeks she began to have a little spotting. Because of the previous miscarriage, her OB, Dr. Lamb, did an ultrasound. After school I went to meet her at work. She had some news. We stood there on the walkway just outside the mailroom where she worked and with a huge grin she told me, "They saw two hearts on the ultrasound." Clearly, my years of medical training had not prepared me for this moment. I mumbled my incredulous response: "Our baby has two hearts?" She laughed and replied, "No, we're having twins!"

Life changed drastically in July of 1986 as I began a surgical internship at UC Davis Medical Center in Sacramento. I was required to work in the hospital for about 110 hours a week. We had a mortgage to pay, and Barbie was home with two newborns and no husband. The honeymoon was over.

Things eventually got better. Rebecca was born 2-½ year later when I began my Urology residency and Caitlin was born in 1993 in St. Louis during my laparoscopy and endourology fellowship at Washington University. Our children have always been the joy in our lives. Barbie and I were blessed with the best children. Of course, they all had their moments, but when it came to the important things in life, they have always made the right choices. Eventually, children grow up and fall in love; however, not usually all at the same time. But in 2008 that's just what happened. Our three eldest, Jeremy, Samuel and Rebecca all fell in love, got engaged and were married. It was a busy year.

Jeremy met Alexandria while at Brigham Young University in Provo, Utah. They were married in the Sacramento Mormon Temple. It was an unusually hot day in May, at 104°. The next day, Samuel proposed to his sweetheart Michelle Moran from Ridgecrest, California. They set their wedding date for August 16, 2008, only three months later. We began preparations immediately. They had decided to be married in the San Diego Temple, which is in La Jolla, about ½ mile from where we lived when they were born. Life was already moving at a hurricane pace when Rebecca got engaged. Her young man, Corey, had joined the church as a new member in October of the previous year and was waiting for Rebecca to return from her sophomore year at Brigham Young University.

The day had arrived when he had planned to propose: June 13th, 2008, the day of my diagnosis. I was part of his plan, so I put aside the news of my heart condition and focused on helping my daughter get engaged. I was to take the family to a nice restaurant, but after leaving the house, I was to drive a mile away and then realize that I had forgotten something. This I did and then asked Rebecca to go in and get the gift certificate that I had forgotten.

Corey was waiting in the courtyard with the ring, and when she arrived he executed his carefully planned proposal. Barbie and Caitlin were in the car with me and heard the scream. Barbie immediately looked at me with major concern, but my smile gave it away and she realized that the outburst was one of joy. We all went out to eat at Biba's, a famous Italian restaurant in Sacramento, to celebrate the occasion. I ordered whatever I could find that had the least amount of salt. The food was great, but in my mind lurked the heavy news of my diagnosis; restrictive cardiomyopathy. I decided not to mention it to Barbie that evening, to avoid spoiling the celebration.

The next day began like any other Saturday. There was always plenty to do. Barbie was outside in the backyard with Rebecca talking about, what else, the wedding. It was decided that it would be on October 25th. As does every patient who is given a new diagnosis, I decided to research '*restrictive cardiomyopathy*' on the internet. Being a physician helps a lot, but there are many things that I have not really dealt with in many years, *cardiomyopathies* included. I began reading through the sites which outlined etiology, incidence, differential diagnosis, treatment and then finished with prognosis. Prognosis; I sat there shocked. I quickly checked another site; it was from the Mayo Clinic. There it was again: prognosis 5 years/ 50% mortality. I looked for treatment. There was no cure, only management of symptoms.

I walked into the backyard and as Barbie looked up at me I began to cry. These were the first of many tears to come. Concerned, she inquired as to my emotional state. I related to Barbie, Rebecca and Caitlin my diagnosis and then I quietly said to Barbie, "The life expectancy is 5 years." She hugged me, her tears now added to mine.

There was still so much I did not know. What had caused this to happen to my heart? Dr. Khurana had mentioned a few conditions in the differential diagnosis that were diseases that I really had not heard of since medical school, including infiltrative disorders like *sarcoidosis* and *amyloidosis,* (conditions in which proteins damage tissues.) Additionally, she mentioned that it could be *idiopathic,* loosely translated as 'unknown etiology' (cause) or as we liked to say in medicine, "The idiots don't know the pathology." It was a lot to absorb. How would this affect my future life? How long would I continue to work? The surgeon in me tackles every problem as fixable as long as I can take it apart and understand the pieces. But I still did not have all of the pieces. I would have to wait. Of the potential etiologies, she felt that *amyloidosis* might be one of the causes, but that we would need to do some tests first, such as a fat biopsy, and suggested that I schedule them. I replied that I would have to wait a week, since I was heading to higher altitudes within the next few days.

CHAPTER 3

Every summer our church sponsors a Girls Camp for the young women from age 12 to 17. For many years Barbie and I have also attended as adult leaders to help with the camp. One of the outdoor experiences includes backpacking and overnight camping in the wilderness. The camp is run by the girls and women leaders, but a few men are always invited, generally to do the heavy lifting. The hike also includes men, and participating in these excursions has always been a highlight of my summers. The hike was specifically for the 15 year old girls and Caitlin was 15 this year. I had been looking forward to this for quite a while. It had become clear to me in January that I was not in adequate physical shape to go backpacking. At that time I had figured that I had five months to improve my stamina through a program of regular exercise. It did not take long to realize that not only was I not improving, I was getting worse. I ultimately accepted the reality that I would not be going on the hike. For years Caitlin had watched her parents leave her to spend a week at camp. Now it was her turn to have us with her. I did not want to disappoint her. Barbie, of course, also realized this and made arrangements so that she could be one of the leaders to go with the girls. Caitlin would at least have one of her parents there.

Soon that sad Saturday morning moment of discovery gave way to preparations for the Monday trek. I still planned on going to the main camp and helping out there while Barbie and Caitlin were in the woods for two days. The Girls Camp was always held at Camp Marin Sierra, about 20 miles west of the summit of the Sierra Nevada, at the junction of highway 20 and interstate 80. It was the same Boy Scout camp that I had attended when I was a boy from 1971 to 1973. Early Monday morning we arrived and set about getting the backpacks ready. An hour later all of the girls and adult leaders gathered in a circle to prepare to leave. As I watched their excitement I again settled into that emotional resolve of accepting another personal passion that was no longer mine to do. After the usual prayer, they moved toward the trail. We hugged and they were on their way.

Dr. Khurana was worried about me camping at 5500 feet. I said that I would be fine, but I always say that. It turned out to be a very difficult week for me. First of all, nobody knew that I was sick so they expected me to work like all of the other men there. I still was not ready to share my embarrassing weakness with others. For over a year and a half, I had slowly become more ill, but I always felt that I could not divulge this to anyone else until I knew why. I was afraid that if I failed to give them a reason for my decreasing activities, people would see me as sickly and weak. As chief of the urology department, I did not want people to alter or filter their responses to my role and responsibilities out of deference to my illness. Looking back it is hard to imagine how obstinate and naïve I was. Even worse, I was completely blind to the true victim of my silence, my beloved wife Barbie.

All my life, I have been the strong one. Others have looked to me to remain calm amidst chaos. A surgeon does not give up. We fix things. That is who we are. Ask any surgeon and they will regale you with tales of carrying on no matter what assails them personally. I have seen residents so sick that they had to have an I.V. placed to give them fluids while they were operating. In fact, I once found myself in that very situation. One day, during my tenure as a faculty member at Yale University, I was scheduled to do a ureteroscopic laser lithotripsy on a major V.I.P. of the Yale University upper echelons. He shall remain nameless; suffice it to say that the dean of the medical school called me at home the night before to stress the importance of a successful outcome.

The case involved passing a tiny (2.7 mm) telescope up the urethra, through the bladder and ureter, and into the kidney, and then to utilize a Holmium laser to disintegrate an obstructing stone. It was a routine case. I spent the morning with my boss, Dr. Weiss, laparoscopically repositioning a testicle from the abdomen into the scrotum of a two year old boy. As I walked from the pediatric OR to the main OR I began to feel pain in my left flank. As a urologist, I immediately knew that I was passing a kidney stone. Within five minutes the pain escalated to severe proportions. If I were to rate my pain, as I often ask my patients to do, I would have given it '4 stars' and two enthusiastic 'Thumbs Up'. It was at least an 8 out of 10. With pain like this, and an important operation only 20 minutes away, I saw only one option; get an intramuscular shot of Toradol from the anesthesiologist and proceed with the planned surgery. Toradol is a very strong non-narcotic pain reliever that kills the pain without making you loopy. Within fifteen minutes the pain was tolerable and I did the surgery. It was no big deal to me; this is what surgeons do.

Unfortunately, that mentality does not always serve us well when we surgeons suddenly find ourselves on the other side of the table as a patient. My silence with regard to my mysterious illness was a side effect of my ego at the time. As someone who always had an answer for everything (or at least thought he did), how could I explain to other people what was happening to me when I did not know myself? In my career I have seen so many people whose lives were paralyzed by some unknown untreatable malady, in many cases exacerbated by their fragile psychological state. I resolved to be much stronger than that. If I could not explain this to myself, I did not want to try to explain it to others. I did not stoop to lying. I simply refocused their attention on something much more benign: salt.

CHAPTER 4

One episode, three months earlier in March of 2008, painfully illustrates how my silence, and tendency to minimize, affected my care, and even my chances for survival. At that time I knew that my heart was not functioning well. I had various arrhythmias, some benign and some more serious, but they were not consistently present and therefore were rarely documented when I was being evaluated by monitors. I knew, however, that there were times when I would have a short burst of a very unhealthy heart rhythm called *atrial fibrillation*. The rhythm occurs when the atrium of the heart jiggles like Jello instead of providing a normal equally timed beat which serves as the natural pacemaker for the heart. The atria on the right and left receive lower pressure blood from the body and lungs. Between beats when the main pumps of the heart, the ventricles, relax, the atria push their collected blood through one-way valves into the meaty ventricles. These full ventricles then contract, pushing blood back to the lungs and entire body. The entire process depends on the regular and synchronized contraction of these four chambers every second of every minute. It cannot stop or we die.

During this time, when I overexerted myself by riding my bike up a hill or trying to run across a street before the light changed, I would fall down if I could not lie down fast enough. In those moments, when I checked my pulse, I discovered what we call an irregularly irregular heartbeat. This is *atrial fibrillation*. The ventricles, not knowing what to do without the signal from above will eventually trigger spontaneously. But it is as if no part of the heart can decide who's boss and whoever fires first gets the beat. This leads to a very irregular pulse. Unfortunately, it also leads to a more serious consequence. The 'jiggling' of the atrium results in a pool of stagnant blood, eventually coalescing into a clot. The writing is stuck to the wall. "Clot breaks free! Man has stroke," headlines the evening edition. Within seconds a free clot (now called an *embolus*) can travel from the heart to any of hundreds of small vessels in the brain, thereby choking off the blood supply to the brain. The resulting injury is called a stroke (if it leaves permanent damage) or a *transient ischemic attack* (TIA) if the patient recovers without ill effects.

On the 1st weekend of March, Rebecca had flown home from her fourth semester at BYU to be with Corey and to visit us. Friday evening we all went out to have pizza (definitely not on my diet at the time; two slices exceed the recommended daily salt intake). I have no self-control if pizza is placed in front of me, and this pizza turned out to be delicious. When we got home Corey and I went out back to the pool house to shoot some pool. He was soundly trouncing me. During the second game, as I stood watching him make yet another shot, I suddenly saw only the upper half Corey's body. As my gaze fixed upon him, I could not see his legs. I knew that he was still intact so I figured that my vision was somehow messed up. Additionally, I also felt a very strange and unsettling lightheadedness. This feeling persisted, and I began to get concerned. I did not say anything. It was my turn and I got two balls in the pocket. I guess I play better with half of my vision. I excused myself and went inside to call the emergency department.

As I sat in my office waiting for the ED doctor, I would alternately cover each eye with my hand and realized that the upper right quadrant of each of the visual fields was missing. This told me that the problem was not in my eyes; rather it had to come from the optic cortex of my left brain. (People always confuse Urology with Neurology, I guess that evening I saw myself as a Neurologist). I described my symptoms to the ED physician and asked if he thought that I should come in to be evaluated. I really did not want to go, but I was a bit concerned. He said to come in and confirmed that I would not be driving myself.

I walked into the family room and asked Barbie to excuse herself from the animated conversation she was engaged in with our prodigal daughter. She took one look at me and knew something was wrong. I told her what was happening; I verbally said that I was not sure if I really needed to go, but deep down I knew that I did. Barbie just said, "Let's go." We briefly told the kids that something was wrong but not to worry and that we were going to get it checked out.

Soon we were checked in at the emergency room at Kaiser in Roseville. I was hustled off to a room and the curtains were drawn. I wanted to keep a low profile. I knew quite a number of people that worked there, since I was often called in as the consulting urologist. Now I was the one on a gurney.

Various doctors performed tests and examinations to see if they could recreate the scenario. It turned out that the defect went away when I was sitting down, but returned every time I stood up. This pattern repeated itself six times that evening. A CT Scan did not show evidence of a major stroke. But eventually I was admitted to the intensive care unit for observation. This was the first time I had been admitted to the hospital since the age of four, when I went for the traditional tonsillectomy popular in the early sixties.

Within six hours the symptoms left, never to return again, but I was stuck in the ICU. ICU nurses are more comfortable when the care they are expected to give actually turns out to be intensive. They did not know what to do with me and my lack of medical needs. I had brought a book from home to pass the time. Every 15 – 20 minutes the nurses would peak around the curtain to ask if I needed anything. I really do not like to bother people so I always say no, always have.

The next morning my boss showed up. Everyone has a boss, but most people do not end up in the embarrassing position of hapless patient of their own boss. Even though I was the department chief, I reported to the Physician-in-Chief of the hospital. He also happens to be a neurologist and was on call that weekend. Dr. Rozance is a wonderful man and a good doctor. I wondered if it was strange for him to see me in that bed. He examined me and asked what had happened. I have a horrible habit of minimizing and correlating as I speak, and at this moment I fell into my old pattern, describing my symptoms and simultaneously ascribing them to what I thought might be the cause.

Dr. Rozance said it might have been a stroke, but it also could have been an atypical migraine. Reflective of my healthy state and absence of sequelae (permanent side effects) he settled on the latter diagnosis, but recommended a daily aspirin to be safe. He left, but I did not. Protocol required that they observe me for at least 24 hours and I was soon transferred out of the ICU to the floor. Fortunately, it was not the surgery floor where all of the nurses know me. I really did not want anyone to discover that I was there, so I hid in my room. An MRI was ordered which did show a very tiny lesion in my left occipital cortex. On a repeat MRI a year later, however, it was gone. Sunday night I left the hospital on 81 mg of aspirin daily as my treatment and prevention. The next morning I was back at work. No one ever knew that I had spent the weekend in the hospital. Except that, ironically, as I was walking into my office building, my cardiologist was walking out to go to the hospital to see me because she had received a message that I was admitted. I remember the shocked look on her face as she questioned the wisdom of my going to work that day. I assured her that I was fine and went to work. Of my family, I had called my mom, but only after it was clear that I was fine. To this day I continue to believe that I had suffered a transient ischemic attack from a short period of atrial fibrillation. I have been on aspirin ever since. It has never recurred.

CHAPTER 5

The girls' camp was nestled not far from the Yuba River near the summit of the Sierras. We had our own little lake there at the scout camp with canoes and sailboats. The men helped with security at night and many other jobs during the day. The showers were heated by wood-burning boilers that had to be stoked throughout the day. My saving grace was my brother-in-law Craig. I told him that I had just been diagnosed with a heart problem and heavy lifting would be difficult for me. He looked out for me and helped me with what chores I was assigned.

Chubb Lake held many memories for me. As a boy scout I had earned a number of merit badges there, including my favorite, canoeing. Hiking was now no longer an option; at least I could still take out a canoe, or so I thought. The Boy Scout of America rules require anyone using a canoe on the lake to pass a swim test, even the adults. This involves swimming out to the floating dock and back twice, (100 yards) and floating on your back for one minute. Something that was so easy at age 12 now seemed impossible. I knew that if I swam to the dock, I might not make it back, so I asked if I could do my test in the intermediate swimmers area which was shallow. I made it one and one half laps and could go no further. I was gasping for breath and holding on to the dock. It took five minutes just to pull myself out onto the dock. The waterfront staff person testing me was somewhat surprised at my failure. She had seen me in the past push a handcart up a rock strewn path. I am sure she wondered at my weakness.

As I walked off the dock, I asked the waterfront director if I could still take out one of the canoes. She said no, it was not allowed for non-swimmers. Now I was a non-swimmer, a non-canoer, a non-hiker, and a non-worker. I slowly walked back to my cabin, holding back the tears. I was broken and could not be fixed. Even the simplest of pleasures, floating in a canoe, was denied to me.

Two days later, Craig and I (mostly Craig) were loading wood into a boiler and the waterfront director was walking through that part of the camp. She saw me and came over to where we were working. It had been decided that it would be OK for me to take out a canoe if I had a certified swimmer with me. It is not typical for people to bend the rules in a camp like that, but I was so grateful for that gift. Barbie and Caitlin had arrived back from their hike earlier that day. When I saw Barbie at lunch, I told her that I got permission to go out on the lake canoeing, but that she would have to take the swim test so that she could be the capable swimmer in the canoe with me.

Barbie is not a fan of cold water; she hates it. But she was willing to sacrifice her personal comfort for me. I sat there on the shore watching her complete the swim test for me. She was my proxy. As she finished, shivering as she toweled off, I felt so much love for her. Within minutes we had our life jackets on and were floating beneath the most brilliant blue sky surrounded on all sides by majestic evergreens. I felt so close to heaven in that moment. Against canoeing protocol, Barbie, in the front seat, turned around to face me so we could talk with greater ease. It was a beautiful moment in a very difficult week. Beautiful moments; those are the jewels that punctuate the otherwise rock-strewn path that is adversity. A million ripples of light reflected off the uneven surface. The strong aroma of pine filled the air. Quiet abounded, gently touched by beautiful sounds: wind in the trees, the paddle dips that broke the surface, birds above, the muted laugher of a hundred girls along the shore, and Barbie's sweet voice. Her perfect voice has always been music to me. My sister-in-law, Rachelle, just happened to be strolling along the bank and recorded this moment with her camera. I see this photo every day as it hangs above my desk. I close my eyes and I am there again.

I left camp one day early to attend the chief resident graduation dinner in downtown Sacramento. As the representative from Kaiser, tradition required that I say a few words about the finishing chiefs and the four years that they had spent training with us. The temperature that day was again 104°. Although such heat is common in Sacramento, I did not feel acclimated. The walk from the parking garage to the hotel was daunting. I do not think that I have ever felt weaker. Later, many who saw me that night told me that they knew something was wrong with me. I said a few words about what wonderful doctors were graduating that evening and promptly left to go home and sleep. I was exhausted.

The next morning I drove an hour up to the campground again to pick up Barbie and Caitlin. Once back at home, while they were unpacking, I started to search the internet. One of the causes of *restrictive cardiomyopathy* was *amyloidosis*. I had no memory of anything that I had learned in medical school about "amyloidosis." I was supposed to get a fat biopsy soon to see if amyloidosis was my diagnosis. But I could not even remember what the word meant. I looked back on the many times when my patients had taken their disease to the internet and returned with reams of paper and lists of questions. My role as a doctor had always been to filter out the bogus postings and keep them focused on the important stuff. I would help them properly weigh the data and understand the answers they had found. I decided to take a peek behind the curtain. Now it was my turn to dive into the black hole of internet data. It is simple. Up in the right hand corner where it says 'search' you simply type in *"amyloidosis"* And then wait for the answers to appear. I was completely unprepared for what ultimately surfaced. It was not unlike sitting across a table under a grease stained circus tent while an ancient, chain smoking gypsy holds open your hand and tells you your future.

The first page opened to the Mayo Clinic site. Diseases are always presented in the same order on the site: a brief description of the disease, incidence, etiology, symptoms, physical findings, laboratory exams and histology, diagnostic imaging, treatment and prognosis. I stared at the entry.

AMYLOIDOSIS
Symptoms: I had all of them
Treatment: Incurable
Prognosis: One to one and a half years.

I immediately checked another site and went straight to prognosis. Again it stated 1-2 years. Under work-up it mentioned a typical 1.5 year average for delay in diagnosis from the time the first symptoms began. The magnitude of these numbers began to settle into my brain. I indeed had been suffering from these symptoms for a year and a half. So, how much longer did I have?

Once again, I walked into the family room where Barbie was sitting. Last week we had anguished over a life expectancy of 5 years. My prospects had now gone from bad to worse. It was too much to absorb. We rationalized; the work-up was not finished, maybe it was still idiopathic (of unknown cause) and I did have 5 more years. As Barbie and I spoke in depth about this, one thing became clear. We could no longer do this alone. It was in this moment that she shared with me that even though she respected my desire to keep my health issue private, she needed the support of others and felt that it was time to let our family and close friends know about my problem. Until then, I had understood nothing of how much Barbie was suffering in my silence. Now I was utterly unprepared for the incredible impact on our lives that would come from sharing our burden with others.

CHAPTER 6

How had the path of my life led me to this point? Barbie has a favorite song by Alison Krauss that reminds her of me. It is called "The Lucky One." People have often commented that I lead a charmed life, that I am very lucky. It is true. Things have always worked out for me. Acquaintances have actually said to me, "Your life has been so good, God must be preparing you for something bad in your future." These presumptions have always baffled me. I do not believe that God has some celestial scale that must balance fortune and disaster. Sometimes bad things just happen. It is nobody's fault and often inexplicable; therefore questioning why, in a cosmic sense, is *moot*. However, the timing of my sudden change in fortune is fascinating to me. In 2003 I was very healthy. My life was as fulfilling and joyful as I could imagine a life could be. I was in my tenth year as a faculty member in the department of surgery at Yale University. I remember driving to work one morning from Hamden to New Haven, a distance of about five miles. There were at least 20 different routes to get to Yale-New Haven Hospital. In all my years of commuting I had tried them all. It did not matter. Driving in New England is never direct and each of the different routes required 18 – 25 minutes. The drive gave me time to think. On this particular morning, I was taking a new route over East Rock. I saw a billboard that made me think of my family. As I pondered my work at Yale, my work at church and my responsibilities as a husband and father, it occurred to me that my life was not my own. Rather, it was a delicate balance of my responsibilities to others.

Other people told me where I needed to be. My job was simply to show up and do what I had to do.

My secretary, Lucille, reminded me of my surgery schedule or where I would be giving a lecture on stones to the 3rd year medical students. The executive secretary at church left emails for interviews and meetings that needed my attention, and, of course, Barbie kept a family calendar of all of the kids' activities that needed a chauffeur. My life was not my own and yet it was exactly what I wanted. As I reflected upon these things an overwhelming feeling of joy filled me and I realized that there could not be a happier man on the face of this earth. I was 44 and had witnessed more amazing experiences in my life than I could have ever hoped or dreamed. I casually mused that if I were to die in that moment, I would have lived a fulfilled life with almost no regrets.

However, within a year's time, things were different. Both Barbie and I had developed a sense of restlessness and an intuition there was a change coming. Ultimately we decided to move back to California and take a position at Kaiser in Roseville. Neither of us was completely sure of the reasons for this move, although we proffered many different explanations to those who asked. My father was ill from *multiple myeloma*. He had been diagnosed three years previously and was getting worse. Barbie was ready to leave the cold weather, and the thought of another seven month winter of dreary days depressed her. Jeremy and Samuel were graduating from high school and would be attending Brigham Young University in Provo, Utah. We knew that once our children went west, they would likely not return to the east coast. The idea of being closer to them appealed to us. The sum of all of these reasons made logical sense. However, deep inside me was something I had never felt before: doubt. I knew we needed to move, but when I was secretly honest with myself I did not know why.

Finally, in August of 2004 we moved. Despite growing up in California, I felt like a stranger upon my return. I took up cycling. Bike riding in California is such a pleasure. They build actual bike lanes and the asphalt is smooth, allowing for the use of a road bike. In Connecticut, commuting on a bike from Hamden to New Haven was a death-sport. The roads were narrow and poorly maintained, the drivers resentful of a bike in their way. Quick reflexes were required even just to avoid getting killed. In California, however, I could bike the 12 miles to work without hearing the constant honking of horns or employing rapid-curb jumping to prevent collisions. In October of 2005, I even entered to ride in the Foxy's Fall Century road race. This is a 100 mile ride from Davis, California across the western central valley through Vacaville, Fairfield, Lake Berryessa and back to Davis. I made it, but I was almost the last one in. I silently wondered why I could not keep up.

In April of 2006 I was asked to be the chief of the department of urology. I would be responsible for a department of 12 urologists and a staff of about 30 nurses, medical assistants and support staff. I had always thought of myself as a very easygoing guy and tried to be friendly to everyone. Somehow this was not the way I was perceived by others. Unfortunately, I have tendency to speak with an authoritative tone in my voice, which conveys the notion that I think I am always right. It is not intentional. Occasionally, people who do not know me well derive from this that I am arrogant and condescending. For this reason, it was not a smooth transition into my role as chief. Simultaneously I found myself not connecting as well as I should have with my patients. I just was not in top form.

CHAPTER 7

About this time, I was riding my bike home one day and had great difficulty in riding up a prolonged steep hill, such that when I got home, I collapsed on the couch for ten minutes. Barbie was very concerned; as usual, I made some excuse. However, that was the last time I rode my bicycle to work.

The onset of some diseases is so insidious that it can be many months before you realize that what you are experiencing is more than just indigestion or fatigue associated with a normal, healthy life. My first indication that something might be awry was in the spring of 2006. I had a habit of walking at lunch time. At Yale, lunch was a walking experience; in California you get in your car to cross the street. There were at least 100 eating establishments within walking distance of the hospital in Roseville. I would try to walk to a different one each day that I was in clinic, as I had an hour for lunch. Soon I noticed that as I returned to work after eating I was walking very slowing and felt out of breath. I also would experience pain in my upper abdomen. This would slowly resolve once I arrived at my office and sat down. Over the ensuing months this continued to occur and become a daily experience. However, the true measure of my decline was a particular staircase. As I entered the hospital to go to the operating room, I met a staircase ascending from the first to the second floor. This short staircase would become my nemesis, and a daily test of my endurance. For 48 years I had been in a habit of climbing stairs two steps at a time; clearly a more efficient use of energy. Now, I was reduced to one step at a time. And when I made it to the top, I had to stop to catch my breath.

I tried to keep exercising but found myself struggling at the slightest effort. I would occasionally even feel irregular heartbeats after exercising. Finally, I decided to call my primary care physician, Dr. Edwards. I described my symptoms to him and we decided to keep an eye on my condition. By October of 2006 I began to feel some tightness in my chest and called again. He ordered an electrocardiogram that came back with some mild abnormalities. The results concerned him enough to order an exercise stress test. As is so typical when you bring your disease to your doctor or take your car to a mechanic, everything works normally that day. The test was negative, no ischemia (poor blood supply) with exercise. A nuclear medicine heart perfusion test confirmed that my heart muscle remained well perfused (good blood supply). It did not appear to be a problem with my coronary vessels.

Time passed.

I accepted that the problem was not with my heart, but continued having the same symptoms. I slowly worsened but remained functional. Whenever my mind was free to wander, it wondered what might be the cause of my inexplicable weakness. I would work around the house and get completely out of breath bending over to pick up anything over five pounds. Using a pick to dig a hole was torture.

Barbie had noticed that I was experiencing periods of sleep apnea. For many seconds I would stop breathing while I was asleep. She would lie there awake waiting to hear my next breath. Finally in April of 2007 I made an appointment to go see my doctor.

I informed him that I did have a history of high blood pressure and *gastroesophageal reflux disease* or GERD. Acid reflux is a very common diagnosis and is made worse by stress. I did not feel particularly stressed. I also described the following symptoms:

"Hoarseness, jaw pain, difficulty swallowing, (*dysphagia*) abdominal bloating, early satiety (fullness with eating) *periorbital petecchiae*, (red spots on my eyelids), chest tightness, nasal congestion, palpitations, sensation of a fast and/or irregular heartbeat, sleep apnea (noticed by my wife as short periods of breathing cessation at night) a pounding heartbeat lying down at night on my left side and I would get dizzy getting out of a car after sitting for a while"

Dr. Edwards examined me and we discussed my symptoms. Ultimately, following my lead, he ascribed my symptoms to GERD and allergies.

I do not ever blame my doctors for missing the diagnosis. We have a saying in medicine: "Common things are common." However, the contra-positive to that statement is equally true, "Rare things are rare." The last time that most physicians have heard of *amyloidosis* was in medical school, me included.

Then things got worse.

In May of 2007, our family went on a hike to some waterfalls. Samuel and Jeremy had just returned from serving as missionaries for two years in Argentina. With our entire family together again for the first time we set out to enjoy the day sliding down the amazing waterfalls just outside of Georgetown, California, about an hour's drive from our house. Nature had created four natural waterslides. The first three were relatively safe and emptied into deep pools of snow-melted water. The fourth was suicide and to be avoided. Barbie and I had done this hike 25 years earlier as newlyweds and were excited to share it with our children, now grown. On the two mile hike back up the hill I got severely fatigued. I tried in vain to hide it by forcing myself to try and keep up with my kids to the point that I almost fainted. I continued trudging forward and then things started to go black, as if I were looking down a tunnel that was rapidly getting longer. Finally I sat down, breathing heavily, and waited. My boys were no longer in sight, unaware of my plight. I finally made it to the car, but the incident really scared Barbie. I was terrified.

As a result, I decided to see a cardiologist. Dr. Anu Khurana was a cardiologist whom I knew. I asked her if she would see me. She began an extensive workup: ECG, Holter monitor, echocardiogram and cardiac catheterization. The tests showed various supraventricular non-specific arrhythmias (weird heart rhythms) but nothing to point to a specific etiology. The cardiac catheterization showed clean coronary arteries, but the machine that assesses cardiac output, measuring the amount of blood the heart pumps per minute, was not working that day. The echocardiogram showed only mild changes, with some borderline thickening of the intraventricular septum (middle of my heart). The thickening was not sufficient to diagnose restrictive cardiomyopathy. She used the term right heart dysfunction or diastolic dysfunction, but for me this had no particular frame of reference. I knew that my right heart pressures had to be high because every night a tri-phasic bounding venous pulse would beat this into my brain as I fell asleep. In desperation, I ordered an abdominal CT on myself to rule out anything else. Of note was the finding of perihepatic vein edema (there was fluid around the vessels in my liver). I tried to get someone to comment on this, but to no avail. However, this finding always worried me. Ultimately, it turned out to be an early sign of my high venous pressures from right heart failure. My gut was also under back-pressure from a failing pump downstream.

In addition, I had a blood test called a BNP, which checks for congestive heart failure. Mine was in the mid 200 range: elevated, but not enough to make the diagnosis.

The focus became the arrhythmias and we made an attempt at beta-blockers, with disastrous results. Beta-blockers are a class of drugs that lower blood pressure and can normalize irregular heart rhythms. They just made my abdominal pain even more severe. My doctors thought this was a drug reaction, but other beta blockers had the same results. We tried calcium channel blockers, another blood pressure drug, and those seemed to work. For a while my arrhythmias stabilized and I felt better. I did note that when I exercised, I could never get my heart rate to go above 110. However, at rest, it would never drop below 85. I seemed to have a very narrow range of rate where my heart wanted to live. I would later understand why.

CHAPTER 8

By January of 2008, I was getting much worse; I was dizzy all of the time. Dr. Khurana had told me that I had diastolic dysfunction, etiology unknown. I asked her if this was congestive heart failure and she said it was similar. I asked her if there was anything I could do to improve it or stabilize the condition and was told maybe. This was depressing. I thought that I would never run again. I gave my bikes away. I would see older people running, I would see obese people climbing stairs and think, "This is not fair, why can't I do that?" But I continued to hold my peace, not complain and stay silent.

Dr. Khurana, however, did two things that helped quite a bit. She started me on a low dose beta-blocker that I could handle, Coreg, and a low sodium diet. Within one week I lost 10 lbs and felt much improved. The low sodium diet then became my mission. How I felt daily was directly related to my weight and salt intake. People began asking, "You look great. How are you losing the weight?" I said that I was on a low sodium diet for high blood pressure. What they did not notice was that I was always sitting or leaning against a wall as I chatted with them. And what *I* did not realize was that I was in a state of malnourishment from abdominal edema caused by my right heart failure. My stable weight was the zero sum gain of increased fluid retention minus fat and muscle loss. Over the next four months I lost 30 lbs of fat and muscle without realizing it. I finally figured something was wrong when sitting became painful due to a lack of fat 'padding' on my gluteus maximus.

Saturday, July 26, 2008
The cost of salt

The bible says that we are the "salt of the earth." This reminds us of how salt is an essential part of life. However, as with all aspects of our lives, balance is essential. This is no more evident than the critical balance of salt in our bodies. We must maintain a level of sodium of exactly 140 meq/dl at all times. If we deviate, even 10 meq in either direction, we can have a seizure and die. This is handled beautifully by our kidneys, which I have always believed to be the most important organ in the body. (I am having serious second thoughts, of late, as to the kidneys importance compared to the heart).

For years people would comment to me of how salt was a poison and to avoid it in the diet. My response was typical of a scientific 2-dimensional view of the body as a chemistry lab. I would say, "You do not need to worry about salt, as long as you have a good heart and good kidneys, you'll be in balance." Although this, en faze, is true, it belies the insidious nature in which this delicate balance can be disrupted.

About a year ago, Barbie bought me a book on the history of salt. It was fascinating. I realized that until 100 years ago, salt was considered a rare commodity and was often rationed. Now it is ubiquitous. It is in everything. Even while I was reading the book, I had no idea that my body was struggling to maintain my salt balance.

I love salt; pickles, pizza, pistachios, potato chips and pancakes were among my favorite poisons, and those are just the "P's." What I did not realize was that my constant abdominal upset was related to this. Finally, in February of this year, it became evident *that I was in mild heart failure and I was told to go on a salt-restricted diet. The effect was immediate. In one week I lost ten pounds and felt wonderful. However, I then became obsessed with the sodium content of everything.*

Salt-restriction is actually a misnomer. I was told to stay within the daily recommendation of sodium intake for all Americans, not just those with bad hearts. This is 2000 mg a day (the equivalent of one teaspoon of salt). Salt became my adversary. It is in everything: all prepared foods, anything from a can or package, all soups, anything brined or marinated, all restaurant food. You cannot escape it. Why did I lose weight? Two reasons: first, by eating less salt, I stopped retaining water and second, it was hard to find low sodium foods, so I ate less.

Which brings me to this amazing revelation. Yet another in the myriad of weight loss plans. Try eating 2000 mg of sodium or less per day for two weeks, and I guarantee, you will lose weight. Not that I wish to make light (pun intended) of my situation. However, I have learned over the years that my original simplistic view of nutrition and chemistry was inadequate. Our bodies were originally designed for a world in which calories and salt were in short supply. We had to extract minimal nutrients from fiber rich/calorie poor foods. That is all reversed now that food-processing removes the fiber for us and adds salt, fat and sugar for taste. We were not designed for this.

I guess you can teach an old dog new tricks. In the end, salt, which is now the cheapest of food substances, has cost me a lot.

Just a thought.

Kevin

I thought I was fooling people when I told them that my weight loss was from a low salt diet, but I was only fooling myself. I think that many people close to me suspected that something might be wrong and kept quiet. I began to retreat emotionally as well. Activities at church that I used to enjoy, I now avoided. Barbie tried to get me involved, but I was always tired. I would get home and crash in front of the TV or computer. Tensions built up between us, but I assumed it was because of her. I had always been as stable as a rock. How could it be me? I remember one day we had a disagreement. I felt confused afterward and quietly slipped out of the house for a walk. I meandered down to a pond near the entrance of our community. Often, when we disagree, I will ruminate over why my logic was not so blatantly obvious to Barbie, but not this time. I began to wonder if I could actually be depressed. The thought made me shudder.

How could I be depressed? And yet, I was tired all the time, found no pleasure in activities I used to enjoy, and just wanted to sleep. I sat under a willow tree at the edge of the pond. The Canadian Geese were migrating north and a few had landed on the pond. The early evening was brisk and as usual, I did not have on a jacket. I sat alone, lost and incredulous, thinking, "This is not me." My confusion was accompanied by tears. I sat for a while and then walked home. A few days later I looked in the mirror. I thought to myself, "I look really old. Have I aged so much in the last year?" I then tightened my neck muscles, revealing every muscle, tendon and ligament. Devoid of fat, I looked like a skeleton. My reflection scared me. Then came that day in Idaho where I could no longer walk a short distance without sitting on a curb or leaning on a wall to keep myself from falling down. I was broken; the question was, could I be fixed?

Mortality awareness event #3

If my middle name weren't Ray, it would be Tenacious. When I have a goal in mind, I will generally find a way to accomplish it. If along the way it becomes clear that I should stop, I will.

I am not stubborn and I am not stupid. But sometimes I do push myself beyond what reason would
prescribe and, generally, I am not afraid of much.
So it was that our patrol in our Boy Scout troop won
the contest and earned a special trip to hike a volcano, Mt. Lassen in Northern California. The trailhead begins around 8000 feet and climbs to near
10,000. It was a beautiful sunny day; the sky filled
with billowing white clouds. Many people were on
the trail that day. About half way to the top of the
volcano, the wind started to blow. With a rapidity
that I had never seen, dark clouds began to race
from the west to where we were. Our scoutmaster's quick reflexes caught the back of his young
son's jacket before he was blown off the trail. He
decided to turn back and suggested that the other
scouts do the same. I was a little ahead of them
on the trail and was told this by another scout who
ran up to inform us. I assessed the situation. I had
already come halfway. It would be a shame to turn
around now. I decided to proceed. My senior patrol
leader, Erik Bergquist, (age 15 and two years my
senior) seeing my determination felt that he should
accompany me so that I would not be alone. And
then it began to snow. Growing up in California,
this was the first time I had actually seen the white
stuff fall from the sky. It was the coolest thing that
I had ever seen. Within a quarter mile we encountered a park ranger escorting a group of terrified
hikers down the mountain. He strongly urged us to
turn around immediately. My mind reminded me
that if I gave up now, I would not be able to claim
that mountain. Something was driving me to get to
the top. What I was trying to prove, and to whom, I
still do not know. Erik and I continued climbing. The

snow was falling hard now and it became difficult to see.

Eventually, we came upon an outcropping of rock which began the final short ascent to the peak. Huddled in this temporary shelter from the wind, it became clear that from here the trail was directly on the rim of the volcano with a precarious drop on either side. At this point, with a concern for our safety, we decided that it would be too dangerous to walk as the wind would blow us over the side. So we crawled.

The peak was marked with a plaque. We scribbled our names on a piece of paper and buried it under a rock, thereby proving our prowess, and immediately began the journey down. Again we crawled to the rock outcropping for protection against the driving snow which had now become a whiteout. I was freezing at this point. I was wearing only the nylon school jacket that was more than sufficient for the coldest day in Marin County, but afforded me no protection at 10,000 feet in a blizzard. My unprotected hands were freezing. I could not fit them very well into the pockets of my jeans. I would have to warm them first. Our scout survival skills reminded us to place them in our armpits to warm them up. Finally, with some effort, I pushed my hands deep into my pockets and we began the journey down the mountain. Once outside the protection of the rock shelter, the driving wind was blowing the snow horizontal in front of us. We could see nothing ahead of us. Since there was no snow accumulating on the ground, we could still see the trail by looking straight down at our feet. Erik and I stayed together and slowly made our way down. As we walked it occurred to me that others might be worried about us. I thought, "maybe they'll send a helicopter to rescue us," and then immediately understood the absurdity of the thought.

As we rounded the last switchback, I could see my scoutmaster standing below at the trailhead. The closer we got the clearer the anger on his face became. With a tone of complete exasperation coupled with relief he told us how incredibly stupid we were for attempting such an idiotic stunt. He grew up in the Midwest and knew the unforgiving power of nature. I apologized, but could only imagine the warmth of his car, now visible only yards away.

CHAPTER 9

The Sunday after girls' camp Barbie opened up to me about her worries. We could no longer face this alone. Now with a diagnosis of restrictive cardiomyopathy and the possibility of amyloidosis as the cause, it was time to tell others. Barbie made some calls to my family. I think I made one call, to my Mom. Barbie heard my conversation and realized that I was still trying to downplay the seriousness of the situation. Additionally, she sent emails to our friends in Connecticut and a few others. I asked to whom she had corresponded and she listed a number of people, including Markell Fluckiger. While living in Connecticut, Markell and I had served together in the Stake Presidency. President Fluckiger was my Stake President and I served as his first counselor for four years until we moved from Connecticut to California. When Barbie mentioned that she was also going to write to President Fluckiger, now living in Colorado, I simply said, "Boy, I could really use a hug from him right now." And thus began the first of many miracles.

The truth is the truth and remains the truth, regardless of human capacity to discover or comprehend it. Truth does not recognize terms such as science or religion. These words are created by us in an attempt to define whence we discover truth. I am a man of science and a man of faith. With regard to my own personal comprehension of the universe in which I have consciousness, I stipulate the following two facts: first, there is only one all encompassing universal truth, and second, I am incapable of discovering or comprehending all of it right now. These realizations are critical to how naturally I can apply the rigorous requirements of the scientific process while simultaneously accepting the existence of God and His influence in my life without conflict. Faith and science coexist quite comfortably in my mind.

My understanding of God--my theology, as it were--comes from my upbringing and life as a member of the Church of Jesus Christ of Latter-day Saints. A cursory glance at my genealogy reveals that I am a fifth or sixth generation Mormon through all of my ancestral lines. Most of my ancestors joined the church somewhere between 1840 and 1860 and then immigrated to Utah. Clearly, there is considerable genetic pressure for me to be Mormon. There has not been a moment in my life when I did not believe in God. There also has not been a moment in my life when I have not been immensely curious about the world around me.

In the Mormon Church we have a lay ministry. This means more than simply saying that the leaders are not paid for their service and must thereby work to support their families; it also reflects that we are not formally trained for the ministry. If I were to receive a PhD in theology from the Yale Divinity School, it would in no way elevate my standing in the church or allow me to claim any right to serve as a bishop. One of our articles of faith states that a man must be called of God, by one in authority, to serve in the church.

That is how I was called as a bishop in 1994. At the time we had lived in Connecticut just over a year and I was beginning to establish myself in the surgery department at Yale. At church I was serving as a scoutmaster to a troop of two boys. One Wednesday evening in the Fall I got a call to meet the following evening with the Stake President, President Seeley. I was told to bring Barbie with me. With some trepidation we arrived the following evening at his office. With very little small talk as a buffer, he simply called me to serve as bishop of the Woodbridge Ward and then asked Barbie if she could support me. There are certain moments that change your life forever. This was probably number 13 of 19. We, of course, accepted the calling without any idea of the immense impact that it would have on our lives. On October 30, 1994 I was ordained a High Priest and a Bishop. I was not only responsible for a congregation of approximately 500 souls, but also any individual living or passing through the greater New Haven area who needed church assistance. I had no idea how to do this, but I had faith. Although we are not formally trained to be ministers, our informal training begins at the age of three when we are first asked to speak in church on an assigned topic, and continues with increasing responsibilities. For five and a half years I balanced my life as a surgeon, as a father and husband, and as a bishop. It was both the most difficult and greatest experience of my life.

It was during this period that the true purpose of my life began to be fulfilled. My role was to alleviate pain, both physical and spiritual. To accomplish this, I needed to be that man of faith and the man of science. I truly learned that the lines between the two are often blurred as I used the skills that I had developed in both to accomplish my purposes in the other.

Markell Fluckiger and I have had parallel lives in many ways. We are the same age. We both grew up in the Bay Area. Our wives agreed to marry us in the Oakland temple exactly one year apart (they got married first). We both spent time in St Louis and then eventually arrived on the East coast. We became bishops on the same day of geographically adjoining congregations. Over the duration of my bishopric I had many opportunities to interact with Bishop Fluckiger and learned what a compassionate and kind man that he was. He is what I would call a bishop's bishop because he always remained focused on his purpose and was a wonderful example.

Fast forward six years. I had been released as a bishop six months earlier and a visiting general authority of the church was there from Salt Lake City to call a new Stake President.

This new leader would be responsible for directing the affairs of the church in a geographic area consisting of one third of the state of Connecticut. Elder Tingey, the visiting authority, would need to choose a new leader from a group of men that he had never met. He chose the man that I most admired, Bishop Fluckiger, But then in life-changing moment number 14 of 19, I was called to serve as his 1st Counselor. This came at the end of one of the most difficult weeks of my life to that point. However, when Elder Tingey asked me if I was willing serve in any calling in the church, I had to respond, "Yes."

Thus began four marvelous years as I served with the most spiritual, wise and humble man that I have ever known. When I think of the Love of Christ, it is personified in President Fluckiger.

The day that Barbie and I announced that we were leaving Connecticut to return to California, I had to tell the two men whom I most respected and most did not want to leave: Dr. Weiss, the Chief of Urology at Yale, and President Fluckiger, both my mentors and friends. It truly broke my heart that day and I was never the same.

You spend years developing relationships based on trust and respect. And then you move to a new place and you are an unknown; a cipher. I was the same, but people in California just did not "get" me. About a year later, we returned to Connecticut for a vacation to visit friends there. We attended church that Sunday in our "good old" Woodbridge Ward and felt as if we had come home after a prolonged absence. After the Sacrament meeting I was wandering the hallways of the building that had been my second home for eleven years. I thought of the countless hours I had spent there with thousands of individuals who had all touched my life in some way. As I passed the stake president's office, there standing in the anteroom was President Fluckiger. As he saw me a large grin filled his face as he exclaimed "Kevin!" and gave me a big hug. He is a large man and his hugs tend to envelop you. In that moment I felt the love that he had for me and all of my anxieties melted away. I have often reflected that some day in the future I hope to receive a similar hug from my Savior and I know that it will fill me with that same sense of being loved for simply being me. I feel that He too will recognize me, smile and call me Kevin. Therein lie the seeds of all my faith and hope. Oh, the power of a simple hug.

Now, thinking about President Fluckiger and sitting there on the couch, my mind was in chaos. We would now tell the world that

I was sick. As Barbie began the process of calling our immediate family and close circle of friends, I quietly sat and listened to one side of a repeated conversation. "Yes, his heart is not working well", "We do not know yet, he is supposed to get a fat biopsy this week." "He's doing OK, he gets tired easily" "They think it might be amyloidosis ….. I don't know ….. Yes, it is serious, but we've read that there are some new treatments."

As I silently sat and listened to her describe my situation, I began to panic. I felt that maybe we were premature in our decision and should not have told anyone. Between phone calls I blurted out, "We should have waited. What if it really isn't that serious and I am going to be OK? We would have worried everyone for nothing." This comment was returned with a stare of incredulity. "If it turns out to not be that serious, they will all be thrilled," Barbie flatly replied. I kept quiet after that. About an hour later I got a call. It was Markell Fluckiger. It was great to hear his deep baritone voice. He asked how I was doing. For 48 years people have asked how I was in the habitual pleasantry that we all use. This was the first of a thousand "How are you's?" that would follow where I could immediately sense the concern and sincerity in the timber of their voice. I always try to respond with the appropriate combination of honesty and hope in which the question is tendered.

"I am OK," I responded. He went on to tell me that he had a trip planned that week that took him to the Bay Area. He had a free evening on Wednesday and asked if he could pay us a visit. With astonishment, I welcomed his request. Three days later a knock came on our door. He had driven two and a half hours to see us. What I did not know at the time was that in the email Barbie sent out, she had specifically mentioned my comment of a need for a hug. We sat down for a few minutes and reconnected. I had not seen him in over three years. He gave us an inspirational book on dealing with adversity and what we can learn from it. I think he sensed in Barbie her quiet torment and asked if she would like a blessing. One of the great things that exists in our church is that we can use our priesthood to bless others who are sick or have difficult challenges in their lives. He gently laid his hands on her head, and I placed my hands over his hands. He voiced a wonderful blessing full of hope and comfort. Many years had passed since he and I had blessed another person together and it felt good to be at his side again. When he was done, Barbie got up from the chair and gave him a hug. I thanked him and also gave him a hug. Once again, I felt the embrace of his love for me as his friend. The moment may have been brief, but time is irrelevant during a flash of eternity.

Our parallel lives eclipsed in that moment and all of my fears melted away and vanished. I was left with an overwhelming sense of hope. No matter the outcome, it would be right and true; the same type of true that describes the straightness of an arrow. This path we were now on would be difficult, but valuable. The path would lead straight through to the things that mattered most. I did not need to be cured or live forever. I just needed to stay on the true path as long as I was needed. What a gift it is to feel no fear. It would be almost a year to the day before I would feel fear again; and that would be short-lived. We thanked Markell and he left to drive another two and a half hours to San Jose.

I did not sleep well that night. I had a lot on my mind, not the least of which was the big surgical case that I was to perform the following day. In urology the longest case that we do is a radical cystectomy. They can take between six and eight hours depending on whether you build a new bladder out of the patient's own intestines or simply use a short segment of bowel to connect the ureters to the abdominal wall. Additionally, this happened to be the only night that I suffered with severe orthopnea. When you have congestive heart failure fluid can back up into your lungs and make it difficult to breathe. This becomes worse when you lie flat because the fluid tracks up to your shoulders. I tried to sleep, but I kept coughing whenever I attempted to lie on my back. I spent the night mostly awake, sitting up in bed. I knew that it would be tough to get through the following day. Fortunately, I was not doing the case alone.

CHAPTER 10

D r. Eschelle Stapp is my partner and a really great surgeon. I had asked her to assist me on this case since I knew it would be complicated. The patient already had evidence that his invasive bladder cancer had grown beyond the bladder and into his left pelvic wall. It would be a difficult dissection on that side to separate a good margin of cancer from the major vessels going to his leg. The case moved along quickly and soon the bladder was on its way to the pathologist. All that was left to do was build him a conduit through which his kidneys could drain into a bag glued to his abdominal wall that he would wear for the rest of his life. I began to feel a bit tired so I asked the nurse for some juice. Since we are scrubbed-in and sterile, the nurse had to slip the straw under my mask and hold the juice box while I drank--very high tech. The two juice box pit stop was enough to keep me going for the next two hours.

We finished in only six and a half hours. I went out and spoke to his daughter to let her know that he was fine and we had been able to remove the bladder without event. She was visibly relieved and gave me a hug to express her gratitude. A minute later I was stumbling down the staircase and dragging myself to my car. I got home and went straight to bed. Barbie and I had a meeting with my cardiologist the next day.

The appointment was set for 10:30 AM. I saw patients until 10:15 and then took the elevator up one floor. Barbie was already waiting in the hallway outside the Cardiology clinic. Soon we sat in the office with Dr. Khurana. She had reviewed the echocardiogram with her fellow cardiologist and the consensus was that this was restrictive cardiomyopathy probably due to amyloidosis. I still was not exactly sure what amyloidosis was. I do not believe that Dr. Khurana had ever seen another case of this rare condition. She asked if I had already gotten the fat biopsy to make the diagnosis. Unfortunately, the surgeon had only been available the day before while I was involved in my all day case removing a bladder. We had rescheduled it for the following Tuesday, July 1st with Dr. Dugoni. We asked about the prognosis and treatment options for amyloidosis affecting the heart. She really could not verbalize a cogent response, but did hand us a review article about my disease. I asked if I would need a heart transplant and she responded, "you are not that sick yet." I then presented the question whose answer I feared the most, "Will I be able to continue working?" She looked down and quietly said "I don't know." I began to cry. The emotion was infectious, and both Dr. Khurana and Barbie began to shed quiet tears.

She then informed me that I needed to have a heart biopsy to confirm the diagnosis. It could be done locally in South Sacramento, but the regional Department of Transplant Cardiology was located in the Santa Clara Kaiser facility 150 miles away. We chose to go to the latter. I was also in need of a bone marrow biopsy to look for amyloidosis in the bone marrow and assure that I did not have a cancer called Multiple Myeloma. I knew just the guy to do my biopsy: Dr. Philip Sardar, an excellent hematologist/oncologist and a close friend.

The following week saw me in and out of clinic and in the offices of many doctors every day. The search was on. I was now a part-time patient. Friday afternoon I got the call from Santa Clara that I had an appointment to see Dr. Nishime at 11:00 AM the following Monday. We were very anxious to get the process started but still had no clue about its direction. We read and reread the article that Dr. Khurana had given us twice on Saturday. It did not give us hope. There is no cure, some people need dialysis or a kidney transplant, and few patients actually qualify for a heart transplant. The median survival rate is 1.5 years from diagnosis. I did not yet have the diagnosis and I held on to the hope that my heart condition was idiopathic, and not a product of this rare, deadly disease.

The next day we got a call from a friend and learned that our entire Stake in Connecticut, which included 10 separate congregations, was going to fast and pray for me on that following Sunday. It is indescribable the feeling of humility, love and peace that I felt from the kindness and faith of thousands of friends. I reflected on the years of fellowship, sacrifice and joy that we had shared during our time together. Our spirits were lifted and we were ready for whatever lay ahead in our path.

CHAPTER 11

Mortality awareness events # 1 & 4

The first event I do not remember. But it became early childhood lore for me. At the age of two I became thirsty one day. I spied a glass of what I presumed was water sitting on the window sill above the sink. Somehow I managed to climb onto the counter and gulped down the liquid. Earlier that day, my Aunt Carol had been doing some laundry in the sink and had left the glass of Clorox which I had just consumed. My mother quickly recognized my peril and ran me across the street to a neighbor who was a county sheriff. I only regret that I do not remember the ride to the hospital as, according to my mom, "With the sirens wailing, we flew through intersections all the way to the hospital." They pumped out my stomach and found a half eaten muffin, which my mother claimed probably absorbed the Clorox and saved my life. They also claimed that I became blond that day, having been bleached from the inside. I believed them for years.

Event number four had me flying in the air doing a somersault and eventually landing on my coccyx as a car came wide around a blind corner causing me to hit him broadside at about 25 miles an hour on my bike. A sophomore in high school, I was on my way to work as a pantry chef in an Italian restaurant. I sat stunned on the pavement as he, seeing that I was still conscious, promised to buy me a new bike and drove away. I never saw him again. I am glad that I was able to do a 360° in the air instead of landing on my head. I landed like a cat. I guess I must have nine lives. I dragged my deceased bike to the back of the kitchen and started my shift.

Dr. Nishime welcomed us with a smile and began her interview. She asked about every aspect of my life, my condition, my symptoms and my limitations. Her exam was the most complete that I had ever had. I got the distinct impression that I was not the first amyloidosis patient that had come through their clinic. In the end, we talked about a plan. Ah yes, the all important plan. Without a plan, I am lost. I would need a fat biopsy to look for amyloidosis fibrils in my fat. I informed her that I would have that the following day; check. I would need a heart biopsy, which was scheduled for Wednesday, July 2nd back here in Santa Clara. Dr. Dana Weisshaar, the chief of the department, would do the task of ripping out tiny pieces of heart tissue and then send them to Stanford for pathologic analysis. I would also need a bone marrow biopsy. I added that Dr. Sardar in Roseville had me scheduled for Thursday. Soon she left to retrieve the paperwork relating to the myriad of tests that I would need in preparation for the next step. The next step? This was somewhat nebulous. So far nobody had told me what the plan was to make me better. While she was out, at least one nurse and one medical assistant popped their heads into the room to assure me that Dr. Weisshaar was really good at doing heart biopsies.

Dr. Nishime returned and handed me a list of X-rays, lab tests, pulmonary function tests echocardiogram, ECG etc... I was told that these examinations were required by the Mayo Clinic. It finally became clear in that moment that I might need to have a heart transplant. Stanford Hospital did not do heart transplants on patients with primary amyloidosis because they generally did not live long enough to justify using up such a rare commodity as a human heart. Mayo Clinic, on the other hand was willing to take this risk, but only on well screened and highly selected patients. Would I fit their profile?

Dr. Nishime left the room one more time and Barbie asked, "Doesn't a bone marrow biopsy really hurt?" What she heard me say was, "Nah, feels good" Incredulous she exclaimed "What?!"

Realizing her misunderstanding, I then clarified, "No, Phil is good," meaning Phil Sardar. Recently Dr. Sardar had performed a bone marrow biopsy one of my own patients. My patient commented that it had not been as bad as he had suspected it would be. I knew that I was in good hands.

By the time we left that day to drive home we had been given a lot of information and a long list of tasks to be performed during the next two weeks. It was going to be a challenge to fit this all into my work schedule. Because of the Wednesday biopsy, I had to reschedule the laparoscopic nephrectomy that I was to do that day to the following week.

July 1st, 7:30 AM was our monthly urology business meeting. As the chief, I began the meeting with an announcement. Up to this point I had not mentioned my condition to my colleagues at work. The silence would now end. In a matter-of-fact tone, I simply informed them that I had been diagnosed with restrictive cardiomyopathy probably due to primary amyloidosis. I would get a heart biopsy tomorrow and would likely need to limit my work schedule to accommodate doctor visits. The room was stunned. There were promises of support and Dr. Gajendran immediately informed me that I would not be taking any more call. I refrained from arguing and thanked him. Back in my office I gathered together my medical assistant, Dina, and my head nurse, Anne, to restructure my clinic schedule so that I would have Fridays off. I truly believed that I could still balance my practice and my disease. In my mind I was still the surgeon, not the patient.

At 1:30 PM I walked across the hall for my fat biopsy. As I sat in the tiny waiting area, I noticed how close it was to the main exit for the building. Dozens of my colleagues wandered by with puzzled smiles as they greeted me. I am sure they were wondering, "what is his problem that he has to see a surgeon?" It felt strange to be recognized in that fishbowl. Soon I was lying on an exam table. Dr. Dugoni numbed me up over my lower abdomen with lidocaine. He used a biopty gun to sample the subcutaneous fat. This is the same device that I daily used to get prostate biopsies. It employs a spring-loaded needle that rapidly shoots forward, traps a piece of tissue, then retracts. After taking four samples of fat, he was done. A bandage was applied and I walked back across the hall to finish my clinic.

Tomorrow was the big day. The heart biopsy was scheduled at 7:30. We needed to find a hotel nearby. Both Barbie and I sensed that whatever happened tomorrow, our lives would likely change forever. I felt strongly that I needed some spiritual guidance at this juncture. During this time, Barbie and I attended church in the Spanish branch because of my fluency in Spanish. My spiritual leader was Mark Perez, the Branch President. Before driving to Santa Clara, we stopped at his house to receive a priesthood blessing. Mark is a very dedicated and spiritual man and I have great respect for him. I sat in a chair and his son, also an elder, anointed my head with consecrated pure olive oil. Mark then sealed the anointing and pronounced a blessing upon me. Initially I felt the words just as words, more hopeful thinking. Then he paused and began anew. "Expect to receive miracles, many miracles that will preserve your life." He uttered. Suddenly the power of those words washed over me and I knew that he had voiced the will of God and it was true. Clearly, we needed some miracles in our lives. I truly needed that special support, not yet aware that tomorrow would become one of the most emotionally wrenching days I had ever experienced.

CHAPTER 12

We were told that we would need to check in for the biopsy at 6:45 in the morning. Drive, arrive, wait, computers checked, license checked, wrist band applied, redirected, walk to cardiac catheterization lab; this would become a routine to repeat many times over. Prior to any procedure you have staff and nurses go over you again and again. You remove your shoes and clothing and place, or rather stuff, them into a bag. Every time you move to a new location it is assured and reassured that you still have vital signs: blood pressure, pulse, temperature and oxygen saturation. Finally, the cath lab nurse arrived and said, "Mr. Anderson, we are ready for you now." I got up off the stretcher to follow her. I gave Barbie a quick kiss and she left to go wait in the car where it was warmer.

The catheterization lab was like a thousand other operating or specialized procedure rooms. The walls are always tiled and the floors are seamless (easier to wash the blood off quickly.) The space is filled with equipment on stainless steel tables. The table nearest where I will lie is covered with a blue paper sheet that allows all of the sterile equipment to remain sterile. Always, in the center of the room is the operating table. This is where I became the center of attention, but as a patient now, not as the surgeon. Normally I am in charge when I enter the room. On this day I was passive. I did whatever they told me: "Lie down, arms at your sides, turn your head to the left, legs raised, do not speak, hum, keep humming." I implicitly obeyed. I was no longer in control of my life. I was the patient. I needed to be patient.

Dr. Weisshaar is one of the nicest people you could ever meet. She greets all of her patients with a hug. "Hi, I'm Dr. Weisshaar,

I am a 'hugger'," she began with arms wide open. "I am Kevin Anderson," I responded. (I had made the decision to always refer to myself as Kevin in my journey as a patient. I preferred that my caregivers not know that I was a doctor. I did not want to cause them to alter their normal routine or be a source of intimidation. I knew from experience that mistakes are more likely when we take short cuts. Those who demand to be treated as V.I.Ps ultimately can receive substandard care.)

I lay there on the table and Dr. Weisshaar described each step as she performed the procedure. A heart biopsy is done by removing small pieces of heart tissue using a long thin flexible cup grasping forceps. One end is a forceps with a hinged cup. At the other end there is a scissor action handle which allows one to open and close the cup inside the heart. The heart is like a four room house--it has inside walls and outside walls. The goal of the biopsy is to sample the inside wall between the two ventricles. If the doctor were to sample the outside wall and inadvertently punch a hole in it, then the patient would rapidly bleed to death. This would be undesirable. As it is, when you biopsy the heart muscle at the septum or inner wall, the muscle bleeds, but only back into the heart.

Dr. Weisshaar inserted a needle into my neck on the right side and injected lidocaine to numb the area. Then, she palpated my carotid artery and sternal notch as landmarks to direct the next needle puncture into my right internal jugular vein. She knew when she was in by the color of the blood aspirated: purple rather than bright red. She advanced a flexible wire through the needle down into my right heart. Hanging from the ceiling over my chest was a large fluoroscopy camera so that she could use X-ray to verify the position of the instruments inside my chest. She could see that the wire had travelled down to my heart and not up to my brain. She told me that it was unusual for her to do a biopsy in someone who had not already had a heart transplant, explaining that my heart was still innervated. When you transplant a heart, you do not reconnect the nerves, hence, there is no sensation. This meant that I was going to feel this. She inserted the biopsy forceps and grabbed hold of a piece of my heart and yanked on it. As the muscle tore away, I felt a pulling in my chest. It did not hurt, however. I smiled under the sheets at such a strange sensation and uttered, "Doc, you're tugging at my heartstrings." She laughed and said she had not heard that one before.

Soon she had taken four biopsies which would be shipped off to Stanford University to see whether I had amyloidosis in my heart. Next she inserted a Swan-Ganz catheter into my heart. This is a specialized catheter with which I was quite familiar. It is used to measure heart pressures and output. Cardiac output reveals the volume of blood that your heart pumps per minute. This would be analogous to the horsepower of an engine. It is measured by the dilution of cold saline over time. As they injected coldness into my heart, I could feel a strange sensation in the back of my throat that would last two seconds.

And then it was over. The tubes were removed from my neck and I lay there while Dr. Weisshaar looked at the data. She returned a few minutes later and began by explaining that the pressures in my right heart were very high, signifying an extremely stiff heart muscle. She was leaning against the stainless steel cabinets so that I could easily see her from the sheets over my head that had been pulled back. She continued reporting the data quite matter of factly, as doctors often do when slowly revealing bad news. "Your cardiac index is 1.7," she stated. I had not dealt with cardiac outputs since my surgery residency, but some corner of my brain told me that this was an abnormally low number.

"What is considered a normal cardiac index?" I queried.

"Above 3.2," she answered. Strike one, I thought. She continued by suggesting a course of action where I would be admitted to the hospital immediately, have a central venous line placed and begin a continuous dosing of a dopamine infusion to increase my heart function. "Dopamine!!!" my brain screamed. That is what we gave to patients who are "circling the drain" in the intensive care unit in an attempt to raise their blood pressure so that they do not die.

My first thought was, "I don't feel that sick." My second thought was, "I have clinic tomorrow and the man I cancelled today for a nephrectomy is rescheduled for next week. I cannot be admitted, I have things that I still need to do." I was not yet the patient, so I began to bargain. I reassured her that I was doing OK and that I could continue the workup as an outpatient. There was a look in her eyes that I did not yet understand; she knew something that I did not. However, she agreed and added that maybe it would be a good thing for me to go back to work as we prepared for the next step. "Next step," I wondered; Then I asked the question aloud: "Do I need to get a heart transplant?"

Her response caught me off guard, "Only if you are healthy enough."

"Only if you are healthy enough?!" The words seared into my brain. What does that mean? How can one be too sick to get a heart transplant? Internally I was wracked with an overwhelming profusion of confusing thoughts and emotions. Externally Dr. Weisshaar and I were engaged in a very rational discussion about the ensuing workup that I would need to get done. A big part of the remaining question related to whether amyloidosis was indeed the cause of my heart disease. The answer would ultimately determine our course of action. Satisfied that we had a plan, at least for that day, I chuckled and commented how intellectual our discussion had been. She smiled and agreed. Then she left the room to go over some other results. When she left she took with her any pretense of rationality on my part.

As I lay there alone in this sterile environment, my broken heart could no longer contain the built up emotions unleashed by such news. In that instant my own death became an absolute reality to me for the first time in my life. Many times in my past, I had been snatched from the jaws of death. However, in the perceived invincibility of youth I had never once thought that I would die. Today, however, it was unavoidably palpable. I began to weep uncontrollably.

Dr. Weisshaar returned with a list of all of the lab tests and studies that I would need to complete within the next two weeks.

As I heard her coming back, I tried to control myself. I shut down the tears and added a "doctor tone" to my responses. Since medical school I had become adept at the employment of emotional dampers in order to deal with the death and loss that are invariably part of the experiences of a physician and surgeon. My role has always been to instill confidence and hope. During particularly difficult surgeries, emotional detachment is necessary to focus on the urgent task at hand. I now had an urgent task ahead of me: to survive. I needed to stay focused, now more than ever.

I had my work cut out for me. Entire body X-rays, pulmonary function tests, blood work, bone marrow biopsy, a 24 hour urine collection for kidney function and protein quantification and worst of all, a 72 hour stool collection to determine whether I was malnourished from impaired fat absorption. I got up off the table, received my walking orders and, once again, Dr. Weisshaar gave me a hug. This hug felt different. I had met her thirty minutes before, but now my life was in her hands. I knew that she would do whatever she could to keep me alive. I thanked her and went to find Barbie. What was I going to tell Barbie?

I found her reading in the car. She always knows when something is wrong. My face cannot lie. I did not know where to begin so instead, I suggested that we drive to Santa Cruz, 30 miles away, to sit on the beach. There is something about the open ocean that makes me feel at peace. The solitude of nature is far better than valium. I began to unfold the story to her as we drove through the Santa Cruz Mountains. She quietly listened, interrupting only for clarification. And then we were both quiet for a while.

I love the ocean: the brackish mist, the sound of crashing waves, the smell of wet sand and seaweed. Its repetitive and unrelenting rhythm is mesmerizing. Somehow, my place on earth is recalibrated when I seat myself before such a massive expanse. I have had such a wonderful life, full of love and service and so many opportunities. I tried to focus on the good of my past as I looked out at the horizon. The horizon is like the future. You can set sail and try to reach it, but it remains elusive, ever moving away. The horizon is unattainable, unknowable. What is beyond? What would be my future? Finally, one day you see a small cloud covering a peak of some distant island. The future gives way to the present as your course is now fixed on that now visible and ever enlarging destination. My horizon remained empty and unknown. Only faith could take us in the right direction with the hope that we would find our destination.

Barbie sat quietly beside me, as she is always beside me. I could not imagine what was going through her mind. I needed to stay positive for her; I needed to *stay* for her. I knew that I would do everything in my power to stay alive for her. That was my goal, my drive and my purpose for being. One of the things that had originally convinced me to marry Barbie was that I could not conceive of my life without her. You can fall in love with many people, but there are very few that you cannot live without. When you find that person, you need to marry them.

Now I could not conceive of Barbie's life without me. Somehow, deep from the roots of my soul arose a feeling of unquenchable hope. "Bring it on," I thought. Pain, fatigue, nausea; I can handle it. Actually, I had no idea what I was in for. But I was not afraid. With God above me and Barbie at my side, I could do anything.

We began the long drive home. The only CD in my car was Coldplay's "Viva la Vida." The entire CD is themed around death and life; appropriate, I thought. "Cemeteries of London," "Lost," "Viva la Vida," "Death and All His Friends"; this became the soundtrack of our lives. As it played we talked, then cried, then gazed off silent, then cried again. Our journey home felt much longer than the trip to the hospital the day before.

Chapter 13

The work-up began immediately. Dr. Weisshaar's words sounded in my mind like carillon bells counting down the hour. Each new test would reveal how sick or how well my body was. It felt like a final exam. If I was well enough, I would earn a new heart. If I was too sick for a heart, the test would be over soon. That afternoon, rather than going straight home, I went back to the hospital in Roseville to begin the work up. It began with a whole body X-ray, from head to toe. This meant to determine that I did not have multiple myeloma, which can present with bone lesions called *plasmacytomas*. I was familiar with these, since I had seen them develop in my father. As I lay there on the X-ray table I realized I had been in that room many times, but I had always been performing procedure on my patients before; the table had turned and was now underneath me. The radiology technologists knew me as just another patient. I had never realized how hard X-ray tables were.

When I got home, I pulled up my films on my computer and immediately noticed that I had a fairly large right pleural effusion. Half of my right chest cavity was filled with fluid. It was no wonder that I had difficulty sleeping flat. This prompted a new level of anxiety. My mind raced, "Does this mean the amyloidosis is in my lungs too or is this just caused by my congestive heart failure?" Somehow I understood that if too many of my organs were irreversibly damaged by this disease then a lifesaving heart would be withheld from me.

The next day I saw my oncologist, Dr. Sardar. The medical assistant placed me face down on the table as Dr. Sardar numbed a spot in the skin near the top of the left iliac crest on my pelvic bone. In an attempt to numb the tissues deeply, he pushed the needle into the bone to numb the lining called the periosteum. Unfortunately, it is impossible to numb the bone very well. He then plunged a very heavy gauge needle through the bone into the bone marrow. To break through the hard bone required quite a bit of force and drilling motion. And that was the easy part. The real pain (oh, I forgot, we doctors do not use the word pain. I mean "pressure") came when he aspirated. With a syringe he created suction inside my bone marrow. I felt an ache that extended throughout my entire left pelvis. It only lasted about ten seconds and then it was over. The entire procedure took less than ten minutes. He put a band-aid over the site and I went downstairs back to clinic to see my waiting patients.

Part 2

DIAGNOSIS

Chapter 14

July 9, 2008 was the day that my life was completely turned upside down. I had already arranged to lighten my schedule by taking off Fridays each week for appointments and other health related issues. The day before, I had scheduled three patients for future surgery. Despite everything, I still was thinking that I would continue working and get treatment in between taking care of my patients. I reflected on this day 10 days later in one of the first posts on a blog I had begun to chronicle my life and death journey:

Saturday, July 19, 2008
How I got here

Many are surprised to hear that suddenly I am so ill. Those who have seen me for the last year had little idea that I was actually slowing down. I tend to hide things well and minimize my limitations. Some may view this as a fault or pride, but since I did not know what was happening and whether it was reversible, I kept it private. Once I finally did learn the gravity of my condition, I then shared the information with others. The immediate reaction was overwhelming. The emails, calls and cards expressing concern and support formed a touchstone through which I was reminded of the enormous number of souls from all over the planet that have touched my life in some way.

As we daily try to meet all of our appointments and tasks which are driven by our priorities and responsibilities, it is easy to forget the import of where we have been. This was made very evident a week and a half ago on Wednesday. I was scheduled to do two big cases that day, a pecutaneous nephrolithotomy and a laparoscopic radical nephrectomy. The first removes a large stone from a kidney through a half inch hole in the back. The second cures a kidney cancer by removing the kidney through a 3 inch incision at the belly button. I was in my office, awaiting my time for the OR and I got a call from my transplant cardiologist. The heart biopsy had returned positive for Amyloidosis. She told me that I should stop working immediately to prepare for the process of getting a heart and bone marrow transplant.

The call ended and I began to weep uncontrollably. Not because I had been diagnosed with a potentially fatal illness, but rather because I would stop doing what I have done for 20 years. I am defined by my responsibilities to other people. The only true happiness I have ever known was when I was in the service of other people. This is who I am. To suddenly cease doing this is to lose a part of myself. I wondered how, in this emotional state, I would be able to do these surgeries. But then, I am a surgeon. We do what we have to. I remembered how many people were praying for me, fasting for me; and in this moment I knew that their faith would carry me.

The first case went well and we got the stone out of the kidney. As I was getting ready for the last case, it occurred to me that I alone do not have the power to cure myself, but I can cure this man of his cancer. I have the strength left to do that. The surgery went as well as it ever has. Every step proceeded smoothly and in two hours I was speaking to his wife to tell her that her husband would be fine. During the case, all thoughts of myself disappeared I felt no weakness or dizziness. I was carried through. I knew that this was the last operation I would do for some time.

Soon, I was in the OR lounge and saw a woman on whom I had performed the same operation three years ago. She worked for environmental services. It was her job to clean the OR when we are done. I could not do my job without her. She always smiles when she sees me. For some reason this time she asked, "Dr. Anderson, why did I get that cancer?" to which I responded, "It is nothing that you did or did not do, sometimes these things just happen." I could not help think of my own situation in that moment. I then felt to say something much more personal. I said, "Every time I see you, I feel happy because you remind me that what I do has value." She then jumped up from her chair and came over and gave me a hug and said, "Thank you, Dr. Anderson, for saving my life." I could not imagine a more fitting end to such a day.

We all make a difference every day in ways that we do not realize. The sum of all of those moments is what makes our lives worth living. I am grateful for those myriad of moments that have made me who I am.

Kevin

When I finally drove home, I was no longer the doctor. I was the patient. Barbie had not yet heard the news. I could not tell her over the phone. Now we would face it again together as if it were the first time. As I told her, through damp eyes and a stuttering voice, she just held me for the longest time. Words failed us while our love sustained us.

The following day Dr. Sardar had arranged for me to see the pulmonologist to have the fluid drained from around my right lung. The thought was that if my right lung could then completely expand, I would not feel short of breath and would sleep better. Dr. Devendra began with me sitting up on a stool with my arms resting on a gurney in front of me. In order to drain fluid from the chest you need to be upright so that the lung will float on top of the fluid. This allows the needle to drain the dependant fluid without puncturing the lung. Barbie was there as were Dr. Devendra's assistants. He localized the fluid level with an ultrasound and, after numbing the skin and the space between my 8th and 9th ribs, passed a needle into my chest. Through this he slid a small plastic tube and connected it to an empty vacuum jug.

Immediately, straw colored fluid began to drain. However, Dr. Devendra did comment that there was some turbidity which might signify an exudate rather than a transudate. I asked what that meant. He explained that a transudate is merely filtered fluid which you would expect in someone with congestive heart failure as if the basement were flooding because the sump-pump was not working. An exudate, on the other hand could come from some type of inflammatory or malignant process and would have more cells and protein. In other words, an exudate might mean that the amyloidosis was now involving my lungs. This was hard to hear. It could mean I would be excluded from getting a heart transplant.

Mid-conversation, my feet suddenly got cold. The sensation of rapidly being submerged into icy water moved up my body within ten seconds. I asked if this procedure could cause a vaso-vagal reaction and Dr. Devendra said it could. I had never had a vaso-vagal reaction myself, but I have seen it many times. Certain stimuli to the body cause this reflex. They can range from the fear of needles to stimulating organs in the body through procedures and exams. Generally the person will describe feeling suddenly ill. His or her face will become pale and his or her skin cold and clammy. If the person is upright, he or she will pass out and fall down. This occurs as a reflex through the vagus nerve when simultaneously blood pressure and heart rate drop. Often, bystanders will panic when this happens and call 911. However, within a minute the person usually regains consciousness once he or she is lying down and blood returns to the head. Generally, within 15 minutes the person's blood pressure rises as evidenced by color returning to his or her face. If the person was not injured when he or she fell, nothing else needs to be done.

I knew that I was experiencing this, and although I could not see my pale face, I felt the clamminess of my skin. Dr. Devendra said that he was going to stop the procedure and pull out the tube. I asked how much fluid he had drained. Only 300 cc. "No," I thought, "That's not enough." It seemed a shame to go through this and only have a fraction of the fluid in my lung removed. I begged him to continue. But considering my rapidly dropping blood pressure, I probably was not thinking straight. The blood pressure cuff began to tighten on my arm and we all looked at the result once it had cycled. 37/16 mm/Hg. I thought to myself, "how is it possible to have a blood pressure that low and still be awake to see it?" Immediately, they helped me on to the gurney so that I was lying down. Until then I had been still sitting on the stool. Dr. Devendra suggested that a nurse be called to put an I.V. in and give me fluids. I thought to myself, "I have to get back to clinic this afternoon; that will take a long time." From my recumbent position I suggested to the doctor that this was just a vaso-vagal reaction and that I should completely recover in about fifteen minutes. One of the dangers of being a patient who is also a doctor is that sometimes your doctors do not argue with you when they should. However, he must have agreed, and since I never lost consciousness, we just waited and within 15 minutes my blood pressure was back up to its normal hypotension of 95/60. As Barbie and I walked back to the car, I made a tough decision and let her drive me back to work.

On my last day in the office, all of the staff had a lunch in my honor. The menu was salt free. They had scoured cookbooks and the internet for tasty recipes that were low in sodium. I was so touched by their concern as I sampled some very good dishes that could taste so delicious in the absence of that deadly rock. It was their way of sending me off with the knowledge that they cared about me.

I had one last item to resolve which was a tough choice for me but had to be done. How could it be possible for me to continue in my role as chief of the department if I were physically not present? I crossed the hallway to administration where Dr. Chris Palkowski had his office. He was my boss and the Physician-In-Chief of the hospital. I told him what was going on with me, and the expression on his face showed such genuine concern. He, as many others had also said upon hearing my news, promised to pray for me and gave me a hug. I explained that I might not be around for a while and suggested that he allow me to step down as chief. His response surprised me. With calmness and reassurance he told me that I should continue in my role and work closely with my assistant chief, Dr. Chabra, to run the affairs of the department as best that I could. And then he added with a smile, "I am sure you'll be back." I thanked him for his support, unaware of how that decision would provide me with an essential lifeline to keep me tethered to the reality of who I was and still could be. My sporadic involvement as chief-in-absentia would serve me with continued purpose and needed distraction.

CHAPTER 15

Saturday was a rough day. Amyloidosis can affect many organs in the body. It was necessary to see how my gut was working. This is typically done by assessing how well the gut absorbs fat. In order to analyze absorption, the patient must perform a three day stool collection. The total fat content cannot exceed 7 gm/day. This was probably the worst experience of my entire workup. Suffice it to say that the congestive heart failure had caused edema or swelling throughout my entire body, including my intestines. This had led to months of poor appetite, weight loss, and constant diarrhea. For 72 hours I had to carry with me a bucket in a paper bag for the collection. It was a horrible exercise.

We did not know what would be happening even in the next week or how long I would even live. Barbie and I decided that we needed to get our affairs in order rather quickly. We went to my brother Harold's office and he proceeded to write up a trust using Willmaker software to protect us in case something happened. As we sat there for three hours, I felt so sick. Multiple times I would excuse myself, collect my samples and then return. Finally it was done and we went home. I knew that I was deteriorating rapidly.

On Monday we drove to Santa Clara for our two week follow up. We met with Dr. Parekh, another of the transplant cardiologists. After reviewing all of the test results, she left to call the Mayo Clinic. When she returned she told us that they had agreed to see me as a possible candidate for a heart transplant. Even though there was no guarantee, it gave us hope. We asked about going to Stanford instead and she informed us that Stanford did not do heart transplants on patients with primary amyloidosis, although she did not go into detail about why. She did mention that they had done one patient four years prior, but that he had familial amyloidosis which was different. We were told that we would hear within a few days of further plans.

The following day I was supposed to drive to Oakland for a regional chiefs' meeting but decided I probably should not go. This turned out to be a wise decision. At 10:00 AM while at the county recorder's office changing our deed into the newly formed trust, Barbie called to say that we would be flying the next day to Rochester, Minnesota. The Kaiser travel office had already made the travel arrangements for flights and hotel. The ticket was one-way since we had no idea how long we would be there. It was all happening so fast. Caitlin was 15; what would happen with her? Rebecca was back from college and working locally, but we would need extra help. Barbie called her mom in Utah and she agreed to fly out to stay with the girls while we were gone. I was scheduled to do surgery on Wednesday. I arranged for my partner, Dr. Gajendran, to do the cases. I was done.

I had one loose end yet to complete. The pulmonologist, Dr. Devendra, wanted to re-attempt drainage of the fluid in my right chest. I called him and asked if he could do it that day. We figured I would travel better if my right lung were completely expanded. He had me come to his office after lunch and this time he drained 1400 cc with no untoward effects. Fresh with new lung capacity, I was ready to fly.

CHAPTER 16

Bishop Merrill, our local bishop, had suggested a week prior that I speak to a member of our ward, Steve Hargadon, to help me set up a blog. Initially I thought that I did not want to bother anyone with such a request. I was still in my mode of independent thinking. I wanted to avoid as much as possible any form of imposition on others. This personal attribute, which had served me well all of my life, was now a stumbling block. I could no longer do this alone. Barbie and I decided that a blog might help people to know what was happening with us while we were away without having to make so many phone calls. It seemed practical at the time. I had no idea how it would change my life and the lives of so many others.

In the midst of packing for an extended trip, Steve came over and within 30 minutes set up our blog, www.kevinandbarbie.com . I published the first post that night.

Tuesday, July 15, 2008
Big News

Today we got the call that we will be going to Minnesota tomorrow to be evaluated for the possibility of receiving a heart transplant. I will use this blog to try to keep friends and family updated on my progress. Thank you for all of your love and prayers of support.

Kevin

Wednesday morning we kissed Caitlin and Rebecca and did not want to let go as we hugged them. Our bags were heavy, since we carried what we might need for three weeks or three months. Our hearts were heavy in the anticipation of our separation from our daughters. Caitlin has always been a very sensitive child. At fifteen I wondered how she would do without parents around to help her complete all of her responsibilities: homework, piano, golf team, church activities etc. … We were blessed to have Rebecca home from school, now engaged and preparing for her upcoming wedding in October. She would be a huge support for her sister while we were away. Barbie's sister, Kathie, who lives locally, would stay with them until their grandmother arrived on Friday. That was as far as we had planned. They were on their own to find food.

Wherever you are in the world, airports and hotel conference rooms feel the same. Once inside you cannot tell whether you are in Bangkok, Rome or Minneapolis. During my journey, I have learned to notice and be grateful for many small things. On this day it would be moving sidewalks. Somehow, we always have the pleasure of making our connecting flight as far away as possible from the one originating. Finally, we boarded the small plane to Rochester. As I gazed at the world below, hundreds of pools of reflected sunlight sparkled beneath me. It was as if jewels had been woven into a patchwork tapestry. Barbie was quiet, probably sleeping. I felt excitement. There was a chance I might get a new heart. I felt a calm as the sun was setting and the reflected jewels turned from diamonds to sapphires. The sun finally set on the horizon, and so did we. I was ready for anything.

Here are Barbie's thoughts on that first evening,:

Wednesday, July 16, 2008
Big Day Tomorrow

We arrived safely and are getting settled. It seems this will be home for awhile. We have a small kitchen, free wireless internet, a gym, and other amenities that will be helpful.

How to pack for the unknown is not easy. Our suitcases were heavy with books, electronics and all their cables! I even packed some protein shakes and bars. Who knows when I'll get to eat?

I had a hard time leaving this morning. I kissed Rebecca and Caitlin goodbye and held back my tears. I will miss them. But, I know they are in good hands with grandmas and aunts nearby, and might I add, lots of friends who check in and friends to keep Caitlin busy. My sister is at the house now and my mom comes in Friday morning. What a blessing to have a loving family! So many have asked how they can help and truly, I wish I knew.

Tomorrow is Kevin's day to continue as a patient of more "pokes and prodding", this time at the Mayo Clinic. I can't remember how many specialists he is seeing tomorrow, but it's more than three. I have been reading up on what to expect from a heart transplant but I am not so up on the newest treatment for AL amyloidosis. We've been told different things. So tomorrow is a new day of learning more. I am holding up quite well. I am kind of surprised. I didn't know I had this in me. I am not in denial; I know it's just the beginning :)

Barbie

From what I am told, Rochester gets pretty cold in the winter, so many of the buildings downtown are interconnected by either subterranean tunnels or enclosed skyways, our hotel included. It was clear that this town had been designed with the travelling patient in mind. We settled in and I set up the new laptop computer that I had quickly purchased the day before. This would be our window to the world for the next few months. I had ordered two webcams, one for Barbie and one for Caitlin and Rebecca so that we could video chat and not feel so separated. Our only instructions from the travel office were that we were supposed to show up at 6:30 A.M. (4:30 A.M Pacific Time) in the lab on Thursday morning to get further instructions. We called the girls and then crashed and were asleep within 17 seconds of our heads hitting the pillow.

Thursday, July 17, 2008
Let the testing begin

Mayo clinic is quite a place. One might call it an assembly line given how efficient the process is; however, that would not do it justice since everyone is so nice and personable. The facilities are beautiful. The day began at 6:30 AM in the lab and then the ECG followed. Four men or women at a time are called up and sent to gender specific hallways where you remove your shirt and wait in a cubicle made of fine cherry wood. Then you all cross the hall as you would at Disneyland to get on a virtual reality ride. The test is done, efficiently, and you move on to the next station on your pre-printed agenda; Chest X-ray, Exercise tolerance O2 consumption test, Echocardiogram, back to the lab and then back to X-ray.

This morning, we did meet with Dr. Clavell, the transplant surgeon, to discuss my options. He is very nice. He described a week more of work-up (the itinerary is exhausting) and then my case will be presented at their committee to decide if I have a heart transplant first or begin with a bone marrow (stem cell) transplant.

Being a patient here is like a full-time job.

Kevin

Mayo Clinic

Thursday, July 17, 2008
I am not the patient

Not being a patient, I found out today, is still exhausting. I'm tired and my heart is fine and I am not the one who had tests and pokes all day. Kevin mentioned that it felt like Disneyland. I thought so too, but for a different reason. I had the itinerary and for me it was like trying to hit all the shows on time. He had appts. at 7am, 8:20am, 9am, 10:30am, 12:30pm, 2:30pm, 3:30pm. Some were two hours long. Tomorrow and all of next week are much of the same. Many tests he has to repeat. Mayo is extremely thorough.

Barbie

The first day at the clinic was incredibly tiring. The varied tests were spread out through multiple buildings that covered a large section of the downtown area. I would get exhausted walking and have to sit and rest along the way. The buildings were beautiful. They were filled with art and architecture that promoted a sense of peace. I am sure that this is by design. When I first met with Dr. Clavell, I mistakenly thought he was the transplant surgeon. Only later did I realize that he was a transplant cardiologist. His interview and examination of me was even more extensive than the one done by Dr. Nishime. In an hour and a half he knew me inside and out. He mentioned some of the testing that I would receive over the ensuing week and a half, and the process seemed daunting. But what else was I going to do? This was my chance.

You walk, you sit, you wait, a person calls your name. As you approach the desk they smile. (Minnesotans smile a lot) "What is your name?"

"Kevin Anderson," I respond.

"What is your date of birth?" was always the next question.

"August 19, 1959." The password appropriately given and received, I was now allowed to pass through a door and sit in another room. Some rooms were small offices with a desk, computer, sink, window and a clinic table, which is like a small bed with an uncomfortable cushion and a piece of butcher paper pulled over the top. I was the piece of meat. Sometimes a doctor would come in and begin asking me questions: the same questions for me, new questions for the doctors. Sometime a technologist would enter the room and instruct me to lie down or stand or run or walk or swallow or cough or breathe or not breathe or pee or spit.

The first time I went to the lab for a blood draw, they had approximately 20 tubes lined up next to my arm. Each one had a different color rubber cap on the top. The butterfly needle was inserted into my vein in the right arm. One by one the tubes began to fill with my blood. By the time the 15th tube was filled, the needle clotted off. It turns out that I still had a lot more blood in my left arm once that vein was punctured. I wondered at all of the tests that they were doing. It seemed that they checked every possible blood test imaginable. After a few days it began to feel as if at the end of each day some people got together and began inventing more tests that they could do to me the following day.

One day I again sat in the laboratory waiting area. This was a large room that served both the clinical lab and the oncology infusion area. The people in the room reflected a microcosm of the world: every age, every ethnicity. Some appeared wealthy. Some looked poor. Of course, that observation is meaningless. When you are exhausted and in pain, making the effort to make yourself presentable in public seems superfluous. There was a little boy with his mother (or grandmother, I couldn't tell) He looked thin and the bulge under his shirt below the left collar bone indicated a permanent catheter had been placed. "He has cancer," I thought.

My attention was drawn to the center of the room. There sat a young woman, quite pretty, waiting like the rest of us. She was reading a novel. After about 10 minutes her name was called. As she stood up I noticed that she was dressed nicely in what would be described as business attire, matching gray jacket and skirt. Somehow though, it did not seem to fit, almost as if it had been purchased two sizes too large. As she leaned over to pick up her bag, her jacket raised just enough to see the catheter tip hanging down. She was going in to get her chemotherapy. Her well applied make-up almost hid the gray-tan color of her skin.

About 20 minutes later she emerged to leave and walked past me. Her eyes fixed ahead as she moved on to whatever else filled her schedule. I suddenly felt sad. You could see that this was her life now. She was used to it. Come in, get a poison put into your veins and carry on. I wondered why she was alone. Was there no one to accompany her or was everyone in her support network just busy that day. I thought of what it would be like if I did not have Barbie with me. I felt a pain in my heart. I could not do this without her. Without her, there was no reason to do it. I knew that I would endure every test, every procedure and treatment required of me. I could not imagine Barbie being alone. That was my only fear: leaving her alone.

Friday night, Barbie and I took a shuttle to the movie theater to see "The Dark Knight." It was a good movie, but I was in the middle of collecting a 24-hour urine sample to assess my total protein loss. I did not want to drink too much soda because it was a bit strange to have to pull a jug out of a paper bag and empty my bladder into it. I had not really been given many of the results from the many tests, but what I had heard seemed positive. The pulmonologist felt that my pleural effusion (which had refilled my chest within a week,) was likely a transudate and represented a backup from my failing pump. This verdict was extremely reassuring for me. In my mind I was keeping score. I was absorbing fat well from my gut. (I got out of doing another stool collection for Mayo Clinic by promising to give them my report from Kaiser. It was one of those times when being a doctor was very useful. I took my computer to the lobby and printed the report straight from my medical record.) I had less than 7 gms/day of fat. My gut was working. The lung report was positive. I had no neuropathy, and no numbness or tingling in my feet or hands. My teeth and throat were healthy. It was beginning to appear that the rest of me might be healthy enough to justify replacing my heart. I just had to pass the kidney test

CHAPTER 17

Each day of testing began fasting. My blood pressure hovered around 95/60, resulting in acutely noticeable dehydration. Generally, I would not be able to eat until late morning, by which time I was always famished. We found a place across the street that had the best Gyro's sandwiches, Mac's Restaurant. At this point, I had given up caring how much salt I was consuming. Each morning I would get through my tests dreaming of lunch and that meatloaf of lamb and beef with Tzatziki sauce. Friday started with a test to measure kidney function. I personally had never ordered a test like this before. It accurately measured the renal clearance of a fixed amount of a chemical injected subcutaneously. I had to drink specific amounts of water at specific times and lie there for two and a half hours. Finally, I had to empty my bladder within a specific 3 minute window and produce a minimum of 250 cc of urine. I tried cramming all night for the test, but that did not help. The pressure was on and I passed as I pissed. I knew that this was a critical test. The one thing that could really strike me out for a heart was any evidence that my kidneys were significantly damaged by the amyloidosis. I did my best to follow all directions to decrease any possible error. In some ways, this was also a test. They do not give hearts to non-compliant patients. There is too much risk. Keeping a transplant healthy is a full time job. You can never take a vacation from your medications.

Sunday, July 20, 2008
A very long weekend

We had been so busy since we arrived here that we had not had time to stop and think about what just happened to us and our family. I had way too much time this weekend to reflect on the past couple of weeks and the future here at Mayo (or "the clinic", as the locals refer to it.) Though it was good for Kevin to have a few days to recover and get rest.

I try really hard to stay in the "here and now" and not spend too much time thinking about those things that make me sad. When I do, I cry a little and then go for a long walk on the treadmill down stairs. It helped at 5am this morning, as I knew it would.

We were picked up for church by a member of the ward. They were all amazingly friendly, offering dinners, rides, their homes and more. The ward is made up of people who are employed at the clinic - doctors, nurses, techs, volunteers, interns, fellows, and residents. Many of them seem to know what amyloid is and have seen it before. That we are grateful for - it reminds us that we are in the right place. We met the fellow who is training to be a cardio-thoracic surgeon. He is the one who retrieves the heart and brings it back to Mayo and on the side, he teaches Gospel Doctrine. We are pleased we have been met with open arms and by people who are so friendly and giving.

Things I am grateful for:

* Our children are all in a good place in their lives.

* My girls are being cared for (even though Rebecca is an adult - it's good to have grandma around).

* Friends and family at home who are concerned for us and for our children.

* Friends from all over who have contacted us and sent their love.

* A treadmill in the building.

* A beautiful fountain outside the Mayo that allows me to relax. (There is something about water.)

* Modern technology that allows us to communicate and feel connected.

* The "Clinic"

* Kevin

Barbie

CHAPTER 18

It has been postulated that we are connected to every other person on the planet through six degrees of separation. In other words, I am connected to any other person on the planet through a chain of six or fewer people. I believe that in the Church of Jesus Christ of Latter-day Saints there are merely two degrees of separation. When my sister Mindy heard that we were travelling to Rochester, MN, she spoke with her Bishop in Michigan, who then gave us the phone number of the Stake President in Rochester with whom he had previously served. He, in turn, connected us with the High Priest group leader who arranged for someone to pick us up at our hotel and bring us to church. Everywhere we turned, people offered to help. We sat in the back during Sacrament meeting and could just feel the warmth and spirit there. The choir was amazing. Sacred music always touches my heart, but that day my feelings were so close to the surface. Everyone we met treated us as long-lost family. I have attended church all over the world and have found that the Latter-day Saints everywhere share that common trait of Christian love.

When I reflect back on that Sabbath day in the Rochester 3rd Ward, I have often wondered why they seemed so much friendlier than any congregation I have ever met. Of course, they are Minnesotans, and by nature honestly congenial. Yet, I feel the difference was that I had never needed fellowship so much as I did that day. Barbie and I were separated from our identities. We had always been the couple who served others. Somehow those we met that day sensed our isolation and welcomed us with open arms. The feeling of love was overwhelming. I wish I had better words.

Overwhelmed is the biggest word I can use since no other captures what I felt then and feel now. Was this kindness an answer to the prayers that so many had offered for us? And why were so many people praying for me? Who was I to deserve such love? I am just a person like any other.

The bishop welcomed us after the meeting and asked the high priest group leader to see to our needs while in Rochester. We were home here and they were family.

Early Monday morning the process began again. It seemed endless, the tests required. Afterwards we would go back to the Residence Inn and rest, write and talk with our children. It was very difficult not knowing when we might return to California. Samuel and Michelle's wedding was only three weeks away. We brainstormed on how we might fly to San Diego and back if we were still in Minnesota. If I were to get on the transplant list at Mayo Clinic, I had heard that it could take months to get a transplant. Where would we live until then? How would we survive in the winter? When would we see our girls again?

The doctors and technicians endlessly took pieces of me for analysis: testing and measurements, examinations and questions. Yet, very little information was coming back in my direction. My illness took large chunks of me without pity or reason: my health, my strength, my job, my family, my church service and associations. All that was left of my broken existence and broken body was Barbie, always at my side, my indefatigable hope, and the faith I felt from the countless prayers of others. Barbie stayed positive, but I could feel her concern. We would go on walks looking for a grocery store and try to divert our attention to daily tasks in our rented reality, such as cooking, cleaning and planning. The mind, in idle, fills itself with worry of what may be, or not be.

Space, a ceiling, a floor, four walls, but no room. No room to run. No room to work. No room to dream. I was ever moving from room to room, none of which were my own. From womb to room we connect these six planes at right angles to feel safe, protected from the world around us. We call it 'our space' and decorate it with hopes and memories, dreams and passions. Then we are dismantled, who we were becomes dismembered and the walls give way to other spaces; foreign rooms with unfamiliar faces. Still composed of four walls, but decorated with utility. Smiles hiding concern, pleasantries uttered with salutations returned. The unknown remains through the unhinged door that separates the rooms. Home is where the heart is, but where is my heart? In my chest? No, he is at the desk, checking out. My heart must find a rented space until I find a new home. Barbie takes my heart and gives it space, a room within hers, to protect me until I am new again; whole again.

CHAPTER 19

Tuesday, I finally met Dr. Brooks Edwards. I liked him immediately. There was something about his calm, friendly demeanor that conveyed a sense that he truly seemed interested in me as a person and not just a specimen. He is the transplant cardiologist, the same role as Drs. Weisshaar, Nishime and Parekh. They are the ones who take care of you before and after the cardiac transplant surgeon does the deed. He had reviewed all of my tests up to that point and seemed pleased with what he saw. In him I saw the first glimmer of hope among the many specialists that I had seen. It was clear immediately that he would be the one to shepherd me through the chaos that surrounded me. He asked many questions, not just the usual medical ones, but also about our lives, our family and our past. He was sizing me up; weighing me. Could I be admitted to the select few with a fatal disease able to earn a heart transplant?

On Wednesday, they sent me across town to have a cardiac catheterization. When you study the right side of the heart, you place the catheter through a vein and slide it into the right ventricle to measure pressures or take biopsies. I had already had this done by Dr. Weisshaar three weeks prior. It was simple. She numbed my neck, stuck a needle into the right jugular vein and slid a cup biopsy forceps into my heart and grabbed a few pieces. This was followed by a pressure monitoring catheter and Viola! Done in 20 minutes. At the Mayo Clinic they went through my femoral vein. They sedated me and, once in my heart, checked pressures. Additionally, they challenged my heart by giving some drugs to see the effect on heart and pulmonary artery pressures. When they did this, I felt very strange as my blood pressure dropped precipitously. Since I was partially awake, I felt the urgent need to inform them, but of course, they could see it dropping. My heart had lost its ability to compensate.

Plumbing is like electricity. Flow=Pressure/Resistance. (Amps=Volts/Ohms). When my resistance dropped, the flow could not compensate to keep my pressure up and I felt it. It felt like reality was folding in on itself. Everything around me was rapidly flying further away. When I spoke to alert them to my change, I was speaking as if through a small tube, slowly. The word 'ephedrine' filtered down into my brain and between 20 seconds and 16 days later my brain emerged from the rabbit hole, as if they had infused some magic mushroom to make me bigger. My pressure now rose to awake my reality. Their nonchalant tones continued to drone. I was merely a spectator of my own body. The nurse dutifully reported my pressures to the doctor, who made no comment. A few minutes later I was humming as they pulled out the tube from my groin and whisked me off to recovery. The technicians moved on to the next warm body.

For some reason, I was annoyed that day. Why did they sedate me? Why did they go through my groin instead of my neck? And why did I have to lie there a prisoner for so long to 'recover'? For whatever reason, I was very impatient and could not wait to leave the building. Nobody ever came by to tell us what they had found. Finally, a nurse came in and said, "You can get dressed and go." So I did.

That night I went on the internet to do some research on amyloidosis and heart transplants. A national registry compiles all of the data on organ transplants for each institution and OPO. The United States is divided into regional organ procurement organizations (OPO). These were created to ensure fairness in the way that patients receive the scarce commodity of organs. A few days before, Barbie had read a very disturbing statistic. The majority of patients waiting for heart transplants die before they can get one. This worried her. I decided to dig deeper. Which institutions did transplants on amyloidosis patients and how many? Of course, at the top of the list were the Mayo Clinic and Boston University, the two centers currently specializing in amyloidosis. What about UCSF and Stanford? Finally I found the page that listed each institution. It showed how many were on the list for each organ: kidney, pancreas, lung, liver and heart. There was a long wait. Stanford had done only one heart transplant for amyloidosis in the last twenty years, (as far back as the records had been kept.) But I knew who that patient probably was.

The Monday before leaving for the Mayo Clinic, Dr. Parekh had told me about a patient named Leo. In 2004 he too had gone to the Mayo Clinic for evaluation, and ultimately had received a heart transplant at Stanford. This gave me hope. However, I also knew that his condition had been familial amyloidosis, not primary amyloidosis like me. The prognosis for his had been quite different. Familial amyloidosis causes tissue damage much more slowly than primary, since it is a bad protein made only in the liver that ultimately damages the heart. Dr. Parekh had suggested that I talk with Leo, but in the rush of leaving, I had not done it. Now I thought about him. I wanted to talk to him and find out how he was doing. Was he still sick? 2004 was four years ago, and he was still alive. You accept hope wherever you can find it. Sometimes it comes in a funny quip or an aside from your doctor; sometimes in the things that they do not say.

Wednesday, July 23, 2008
Appointment after appointment

I thought it might be interesting to some of you to have a glimpse of Kevin's visits at Mayo. As of today, we have been doing this for a week now and have three more days of testing or visits, including today. Here is a list of some of most of his appointments.
* Labs, labs, and more labs (I will leave out the details)
* Electrocardiogram
* Chest X-ray
* Heart transplant consultation
* Echocardiogram
* Exercise Test
* Skeleton Bone Survey
* Renal Function Test

* Body CT
* Arterial Blood Gas
* Pulmonary Function w/dilator
* Bone Densitometry
* Ultrasound of the Abdomen
* Oral & Maxillofacial Surgeon
* Social Worker
* a Walk test
* two Cardiologists from the transplant team
* Infectious Disease Visit
* Upper Endoscopy
* Pulmonary & Critical Care

Right now he is having a Cardiac Cath. It will be done with local anesthesia, unlike yesterday when he was sedated for his Upper Endoscopy. I have never seen him sedated before. Kind of strange to see him without all his mental capacities working. Sometimes it was a little funny. When he finally felt better after a LONG nap, he asked, "Where did the wheelchair come from?" I chuckled. I had pushed him from the 9th floor of the Gonda building and two blocks to our room. He was quite embarrassed, not because he did not remember, but because I had wheeled him. :)

Tomorrow and Friday he will see: Psychiatry, Dietician, Hematology, another heart transplant evaluation discussion, meet with the transplant surgeon, Otorhinolaryngology, Neurology, and last (deep breath), Esophagus X-ray.

Next Monday will be the BIG DAY when the entire team meets and decides how to proceed. We have heard many options and will be anticipating the call that afternoon.

Love you all and love your comments,

Barbie

Thursday was when we first met Dr. Lacy. Martha Q. Lacy, M.D. (I wondered what the "Q" stood for but did not ask.) She is a hematologist/oncologist who specializes in amyloidosis. I knew immediately that she and Dr. Edwards were the decision makers in my case. I did not know anything else about her. I did not know that she had been studying amyloidosis for years and had written extensively on the subject. I also did not know that as we spoke, she had a paper in press that would be published in two weeks describing the Mayo clinic experience over that last eleven years with the heart transplant and subsequent autologous stem-cell transplant that would soon play a life and death decision for me. All I saw was a reserved but pleasant woman of indeterminate age. She appeared young for someone who had accomplished so much. Among the many things we discussed, one was the timing of treatment. I asked if I should have a stem-cell transplant prior to a heart transplant and she flatly said that my current heart would not survive the fluid shifts associated with that much chemotherapy. Bone marrow transplants come in two flavors. A heteralogous transplant, is one in which the bone marrow comes from a matched donor, usually a family member. Siblings are more likely to match than a parent because their chromosomes are likely closer to the patient's full set than the parents', who each share only half of his or her genetic material. An autologous transplant is one in which the patient donates his or her own stem cells before the bone marrow is annihilated by high dose chemotherapy. Both flavors of chemotherapy leave the patient without white cells, red cells or platelets. It is a big hit to the body and requires a good heart to recover.

No, she said that I would need a new heart first. We also discussed the possibility of undergoing low dose chemotherapy prior to the transplant. Both options had their disadvantages. It was clear that I needed a heart first and soon. She determined not to start me on any chemotherapy at that point. To make her final determination, I would need another bone marrow biopsy. She kept referring to the labeling index. I did not know what that meant. I just had to trust her. I did.

Soon we returned to the cardiac transplant clinic. Again, we briefly met with Dr. Edwards who summarized our progress thus far. He left us in his office to wait to speak with the cardiac transplant surgeon. Our appointment was at 3:00 P.M. We waited, and waited. About every 45 minutes someone would pop his or her head in to ask us to be patient. After 5:00 P.M. no one came in any more. Barbie and I had run out of things to say and sat quietly. Periodically I would stand and gaze out the window from the 9th floor toward the setting sun. To the west, Minnesota stretched out onto the horizon. We were in the tallest building visible. Beyond the trees, beyond the horizon, was home. I thought about our children. Jeremy was newly married to Alexandria and in Utah studying to prepare to go to medical school. Samuel was engaged to Michelle, the wedding date only 3 weeks away while he labored with advanced calculus and physics to prepare for a career in mechanical engineering. Rebecca and Caitlin were even further around the curve of the earth, Rebecca engaged to be married to Corey in October. Fortunately, she was at home in Lincoln with Caitlin. And Caitlin, the 'baby.' Even at fifteen she still seemed so young. How was she doing without us? I wondered when we would be together again. If the Mayo Clinic accepted me as a candidate and listed me, we might be here for a long while. Dr. Edwards had said that the wait could be up to six months. Once done, we would need to stay locally for at least three months before returning home. I wished that I could see beyond that horizon.

The door opened and Dr. Daly walked in. He was a tall imposing figure and, as a surgeon at the end of a busy day might well do, he dispensed with the pleasantries. He simply cut to the core of the issue. "Having a heart transplant will completely change your life. You will never return to a normal life. To survive, you will have to take anti-rejection drugs every day forever." If he was trying to scare me, he failed. The three of us in the room all knew the alternative was unacceptable. This was my informed consent. He soon left. As he did I searched the room for a 'bedside' to see if he had left any 'manner' behind.

As Barbie and I exited the examination room, we found the clinic empty. In Dr. Daly's abrupt manner, we reflected, he had given us both a very valuable warning. We should not ever expect things to return to normal. This brutal honesty is essential in the healing process. No sugar coating, no euphemisms; just the truth. However, he never intimated that I might not get a new heart. Was that an oversight or an endorsement? We walked back to the hotel in the twilight. At least with Skype, we could feel like we were with our children. We both needed to be somewhere else that night.

Thursday, July 24, 2008
A long week

Today we met with the psychiatrist, nutritionist, oncologist and the heart transplant surgeon. The studies are almost completed. I have another bone marrow biopsy tomorrow because the Mayo Clinic does some special studies on it for amyloidosis.

The final decision is made on Monday at the selection conference; however, the surgical director, the medical director and the oncologist feel that I would be a good candidate for a heart transplant. The chief concern in performing a heart transplant in amyloid patients is that even though the transplant would be successful, if the amyloid has already attacked multiple organs, there might be little benefit from the transplant. It appears that my other organs are doing pretty well and show minimal effects.

Dr. Edwards, the medical director, wants to speak with the transplant team at Stanford to possibly get me listed there as well. In that situation, I would be listed at both the Mayo Clinic and Stanford, which could increase my chances of getting a heart. In addition, I would be able to return to California to wait. This

*would be such a blessing. I really do miss my family
and would like to be there for the upcoming weddings.
I hope it all works out.*

Kevin

Friday, July 25, 2008
What matters most

I just went surfing around on the internet about heart transplants, from being listed, to recovery and life changes. I found it helpful and informative, but also a bit overwhelming reading the extremely long list of risks. While I don't believe Kevin will get all of them, there is a chance he may develop a few. I needed to have a picture in my mind of what he will look like in intensive care right after surgery. I have a better idea now and will feel better prepared. It's a wonder how anyone seriously ill survives the enormous stress the body is under during any major open surgery. I am even more amazed and grateful to those who have spent their adult lives researching and studied how the body reacts to medication and trauma and discovering ways to balance the body to its natural state. I truly believe it is a combination of medicine, patient will, and God that heals. All play a vital role in this process.

Having been married to a surgeon for 26 years (in two weeks), I have heard many stories of miracles, healing, death, and pain. At times I feel sympathy for the patient and family, while never knowing who they are. I am happy for those who survive and sad for those who "give up" before they have gone. Life is such a fragile thing; at any moment it can be taken from us. This is why at this point in our lives we are at *peace. I don't feel sorry for Kevin and I don't feel sorry for myself. We face this new challenge knowing there is something we are to learn. I have already changed and will never be exactly as I was prior to this diagnosis. I do not get worried about the "little things" anymore and what gets done, gets done and what does not, does not. I find I do not need "things" right now and also realize since we have been living in a studio room that I don't need much. Though I would not go too far - a computer and a phone are essentials!*

What I have always known, but have truly come to understand is that what matters most are relationships.

Barbie

The weekend was wonderful. Each new day added upon the hope that we had. It just might be possible to return home to our family. The anticipation was electric. Monday we would get the answer. We toured Minnesota, the Mississippi river and Wisconsin on Saturday. Sunday we went to church and the members treated us as if we had been there forever. We were family. We were invited to a gathering that evening at a member's home. Like the east coast and Midwest, there are no fences between houses. This is very un-Californian. As we sat in their backyard, we gazed across vistas of cornfields that filled the valley with the green hills beyond. I felt a calming peace as I nibbled on sweets. Dozens of children were playing on the hill below us as new friends talked and laughed and intermingled. There was an easiness to all of this. People would come up to Barbie and me and ask again about why were we here; about our family and in each case, offer help or prayers or both. It all felt so right. As we left there were hugs from strangers that felt so familiar.

Monday was a day of waiting. I remember in college a girl that I had dated intermittently was walking with me across campus. At one point in the conversation she exclaimed, "Sometimes it seems like the only thing that you truly get excited about are grades." That accusation really stung. I was abruptly forced to focus on a fault that I had theretofore considered a positive attribute. I have since learned how important it is not to overlook people on my way to a goal. That being said, I waited for the results of the bone marrow biopsy and the decision of the transplant committee with the same exhilaration that I would have had anticipating a grade in organic chemistry. It felt as if my life depended on it. Oh, wait: it did.

CHAPTER 20

D r. Lacy was late that day; very late. Finally we were ushered into another non-descript exam room and waited some more. She walked in, sat down and began reporting the results of the bone marrow biopsy. Bottom line; the labeling index was zero. I was still not exactly sure what that meant, but I knew it was good. This was the green light. It either meant that my plasma cell levels were low or that I did not have multiple myeloma. We discussed timing to treat the amyloidosis. There are three chemo-therapy drugs that can help manage the disease: Melphalan, Velcade and Revlimid. Each has specific side effects, some of which would have complicated the heart transplant and some of which would have affected the harvesting of stem cells for the bone marrow transplant. In the end she recommended holding off and hoping for a heart transplant in the very near future.

We thanked her and left. We walked fast (when I run I fall down) to Dr. Edwards office, since we were a bit late. He was smiling. He sat back casually in his chair and said that I had passed. I would be entered on the Mayo Clinic heart transplant list as a level 2. He explained again that the wait could be up to six months. I could wait at home, but if a heart became available, I would urgently need to return by air ambulance. He then paused and thought for a minute. "How would you feel about getting a heart transplant back in California?" he asked. "I would definitely want that, if it were possible." I responded, but I explained that Stanford did not do transplants on those with primary amyloidosis. "Let's see about that," he responded. And he picked up the phone. He asked to speak with a particular cardiologist that he knew there. The cardiologist was not available. Soon he was speaking to the transplant cardiologist on-call, Dr. Ronald Witteles. "Is that right?" "You are?" "Well, he has mostly cardiac involvement and his labeling index is zero, otherwise he is quite healthy." As I wondered at the conversation on the other side of the country, I begin to have a feeling similar to the one I used to get in college as I approached the grade postings on the wall near the professor's door. Next to my social security number I would find a raw score and percentage. I got an "A"; time to move on to the next class. This felt the same.

Dr. Brooks Edwards

As he hung up the phone he turned to us. "I just spoke with Dr. Witteles at Stanford. He is a young faculty member there. It turns out that he has a special interest in amyloidosis and is trying to start a program there for patients like you." We were speechless. He continued. "I will send all of your charts to them. They have a transplant committee meeting this Friday where they will review your case." He added, "If they do not accept you there, I would like you to return here to be admitted and we would start you on pressors to keep your heart going until you get a transplant." Again, I was surprised to hear that I was considered sick enough to need hospital admission. This thought was brief, since a moment later he said something that will echo in my heart as long as it continues to beat. After a pause he looked me directly in the eyes and said, "I just have a feeling that you are going to do well." And then he smiled. He gave me hope. Just as Andy Dufresne in "The Shawshank Redemption" emerges from a 500 yard tunnel of foul darkness to look up at the cleansing rain, so too I felt a kind of freedom in his words; no not just the words, the lightness in his face as he said it. He truly meant it. Was this true intuition based on his experience in comparing me to other patients that proceeded? Or were these just kind words of hope? It felt like the former. We thanked him, hugged him and left the clinic for the last time.

What happened next was one of those pivotal moments that occur in one's life and forever change its course. Usually, in the moment, the event seems small. However, in retrospect, one sees the true magnitude. As we exited the building there was a car waiting for us on the corner. Inside was a friend whom we had just met, a member of the Rochester 3rd ward. He was taking us to his home where his wife had prepared a meal for us to share with his family. Barbie got into the back seat as I sat in the front. As soon as I closed the door my cell phone rang. "This is Dr. Witteles from Stanford. Do you have a minute?" My jaw dropped. Dr. Edwards must have given him my number. He began to describe the new amyloidosis clinic that he was working to develop. It would be multidisciplinary, with a cardiologist, hematologist, bone marrow specialists, etc... He then asked me how I was doing. I felt a sudden need to convince him that I was the best candidate ever to be considered for a heart transplant.

I recounted what Dr. Lacy and Dr. Edwards had told me only minutes before. "My kidneys are working great." That seemed to be one of the code words. Finally, he finished with: "We will present your case on Friday and let you know." I thanked him profusely and said goodbye. As I hung up I turned to Barbie. She was on the phone with the travel office at Kaiser. As I mouthed the words, trying to let my non-verbal facial expressions denote incredulity, "That was Dr. Witteles! From Stanford!!" She smiled broadly as she responded to her conversation, "Yes, tomorrow would be wonderful. What time? As early as possible." Within the space of five minutes everything had changed due to the kindness of compassionate strangers.

I would later refer to this as "The Path of God." I believe that God has a path, specifically for us, which if followed, will lead us to places that we never thought possible. These are often deviations from the path in life that we had planned for ourselves. Often, there is a sense of risk in these unknown uncharted waters. However, God often will provide two things to help us in choosing to follow His path rather than our own. First, he may send a person to suggest or offer an opportunity that we may not have considered or had hoped for, but did not know how to achieve. This person could be a friend, parent, sibling or mentor. However, occasionally the person is a complete stranger: someone, recently met, whose kindness it would be to open a door, hold up a lantern and beckon us on. I have come to see these individuals who have helped shape my life as compassionate strangers. That have no particular reason to help me, but somehow our paths cross at critical junctures in my life. They signal and sometimes facilitate the necessary course correction, and then we part. Only later do I realize the full import of their momentary influence.

The second guide that God provides is the still, small voice that confirms to our souls that "this is right." It just feels right. Many individuals choose not to follow that feeling because of fear. Sometimes it is fear of moving from their position of comfort and safety. They fail to see beyond next Thursday and never lift their gazes up to the horizon to imagine themselves beyond it. These small momentary alterations of course ultimately result in magnificent effects upon our lives. Yet we only truly see them in retrospect. Because of compassionate strangers, I decided to attend medical school in California. I chose to join the faculty at Yale University for 11 years. I met Dr. Ralph Clayman, (my mentor in St. Louis during my fellowship,) who opened up the world to me. I met and married Barbie. And now, there was the chance to wait for and receive a new life-saving heart close to home, close to my daughters and to Barbie.

As we drove to our new friend's house, he spoke of how he would make arrangements for a place to live for us in Rochester if we needed to return and live here. Again, I silently wondered, "why are people so nice to us?" I am sure that by their nature they would be nice to everyone. I was not special. It was just that for the first time in my life I was the weak one. I could not do it on my own. I felt so grateful that I had become ill so that I could witness this goodness from a new perspective.

Wednesday, July 30, 2008
Happy to be here

Barbie and I arrived home last night. I felt like Dorothy from The Wizard of Oz: "there's no place like home." All went well in Minnesota and I was officially listed on the Mayo Clinic heart transplant list. On Friday my case will be presented to the selection committee at Stanford for possible listing. Stanford has only done one transplant on an amyloid patient since their program began. He was done in 2004, and like myself, was a Kaiser patient sent back from the Mayo Clinic as a 'good' candidate. I spoke with him on the phone and he is doing great. He wants to visit me in the hospital when I get my transplant. That would be nice. He invited me to the Amyloid support group that they have at Stanford.

It was so wonderful to see and hug my daughters. When you have a round trip ticket, you always know when you are coming home. Being in Rochester without a return itinerary was emotionally hard. Today, I just sit in the backyard and enjoy the view. California is beautiful.

More to come.

Kevin

Wednesday, July 30, 2008
We wait yet again

We've been home for 27 hours now. I have unpacked, done laundry, found a dress for Samuel's wedding, found dresses for the girls to wear to Sam's wedding, relaxed in the hot tub and best of all, ate Thai food for dinner with good friends, my mom and Rebecca. Some of those items Kevin joined me in - for some reason he did not join me in the shopping! Can't figure out why. While we are home, I have felt the urgency to do as much as I can to prepare for the upcoming weddings. Rebecca is looking at invitations, flowers, and cake. The other BIG things are already done. There are still a few technical details to complete for Samuel & Michelle's wedding. All the other major details were done by Michelle and her family.

We have spent the last 2 months living in the world of 'if this - then that' and we are still here. We've spent a lot of time waiting for the next results or the next plan. Now we wait again for Stanford's decision and then maybe their next plan. And then we wait for a heart. Someone out there has made the decision to be a donor - and that same someone will be a match for Kevin. That is an immense thought. We spoke to the Social Worker at Mayo about this very subject. The realization that someone needed to die in order to give life to Kevin seemed tragic. She reminded us that the donor and their family, in their sorrow, feel at peace in returning life to another. Another great blessing.

Be a donor and donate blood.

Barbie

Part 3

IN SEARCH OF A HEART

CHAPTER 21

To see my daughters was to feel reality anew. We were home. Lydia, Barbie's mom, was there as well. She had left her husband, Lloyd, in Utah so that she could be with Caitlin and Rebecca while we were gone. They could have survived on their own, but given the circumstances it was wonderful to have her there. Rebecca was engaged and working as a dental assistant. (She had taken over Barbie's position at Dr. Boatman's office when we left for Minnesota.) Grandma was cook and chauffer.

We waited, knowing that Friday would bring a thumbs up or a thumbs down. Would Stanford change their policy for me? I knew I had two advocates on my side: Dr. Weisshaar and Dr. Witteles. Having sat on numerous hospital committees in my career, I knew the odds. At Yale, I had been the chairman of the OR formulary committee for many years. It had been my job to control costs. I had served as a gate-keeper to the ever-increasing tide of new technology that continually bled our budget. "Just because it is new, is it better?" I would ask. Recalling my own experiences as cost controller, I could imagine the dissent on the committee reviewing my case: "With so many patients in need of a heart transplant, why give it to someone with an incurable disease?"

This was the first time I would ask myself the question, "How long will I need to live after a heart transplant to justify the cost?" I was thinking not only of the monetary cost, but also the costs to society that are inherent when limited resources must be allocated. My merely breathing did not make me more deserving of a transplant than anyone else. A new heart would be a gift which I would then need to earn. "How many years?" I thought. "How many years would

I need to be a contributing member of society to earn such a gift?"
I was afraid that if I died within 18 months of the transplant Stanford
might think twice before offering one to another amyloidosis patient.
As I thought it over, I decided that three years seemed like a reasonable time. In a strange combination of introspection and calculation,
I determined that if I lived at least three useful years then I might
help to justify such a great gift. I hoped that the selection committee
would feel likewise. Some acquaintances mistakenly assumed that
as a physician I might somehow get preferential treatment. I knew
this to be false. Equality reigns in the world of organ transplant in
the United States. Like God, the organ procurement organizations
(OPOs) are no respecter of persons. We are all equal in our need and
in our chances for salvation.

When a patient is accepted to a particular transplant program,
certain rules apply. First, the patient cannot be accepted to two
programs within the same region or organ procurement organization. For instance, I could not be on the list at the Mayo clinic and
University of Minnesota simultaneously. Second, the patient is listed
at a certain status, which determines which list he or she ends up
on. A patient living at home is accorded status 2. Upon admission to
the hospital for the heart condition, he or she is moved to status 1B
after being placed on a continuous infusion of a drug that improves
heart function. One such drug is called dopamine. This drug, also
referred to as an inotrope, improves both heart contractility and
relaxation, ultimately improving cardiac output. A patient is only
admitted if the he or she is experiencing sufficient heart failure to
preclude functioning without this drug support. Finally, if a person's
heart is so damaged that it can no longer sustain life even with the
assistance of inotropes, a left ventricular assist device (LVAD) is
implanted in the aorta to act as a back-up pump until the patient
can receive a new heart. Such a patient would go to the top of the list
as a 1A. When a new heart becomes available, the regional organ
procurement organization will look at the 1A list first. If no suitable
candidate is found, then the organization moves on to the 1B list.
This procedure assures that each available organ goes to the person

with the greatest or most acute need. A person may begin as a status 2 and then deteriorate requiring hospital admission, and thus move up to a 1B.

Dr. Edwards mentioned that some patients on continuous infusion of inotropes like dopamine can leave the hospital on occasion for a period of time by using a portable infusion pump, similar to an insulin pump. Of course, my immediate thought was San Diego and Samuel and Michelle's wedding. Back when we were still in Rochester, during one phone conversation I had mentioned this to Dr. Weisshaar. At the time, she confirmed that she had treated some patients in a similar fashion as outpatients with pumps while they waited for a heart.

This gave me cause for hope. The wedding was now only two weeks away. Even if I was admitted as a 1B, maybe I could fly to San Diego on Friday the 15th and return to the Bay Area just after the reception on the 16th with my 'heart-kicker' pump on my belt. I love a good plan and was determined to make this happen.

Wednesday and Thursday were a blur. I assumed I would be home for a while and tried to get back to some semblance of a routine. Thursday night, we went to dinner at the Orchid Thai with our friends, Don and Maria Boatman. Maria's parents were in town, and we wanted to get out for the evening. I was feeling quite horrible, but did my best to hide it. I failed. Maria's mother looked very concerned. She had not seen me in a while, and my physical appearance was more obviously changed for her than for my family and others who saw me often. My face was gaunt and thin. My skin was an ashen tan-gray. My hair was a matching gray and my thin, fat-free skin hung over my cheek bones and jaw like a man in late stage starvation. Usually I cannot get enough crispy calamari salad, but that night it seemed such a labor to chew one piece of lettuce. I smiled and felt genuinely happy to be with friends, but when we got home I collapsed into bed, propped up with my usual two pillows to make sleeping easier. I slept in fits and starts. Sometimes I would lie there in the dark and listen to my venous pulse.

Months earlier I had discovered this. A venous pulse can rarely be heard or felt. It differs from the more common arterial pulse which has two phases; systole and diastole, or the contraction and the relaxation phase. A venous pulse, I remembered from medical school, was triphasic. (I did not remember why.) I could feel my venous pulse pulsating in my neck. It had a machine like sound. If I sat up, it went away; lying completely flat turned up the volume. I had known for almost a year that I had right heart dysfunction and assumed that I could hear my pulse like this because of an abnormally high venous pressure. (It is difficult to passively push blood into a hard heart.) In the past I had known it was not a good sign. Now I knew the cause and it was just red noise to rock me to sleep.

Friday morning arrived. Barbie had left for a hair appointment, Rebecca was at work and Caitlin was across the street baby-sitting. I was having a nice conversation with Lydia. My feet were up on the coffee table, as they always were to keep the edema down. The phone rang.

"Kevin, this is Dr. Weisshaar. After a lively discussion it was decided to accept you to be listed at Stanford for a heart transplant." My tongue and vocal cords seemed to be in a different room as I mumbled, "That's great." I was processing so many questions. What should I ask first? Remembering one of the last things that Dr. Edwards had told me, I asked, "Do I need to be admitted to the hospital and be put on pressors?" She responded, "That depends on your symptoms." She then asked a series of pointed questions to ascertain the functional status of my heart. How far could I walk and not stop for a breath? Could I sleep flat? How much swelling was in my legs and how high up the calves? What was my weight? Was I eating well? I answered honestly with no particular expectation, one way or the other. Finally, she said, "You need to be admitted." "When?" I responded. Her response shocked me. "Right now. Do you feel well enough to travel by car?" "What?" I thought, "well of course I am well enough to travel. How sick does she think I am?" Aloud, I simply responded, "Yes."

Then I quickly asked the question that had been plaguing me

for weeks. "Dr. Weisshaar," I began, "My son is getting married in two weeks in San Diego. Do you think it would be possible to get a dopamine infusion pump and fly to San Diego on the 15th and just stay one night? I could be back on the 16th, the very next day." "I don't think that is a good idea," she responded. I was quick to argue my case with statistical illogic. "What are the odds," I retorted, "of a heart becoming available on that particular day?" Her more rational response was immediate. There was no judgment or disdain in her voice. "It is your life; do you really want to take that chance?" I knew she was right. My fears were now reality. I would not be able to attend my son's wedding. I knew I needed to make this sacrifice for the chance at having more time with all of my family. I agreed. We both knew she was right. Continuing the conversation, she asked how soon I could be at the hospital. I replied that we would leave as soon as Barbie returned. "Where is she?" asked Dr. Weisshaar. "Can you call her?" Still unwilling to buy into the urgency completely, I responded, "Well, not really, she is at a hair appointment." There was a momentary silence, which I understood well because I too had experience being the doctor weighing what to say in a moment where crisis conflicts with hair appointments. Finally, Dr. Weisshaar simply said, "Try to be here before five. That is when I get off." "We will be there," I promised.

I hung up the phone. Lydia had been sitting silently listening to the conversation. I looked at her and told her how grateful I was that she was there for us. Then I began to cry. Tears filled her eyes as well as we somberly waited for Barbie to come home.

CHAPTER 22

Friday, August 1, 2008
Stanford said, "Yes!"

This morning around 11 am, Kaiser Santa Clara called to let us know that after a lively discussion at the selection meeting with Stanford, they agreed to put Kevin on the heart transplant list. Once Dr. Weisshaar asked about Kevin's current symptoms, she wanted him to be admitted today. We packed, said our goodbyes again and left. He is now in his room being monitored and on Dopamine to help his heart relax and is now listed as a 1B. Stanford believes he will have a heart transplant within the next few weeks. It is a known fact now that he will not be able to leave for Samuel's wedding. Samuel is understanding and wants what's best for his Dad. We've come up with a video phone chat so Kevin will be able to sort of be present. At this point, he's not even allowed to leave the cardiac unit where there is no wi-fi. He says he will try to sneak out to write a quick blog, if not, I will do a copy and paste. He is comfortable in his bed and forced to rest, thank goodness. He was tiring out more and slowing down.

Barbie

I drove the two and a half hours from Lincoln to Santa Clara. Even sick, I always drive. Barbie knows I am not a good passenger. I am positive that there are numerous metaphors and personality traits couched in the statement: "I am not a good passenger" I will leave that to the reader. Suffice it to say, I like driving and as I lost control of my life piece by piece, this was one thing that I still could do; driving is something that like cooking, oh yeah and surgery, relaxes me. I had explained to Barbie that I definitely would not be able to leave to go to the wedding. We made a promise to each other that no matter what happened, she would be there for both of us.

I parked the car and gave Barbie the keys. We walked to the second floor of the hospital and went to the nurses' station. I was escorted to my room, where I removed my clothing and put on my new uniform, which consisted of the front half of an ugly dress with a pocket in front. Five wires of different colors were glued to my chest and plugged into a plastic device the size of an old 8-track tape cassette. They stuck the device in the pocket and put me in the bed. On the wall opposite me was a clock. It was strategically placed in my direct line of sight to torture me. I began to wait.

Some of the chemicals that we doctors put into the body are rather caustic. Depending on the properties of these drugs, high concentrations would destroy the local tissue as soon as contact was made upon leaving the I.V. To more rapidly mix and dilute this life-saving elixir, it needs to be dumped into a vein with high volume and high flow to immediately mix it just before it enters the heart for total body distribution. Peripheral veins such as in the hand, forearm or elbow have slower flow, insufficient for rapid mixing. The superior vena cava, just before it enters the heart, is an ideal central vein for such a task. The challenge is getting a catheter tip in this location. When I trained as a medical student and surgery resident, we would place a needle under the clavicle into the subclavian vein to allow access to the superior vena cava. Alternatively, anesthesiologists (and cardiologists) prefer to use the internal jugular vein in the neck.

Since my time in medical school, doctors have been utilizing another alternative. Below the biceps muscle in the upper arm runs the brachial vein. Through this a Peripheral Intravenous Central Catheter (PICC) can be inserted. The long plastic tube enters through the skin there, with the tip ending in the superior vena cava. The PICC has two separate parallel tubes, or lumens, within the catheter. A continuous infusion of drugs can be dripped through one tube while blood can be withdrawn through the other. This setup avoids the daily needle stick otherwise required for blood tests while providing a stable catheter for drugs that can remain in place for weeks or even months.

Friday afternoon, soon after I arrived, a nurse who specialized in placing PICC lines began the elaborate cleansing ritual to insure an uninfected insertion with perfect tip placement. The process took almost two hours. An hour later, after a chest X-ray confirmed the catheter tip was just above my heart, the dopamine began. At first I felt a mild tingling sensation and flushing in my face. There was a slight pressure in my chest. That was it. I was now attached to an I.V. pole. The pole was taller than I was and followed me everywhere, so Barbie named him Harvey, my invisible protecting "pooka."

Within a day I began to see the results of the combined effects of the dopamine and Lasix. The dopamine made my heart muscle a little more elastic and a lot more contractile. This improved pump sucked more fluid from my lungs, bowels, legs and tissues and sent the water overload to my waiting kidneys, which were primed with Lasix, a potent diuretic. The flood gates were opened. I would fill the urinal so quickly that the nurses could not empty it fast enough. One particularly important job for nurses is recording I's and O's, or in's and out's. One way to ascertain the health of the patient is through their ability to maintain a physiologic balance of what goes in to the body vs. what comes out. I had been out of balance for almost a year. Now, I was rapidly rebalancing. Within a few hours, I would fill the urinal to over a liter, dump it and begin again. I began charting my own urine output on a dry erase board in the room to assist the nursing staff. As a surgeon, and especially as a urologist, this was quite exciting. For the first time in what seemed like forever, I could see my heart and kidneys working harmoniously; within days I could feel the difference. And soon the difference was visible. My belly was disproportionally bloated compared to my gaunt face. This was from edema in my mesentery, bowels and liver. This is what had killed my appetite for so many months and caused pain after eating. Soon the edema started to resolve.

Every morning I was awake at 5:15 AM, excited with the anticipation of being weighed. The nurse would turn on a single small light so as not to awake Barbie, who had set up her roll-away bed in the corner. I would jump on the scale to learn my 24 hour weight loss. I was losing 5-6 lbs a day. Within four days I had lost 20 lbs. I went from 195 lbs to 175. However, on day five I began to feel incredibly weak. I weighed in at 169 lbs, I had reached my dry weight. At this level, all excess water had been pumped out of me and I was finally dehydrated. I told my doctors and they backed off on the Lasix. I was now at my true weight, 175 lbs. This made things easier on my heart; now it did not have to pump against so much pressure backup. My gut, now freed from excessive water weight, began to digest more effectively. My appetite returned, only to find low-salt tepid, rubbery green beans again in my plastic feeding tray.

The dietician, however, was kind to come and offer me whatever I wanted, within reason. I had lost an incredible amount of protein over the past nine months. My muscles had wasted away as my body cannibalized them for calories. The markers of serum albumin and pre-albumin indicated that I had been in a kind of starvation mode. I knew how critical it was when doing major surgery on a patient to have him or her in "positive nitrogen balance," meaning that more protein was going in than what was being metabolized. I needed to bulk up if I was to be healthy for a heart transplant. Salt avoidance was my watchword for a long time; now it was protein intake. Again, I looked at labels. It turns out that the quickest, cheapest way to get protein is to drink milk. Eight ounces of 2% milk has 11 grams of protein (and very little salt.) Most protein shakes have 15 grams. Got Milk?

CHAPTER 23

Tuesday, August 5, 2008
Living out of my car

Walking to the car 4-5 times a day to pick up or return things seems awful and sleeping in a hospital room on a small bed seems uncomfortable but actually it's not so bad. I am plenty warm and walking to the car gives me exercise. I try to use the stairs as much as I can and take a walk every day around the perimeter of the hospital as well. It helps, as we know.

Kevin and I have spent a lot of time together in the past few weeks and crazy enough, we still like each other and honestly still love each other. I'm not tired of him and he's not tired of me. Tomorrow is our 26th anniversary. It will be an anniversary to remember. He feels bad that he cannot get out to get me anything - I responded that I didn't need anything. We are doing well.

Here is what our day is like:
4am vitals
5am weight
5:30 am blood draw
6am usually a visit from someone checking on something
7am vitals again and meds
8am breakfast, 12pm lunch, 5pm dinner
throughout the day, more vitals, meds, and drop ins

He walks laps around telemetry. That is where he's confined. And visits the John often because of all the lasiks (sorry, Lasix - he is not having eye surgery). I think he has lost 10 lbs. of water since we got here.

We spend our day talking and not talking for hours; reading and not reading for hours; sleeping and not sleeping for hours.

All is well,

Barbie

Wednesday, August 6, 2008
Impatient to Inpatient

It was four years ago this week that we left Connecticut. Many have asked why we left and the reasons are varied, but it was a necessary step to get us where we are today. Among these was the distinct feeling that I needed to make a personal change in my life. I sensed that I was becoming increasingly impatient. I was always looking toward the next item on my agenda rather than giving my full attention to the present. I was impatient in meetings at church as well as at work. I tried my best to hide it, but I felt it. Two hallmarks of my personality have been hard-wired into me from a very young age: Economy of Resources and Economy of Time. These attributes have served me well for my entire life. I wish to accomplish as much as I can in the least amount of time and for the minimum amount of cost, whether it be in dollars or effort. Do not think that this would indicate a compromise on excellence; rather it is more of a desire to avoid distractions and waste along the way. However, eventually, I began to feel a gradual slipping into impatience which ultimately would rob the moment of its innate beauty.

The culture at Kaiser was more structured and required that I slow down to carefully regard the relationships and feelings of others. I was surprised to find that I was not as good at this as I thought I was. There is an inverse relationship of how much control you have in your life with how much patience is required. This was a beginning. The same occurred at church. Clearly, this was a life lesson that was critical for me to learn. But, it was not easy. The first year was very difficult for me. But it was a necessary preparation for what was to come.

Two years ago my symptoms of weakness became apparent, but were not so significant that they were obvious. I continued life as normal, but always with the thought questioning what was happening to me. Not ever wanting to be seen as weak, I kept this mostly to myself, but Barbie knew. Then things worsened.

It has been six weeks since we shared the news of my condition with others. The response was immediate and overwhelming. I have always believed that I am not entitled to anything; that everything I receive in life is either earned or it is a gift. Since I never expect anything from anyone, I am never disappointed. But in a way, I do err. I do need other people. I realized this as the words of encouragement and prayers of concern filled my life. I have never experienced this before. I feel gratitude all of the time to everyone who is helping me.

I am now completely reliant on everyone else.

Dina, my medical assistant is working hard to help my patients get follow up, while my partners have all come together to take care of my patients. My responsibilities at church are fulfilled by my brethren there. Barbie does everything else. The kids are doing great and take care of home. I miss them.

My life is confined to my hospital room and the telemetry unit at Kaiser, Santa Clara. For activity, I walk 5 laps three times a day. I counted the steps and 5 laps is a half mile. I have two constant companions: the I.V. pole on which drips a solution of Dopamine that keeps my heart physically strong, and Barbie, who keeps my heart spiritually strong. My love for her is immeasurable. I could not do this without her. Last of all is the wait. We have no idea how long we will be here. The endpoint is unknowable. There is no economy of time. But time now, means something very different to me.

My patience today is an investment. I need to buy more time. So many others have stepped in to carry my responsibilities while I commit my heart and soul to this goal. And yet, all I can do is be patient and submit to my doctors and to God. My life is in their hands. I cannot imagine being in a better place, especially with Barbie at my side.

If God wanted to teach me patience, I cannot imagine a better path than the one that I am on.

I am so fortunate.

Kevin

Thursday, August 7, 2008
Life Decisions

I found in my life that the most difficult decisions to make are those that are between two goods. Every day I am here with Kevin is closer to the time that I need to leave him for Samuel's wedding. I would not miss his wedding; I couldn't miss his wedding. And yet, I am also struggling with leaving Kevin. I know Kevin will be fine and I know that if a heart is available while I *am away, he will be in good hands. Of course, I wish we both could be with Sam & Michelle, but going without him is starting to feel heavy on me. A good cry always does one well. We cannot be "strong" all the time; we were given opposition for a reason. I am not leaving until next Tuesday night and then driving to San Diego Wednesday morning. It just hit me this morning that it will be here soon. I will enjoy being with our family again and seeing Jeremy & Alexandria and Samuel & Michelle. I look forward to also being with friends who will join us. I guess I'm feeling that if I address my feelings now that my flood gates will be under control at the wedding. I do not want to spoil something beautiful. Funny thing is that I do feel strong most of the time and that last time I cried was on Friday when we arrived at Kaiser Santa Clara. I felt much better after (crying in my car). And I am starting to feel better now as I am rambling. I know a lot of people are reading this blog and as a usually private person, I am not worried at all who reads this. We feel fortunate to have this means of communication to release and inform.*

Thank you to everyone for your continued support.

Barbie

Even as an inpatient, I could not help trying to follow a schedule. Part of that schedule was determined by my doctors and nurses. However, I had a lot of free time to fill. My options were limited. The telemetry device attached to my chest had a limited range. I could not leave the cardiac care nursing unit. The double door linking the unit to the rest of the hospital had a sign above it with a warning: "No telemetry patients beyond this point." On my walks around the unit I would look at that sign and imagine an invisible force field that would discharge a powerful shock if I attempted crossing that arbitrary line, and feel somewhat resentful of my confinement. But I had committed myself to obeying my doctors' orders. I did not cross.

Before I discovered I had internet access in my room, I would use the computer at the unused nurses' stations just outside my room. To add some legitimacy to my accessing a hospital computer, I would affix my hospital ID to my gown. I did receive some strange looks as a passer-by would look at me behind the counter and then look down and see my name badge,

Kevin R Anderson, M.D.
Roseville
Chief of Urology

Since I was still chief of the department, I had administrative issues to resolve. I was late on approving timesheets for July. There were also some member service questions needing resolution. Ultimately, a very serious and official looking nurse, whom I had not seen before, came by. Under her name was an official appellation:

Charge Nurse

She was not smiling. "You are not supposed to be using this computer" she curtly informed me. I explained that I was the chief of urology in Roseville and that I just had a few administrative issues to complete. She countered with the dreaded, "We have a mock 'joint commission' survey today and you cannot be sitting there." Then she softened a bit and offered, "Well, if you wait until 3:00, I can let you into the shift nurses office and you can work there." I thanked her, apologized, and dutifully went back to my room. Later that day I decided to explore the CAT-5 outlets on the wall behind my bed. There were four, each a different color. When I plugged into the blue one my computer suddenly indicated internet access. I was now just slightly freed from my cell as I connected to the outside world from the comfort of my hospital bed.

Friday, August 8, 2008
Amyloidosis

I have found a way to get Internet access in my room. I feel like I can step outside now, at least into the virtual world. I am feeling well. The medication, dopamine, has really improved my heart function. The loss of that extra fluid has greatly improved my lungs and my abdominal organs. I actually feel quite normal. Many of the symptoms that concerned me as possibly secondary to amyloidosis were actually due to fluid retention.

Amyloidosis is a strange disease. It begins in plasma cells. They originate in the bone marrow and circulate through the body. They sense foreign proteins, (such as viruses and bacteria) and produce specific antibodies to fight off infection. Amyloidosis begins when a renegade plasma cell begins producing a faulty antibody protein that does not break down. I guess you could call these cells 'crazy' as it is referred to as a plasma-cell dyscrasia. It is not a cancer because the abnormality is not in the 'immortality" of the cell but rather the cell product. These proteins do not form or fold correctly and pile up in the body. They then get stuck in tissues in various locations; in my case the heart muscle.

This makes my heart muscle stiff and the heart then cannot relax well in between beats. The end result is that there is little time to fill up the heart ventricles so less blood is pumped per beat. What I feel is that any attempt to do any activity requiring greater blood flow is met with an immediate sensation of no energy. It feels like the battery died. Running, walking up stairs, bending over to pick something up all result in immediate fatigue and dizziness. The technical term for this is restrictive cardiomyopathy. My heart pumps about half of the volume that it should in one minute.

Amyloid can go all over the body and affect the gut, liver, kidneys, salivary glands, lungs etc... I had an extensive work-up at the Mayo Clinic and it appears that while other organs are involved, the most significant is my heart. Normally amyloid patients are not treated with heart transplants because they are either too sick with multiple organ involvement or there is a concern that the new heart will fail if the amyloid continues unchecked. The Mayo Clinic is one of the few places willing to combine heart transplant with amyloidosis treatment such as a bone marrow transplant.

However, because I am relatively healthy, and my other organs are not significantly involved, Stanford has agreed to accept me to their transplant list. I will be only the 2nd transplant at Stanford with amyloidosis and the 1st with AL Amyloidosis.

Once I have a new heart, then I can receive treatment for the amyloidosis. Since this is a rare presentation of a rare disease there is no absolute right protocol for me. As it stands now, I will either get chemotherapy with Melphalan, Steroids and Revlimid or a stem cell transplant. They will follow a relatively new blood marker (Kappa light chain levels) to ascertain my clinical response.

I thought this brief summary of my condition might be helpful to some of those following my progress.

Kevin

On my thrice daily walks I would always pause at the east end of the hallway. There I would stand for a long time and gaze out the window at the hills beyond. The golden yellow would stretch for miles, and I was reminded of the true reason California is called the

"Golden State." Across Homestead Avenue, just beyond the parking lot, was a row of trees. As they swayed in the hot summer breeze they transported me away from the hospital, away from my benevolent prison in space and time. The eternal trees, unaffected by alarms and clocks and deadlines, provided me with solace. Three times a day I would stare at them. Three times a day their colors changed as the earth spun against a fixed sun. I thought of my youth, with summers spent in the hills and later the Sierras. The trees I encountered then were oaks, manzanitas, bay and madrones in Marin County; later I roamed through pines and towering Sequoia. I have always found solace among the trees. Now I placed my hand on the glass that separated me from symbols of a solid foundation. I remembered where this arboreal connection had come from and why just gazing at them gave me peace. I was only seven when I nearly drowned for the first time. It was the solid root of a tree that had saved my life.

To save a life:

The Boy Scout motto is "Be prepared." It was at a Cub Scout day camp where I saved a life for the first time. I was fourteen. I was already an Eagle Scout and was working at the day camp for the summer. After the little ones had gone home one evening, I was down at the lake practicing life-saving skills that I had learned for the required merit badge of the same name. I would carefully coil the 50 foot length of rope over my left arm and then throw with my right, allowing the rope to fly untangled as I aimed for a specific spot on the lake. At the time I did not know why I had been brought to the lake to do this, as if by an unspoken need. I had not practiced this skill since my merit badge training the year before. On this evening, once I felt like I had it mastered I left and went to dinner.

The next day the cub scouts were swimming in the lake. It was a cold morning. We could see mist rising from the lake as the sun came over the trees. I was standing in the same spot on the left bank of the lake where I had been the evening before. Dozens of eight- and nine-year-old boys made noise as they splashed in the frigid waters. Suddenly, I saw a small boy too far from the main beach; he was struggling. He was waving his arms and trying to yell for help when he could arch his neck to get his mouth above water. The life buoy was on my arm in no time, and I pitched it out to the struggling scout. The 12-inch buoy just skimmed the back of his head as it landed a foot behind him. He grabbed the line and I pulled him in. Panting, he explained that the cold water made it hard for him to catch his breath and he panicked. I gave him a towel to dry off and within 10 minutes he was back playing with his friends.

Since then I have had the opportunity to save many lives. What does it mean to save a life? Sometimes it means that someone is in immediate threat of dying within minutes from a major injury. At others, it is removing a cancer and adding years to the person's life. However, there is more than just physical death. There are people who are suffering emotionally and spiritually and feel lost. They also need saving. When I served as a bishop, I felt the solid foundation of my faith in Christ as *my* anchor, rock and root that allowed me to help lift another suffering person. Trees and rocks have always been symbols of solidarity in my life. As now *I* was the weak one swirling in disease and uncertainty, I looked to the trees in my life for saving support.

CHAPTER 24

We had been in the hospital for two Sundays, each one bringing visitors, both family and friends, to cheer us up. The room would be filled with laughter and snacks, contraband from the outside. I spoke with Samuel about the wedding the following week. We decided to set up an internet link during the reception so that I could Skype myself there. I could be a talking head on the table next to the punch bowl. Or they could stick me on a chair in the receiving line and I could give virtual hugs and handshakes.

I had developed a reaction to the dopamine and had severe itching in the groin and under my arms. The site where the PICC line entered my arm was driving me crazy and I could not keep from scratching it. My only relief was to stand in the shower. However, to keep the PICC line dry, I had to wrap my arm in plastic and hold it over my head as the I.V. line draped over the shower door. I learned to warn the nurses monitoring my heart so that they would not frantically burst into the bathroom to see if I was dead since I had disconnected the heart monitor leads in order to bathe.

I wandered the hallways and tried hard not to peer into the other rooms where everyone seemed twice my age. I got to where I could walk pretty fast. Occasionally a nurse would chase me down to ask if I was feeling OK. After I reassured them that I was fine they would report that the monitor had recorded a run on ventricular tachycardia. This is a potentially dangerous rhythm in which the heart ventricle sets the pace. I learned that this is one of the reasons that I could not leave the hospital on a pump. Dopamine causes arrhythmias and many other patients waiting for hearts already had implanted defibrillators such that if they experienced an arrhythmia the defibrillator would fire and send them back to normalcy. It was becoming evident that I was experiencing 'runs' of tachycardia frequently. However, I never felt any symptoms from it.

The nurses on the cardiac unit were generally quite good. I always introduced myself as Kevin. However, soon the word got out that the guy in bed 2200 is a Kaiser surgeon from Roseville. Seasoned nurses just treated me normally. However, a timid new nurse and a cocky older nurse were randomly assigned to me on successive days. Both made mistakes, but for very different reasons. The timid new nurse had the job of drawing blood from my PICC line. After drawing the blood, he needed to flush the line. However, in his nervousness, he flushed the line receiving the slow dopamine drip, thus giving me a sudden bolus of the dopamine that was sitting in the tube. The effect was immediate. My whole body felt a vibratory buzz and my face became flushed as my heart tried to leave my chest prematurely. I immediately noted the error to the nurse and utter devastation and horror filled his face. I calmed him down by telling him that I would be alright, but he raced out of the room searching for the charge nurse. I do not think he was assigned to me after that. He made a mistake because of his lack of experience; he will not likely make it again. I do not blame him. He tried his best.

On the other hand was the cocky nurse. He made it clear to me that even though I was a doctor, he was in charge. He knew that he was so good that he was infallible. As I made quiet suggestions about my PICC line care, he would scoff and tell me what an expert he was. To do a blood draw, first you attach an empty syringe to remove the blood that has been sitting in the long lumen of the catheter and discard this. This stagnant blood is bad blood, since it has been out of the circulatory system. The next syringe drawn represents fresh blood sufficient for lab testing. Finally the line is flushed with sterile saline to prevent clot formation inside the tube. My cocky nurse, still in his infallible mode, picked up the syringe with old clotted blood and attached it to my line. Before a word could escape my gaping mouth, he forced the plunger and emptied the syringe within 3 seconds. I could just imagine showers of clotted infected blood racing to my heart and finally lodging in my lungs. I calmly pointed out his error. Incensed, he retorted that he knew what he was doing and that his action was proper protocol. Finally, he stormed out. Which nurse was more dangerous? Fortunately, Nurse Cocky never came into my room again.

As the second Sunday passed and so did the visitors, Barbie and I were alone again. I remember those as sweet days. We were not bored. Sometimes I read, or slept. She read. She would go out to shop, get lunch for herself and I would always smile when she returned. She had not left my side for months. What comfort to have her always near. I was completely dependent on her. This was quite new to our relationship and I think that she enjoyed it.

Both Barbie and I now sensed the impending doom of separation, but we tried not to talk about it. Monday passed quietly.

Tuesday August 12, 2008 – *Our day that will live in infamy*

About a week prior, I had received a notice from the Mayo Clinic that if my status changed, I was required to let them know. Upon admission to Santa Clara for the dopamine infusion, my status changed from a 2 to a 1B. This put me higher on the transplant list. I therefore informed the heart transplant center at the Mayo Clinic, thus increasing my status there as well. I thought nothing of it, since Dr. Edwards had said that it could take six months to get a heart transplant in that region. I also failed to mention this communication to Dr. Weisshaar. I assumed the odds were low that a Mayo heart would come first.

Barbie and I said goodbye at about 11:00 A.M so she could get ready for the trip to San Diego. There were a few tears, but mostly we discussed logistics. She would leave tomorrow morning at 3:00 A.M. for the beach house on Mission Bay that we had rented for all of the family. All of our family would be there, except my brother

Daren and his wife Rachelle. They would stay behind so that Daren could provide me with company until Barbie returned home Sunday morning. That was the plan.

At 12:00 P.M. I was temporarily paroled from the nursing station. The force field was dropped and I walked with my I.V. pole to a conference room down the hall. On the second Tuesday of each month the Kaiser transplant cardiology department held a support group for all patients who had ever received a heart transplant, or were anticipating getting one. Janet Stevenson, the department social worker, always organized the meeting and that day invited me to participate. I sat down at the head of the table since there was a plug nearby to keep my pump going. I had put on a pair of flannel pajama pants to cover my butt when in public. I scanned the room, regarding all of the faces there. All ages, all backgrounds. My eye caught a woman sitting to my direct left. She was pretty with dark black hair, about my age. I could tell that she was also new. As the meeting began, she went first. "My name is Debbie Douglas. I need a heart transplant because I have a rare fatal disease called primary amylosis."

My jaw dropped. She was me, only two weeks earlier. I listened as she described her symptoms, which were identical to mine. However, she had only experienced a short delay in her diagnosis. It had taken only 2-3 months before an astute oncologist in Santa Rosa diagnosed her. Like me, she looked completely healthy.

Finally, I interjected, "Debbie, I am Kevin Anderson. I also have primary amyloidosis and am waiting to get a heart transplant at Stanford." When she heard this, a huge smile came over her face and she spontaneously got up, came over and hugged me with tears in her eyes. I knew exactly what was going through her mind: "I am not alone." Before that point, during my career as a doctor, I had never understood the interest that patients had in support groups. Now I knew. Chronic life-threatening diseases bring with them a certain loneliness that is hard for others to understand. Since words often fail to convey what you are feeling, associations with patients with the same condition allow you to share without words. Each of you simply understands, and that is enough. After she detailed her story I told mine. She wondered if she too would need to go to the Mayo Clinic to be evaluated as I was. I suggested that since I had already opened the door to Stanford, she might be able to forego the Minnesota trip. Our doctors could do the Mayo clinic work-up locally now and potentially get direct access to Stanford for her, if she were a candidate. Ultimately she was, since her disease, like mine, was primarily in her heart. Debbie and I immediately bonded as brother and sister, given the shared state of our damaged hearts. Later she would often refer to me as her big brother because I went first.

I finished my story, sharing that my wife Barbie had left me earlier that day to be with all my family in San Diego for the wedding of my son Samuel to his bride to be. To this day I can never refer to that event without crying. On that first public mention of it, my sadness at not being there as his father overcame me and I wept. I could not finish and Janet moved on to another member of the group. Finally composed, I sat quietly for the rest of the meeting and then was escorted back to my empty room and cold lunch sitting on my tray. I felt so alone.

Chapter 25

For hours I sat on the edge of the bed just thinking. Finally, needing a diversion, I opened my computer and started playing mindless games. To break the silence, I set Pandora on my computer to Coldplay. Random songs played, all from that genre. Then one song struck a chord with my emotion of the moment followed, by a second song, compounding a stabbing sense of wanting from my soul. I turned from my game and opened a blank page in our blog to record my pain.

Tuesday, August 12, 2008
I miss her

She has only been gone a few hours and already I miss her so much. Barbie needed to leave to go to Samuel and Michelle's wedding in San Diego. We have not been away from each other for almost a month. I did not really understand how her constant presence gives me such strength. I have learned over the years that a life-threatening illness is much harder for the spouse than for the patient. If a short, brief absence makes me feel like this, a permanent one would be incomprehensible. I have to get better so I can be with her for as long as possible. This is why I must stay here while Barbie goes to San Diego. Each one of us must sacrifice so that we can realize this blessing.

Music makes it worse. Music uncovers the raw emotions that intellect has buried. While listening to Pandora.com, songs like "Make this go on forever" by Snow Patrol would be followed by "Better Days" by the Goo Goo Dolls. The cumulative emotional wave would sweep me away into past memories and future hopes.

Barbie's presence keeps me in the present. In her absence there is only the future when she returns.

I am so blessed to have her forever.

Kevin
Posted by Kevin Anderson at 7:01 PM

Later she responded to my lament.

Tuesday, August 12, 2008
Our moment

I am done being strong. I don't think I have ever cried for as many hours as I did today. I started an hour before leaving Kevin and then continued my entire 2 1/2 hour drive home. This is a bittersweet moment. My tears have dried up. I have known for a long time that this moment would come and it would be hard. It's hard, very, very hard. Leaving him at the hospital in his sparse room and knowing he is not able to attend the temple sealing of Sam and Michelle is a devastating feeling. I didn't know it would be this hard. And for everything I know about eternity and the blessings of the Gospel, does not make this moment easy. Someday we will look back at this time and see a clear picture of how it all came to be and why. Until then...we move forward, because that is what we do.

Kevin is my life, my breath and my joy. I am who I am because of him. My life without him is unimaginable. I am not ready for him to be anywhere but by my side for a very long time.

Barbie
Posted by Barbie at 8:44 PM

When I read Barbie's post I missed her even more. How could anyone do something like this alone? I felt lost without her. For years I had been the strong one. I was the rock, the solid ground in any storm. I did it as a Bishop, as a professor of surgery, as a father, as a scoutmaster, and as a husband. I made hundreds of decisions every day. There had never been time to waver or wonder. So many people relied on me to know what to do. But as a husband, as an eternal team with Barbie, we had always made decisions together. Until this moment, I had never fully realized how much I have always needed her. I took so much for granted. Now, even though it would only be for a few days, I felt so alone.

Two hours slowly passed, I wanted to go to sleep, yet somehow when she was not near I was not tired. I lay in bed in the dark, waiting for sleep. My cell phone rang.

It was the transplant coordinator from the Mayo Clinic. "Mr. Anderson?" she began. "Yes," I replied. My heart was racing. I was probably in V-Tach at that moment. "We have a heart for you," she continued. "How soon can you get to Rochester?"

"I will speak with my cardiologist here," I managed to say, as my mind was trying to process what this meant. We hung up and I sat stunned in the darkness. I had never expected that the Mayo Clinic would have a heart first. This was not supposed to happen. Dr. Edwards' words again echoed in my brain. He had said it might take six months to get a heart in Minnesota. I grabbed my I.V. pole and made my way to the nurse's station. I randomly spoke to whoever was there; a few nurses and aids glanced in my direction. I blurted out, "The Mayo Clinic just offered me a heart." I was hoping someone might step forward and tell me what to do. They all just stared at me. This was probably a request they had never heard. I knew time was of the essence. My mind was racing, sorting, trying to resolve a cogent plan. Questions emerged. "How long does a heart survive?" I would need to fly from California to Minnesota as soon as possible. Then I thought to myself, "Dr. Weisshaar will know what to do." Fortunately, she was on call. I could call her. She had given me her cell phone number. No nurse moved to help or even respond. I was on my own and needed someone who knew what to do. When I pulled out my phone, they all went back to their business.

"Dr. Weisshaar," I began, "I just got a call from the Mayo Clinic. They have a heart for me. They told me they are still doing tests to see if it is a good heart." I did not say it, but my tone conveys my urgency and anxiety.

"I will order an air ambulance to get you there. I will be there in 20 minutes." And she was gone.

I walked back to my room and sat on the bed. I had to call Barbie. I knew she was at home packing. She would be leaving at 3:00 AM to make the nine hour drive to San Diego. It was now midnight.

I called her. I explained what had happened and that I would be flying that night to the Mayo Clinic to get the heart transplant. We both cried. These should have been tears of joy. But we both knew instinctively what this would mean. She was empty. She had already emotionally given all that she had and there was nothing left. I felt horrible as I ended the conversation. As a husband, I was supposed to reassure and comfort my wife. At that moment, I was failing.

What we did not say to each other was that if I went to the Mayo Clinic, I would be alone. Barbie would eventually join me. I would have to be there for months and would not only miss Samuel and Michelle's wedding. I would miss Rebecca's wedding as well. As much as I knew that I needed a heart, I had never expected it to be like this.

Soon Dr. Weisshaar arrived. She came into the room and sat down. She informed me that she had called the air ambulance company and had a jet on standby. She inquired what my status was on the Mayo Clinic's transplant list. "I am a 1B," I responded. I explained that they had sent me a letter requesting that I update them on my status and that I had. She frowned (something she does not often do.) This did complicate things.

Then she looked up and said that, as she was driving in, it occurred to her that she had not asked me what I wanted to do. I feel she was inspired to ask me this. I tried to convey my anxiety about being away from my family and how I would be alone, since Barbie was on her way to San Diego as we spoke. Yet silently I also felt a loyalty to the Mayo Clinic for having taken such good care of me and a pang of guilt consumed me that I could be so ungrateful as to even consider refusing such a life giving gift. I explained only that I was willing to go, but that it would be hard for me to be away from my family. She understood.

She told me that she would call her counterpart there to decide what to do. In that moment I watched an angel walk out of my hospital room. Suddenly, everything that I had ever been was gone. I had no strength left. My health had failed me. I was no longer working in the career that I loved. I could no longer serve in the church. I was in a hospital miles from my children. The one person who has always been there, Barbie, was now needed elsewhere. The only thing I had left, the one characteristic that had defined my entire life, the essence of who I am, my ability to make decisions, was now gone. I did not know what to do. I was lost; I was empty. I found myself again at the mercy of compassionate strangers. All that was left to me was my faith in God. He would never abandon me in my time of need. All of those times in church I had sung the hymn, "I Need Thee Every Hour" came rushing back into my mind. This was one of those hours.

I lay in my bed (kneeling was difficult) and poured out my broken heart to God. I prayed, "Please let them make the right decision."

CHAPTER 26

Wednesday, August 13, 2008
Things always seem to work out

Answers to life's mysteries sometimes come faster than you think. Only a few hours after Barbie left, I got a call about an available heart. Normally that would be cause for excitement, but this call was from Minnesota. The Mayo Clinic had a heart. This decision was too hard for me alone. I called Barbie and she was distraught. I spoke with my doctor here, Dr. Weisshaar, and she said she would arrange to have me flown there. But then a small miracle occurred. Dr. Weisshaar came to my room to ask how I felt about this. I shared my concerns, about the distance, being alone, Barbie being gone at the wedding etc... She understood and said she would speak with the surgeon there. While she was gone I prayed that the right answer would be found.

She returned (after what felt like an eternity) and said, "You need to get some sleep, we passed on the heart." I felt a huge relief as she said this and knew it was the right answer. Even though it would not seem prudent to pass on an available heart today, not knowing when one might come again at Stanford, she felt that I was very stable and healthy and could afford to wait. The doctors at Mayo were in agreement.

I called Barbie and she was relieved. We both got a restful night's sleep. It turns out that there were many factors in the decision, but I believe that Barbie's presence at the wedding, and thus her absence here, was the tipping point.

It's just another chapter in this surreal journey on which we find ourselves.

Waiting, with renewed patience,

Kevin

I remember wandering the floor the following day. A thought came, briefly, that by turning down the heart from the Mayo Clinic, there was the possibility that I could have a sudden fatal arrhythmia and die. I vanquished this thought immediately. My faith told me this would not happen. I only had to remember how I had felt the night before--what relief I had felt on hearing Dr. Weisshaar's decision. God had a plan for me. It would all work out. It always does. That random thought never returned.

Thursday, August 14, 2008
Sand and waves calm

My mom, my sister, Rebecca, Caitlin and I left yesterday morning at 5am to drive here to San Diego. After the night Kevin and I had, I think I fell asleep around 11:30 pm for a little while after Kevin's first call about the possible transfer to Mayo. I prayed for a while too. It was already too hard leaving him, and then having to face the possibility of not being with him in Rochester during the transplant and recovery was more than I could bear. His final call at 1 am was a relief. None of us (doctors and all) feel badly about the decision to pass on the heart. We still feel good about this and I feel wonderful knowing that some lucky person received a heart that night.

We arrived here about 1:30 pm . I drove the entire way because I did not feel tired at all. Another great blessing. I slept 10 hours last night; I never sleep that long. It did my body good. The first thing we did once getting settled in the beach house was to go to the beach. There is something wonderful about sitting on the beach, putting your feet in the sand and hearing the waves crash. My spirit felt so calm. I called Kevin while on the beach so I could feel him with me. I miss him, but feel so much better. After our experience Tues. night, we can do this!

I wish he were here, but like we all know, it is better that he is where he is. His brother, Daren, is arriving today to spend the weekend with him, while most of the rest of the family will be here for Sam's wedding.

Barbie

In the world of virtual presence, someone had the idea that I could be at the reception as a floating face on someone's laptop computer. I decided I would dress up for the occasion. Daren was on his way to Santa Clara to stay with me over the weekend so I asked him to see if he could find a bow tie at a thrift shop somewhere. On Thursday he showed up with some snacks, games and a bow tie that required a knot. Neither of us had ever tied one so of course we appealed to the source of all useless knowledge: Google. Following the diagrams on the screen, I was able to get a knot, but all symmetry was lacking. It was quite pathetic. Dr. Weisshaar came by on rounds and added her two cents, since she had once helped her husband with a bowtie. It was a fun diversion. For a while, I tried not to think about Saturday morning at 9:00 A.M, when all of our family would be with Samuel and Michelle in the San Diego Temple for the ceremony without me. Every time that image would surface to a conscious level I would tear up and feel sad. I kept wondering how I would get through that Saturday morning.

Daren was great. We talked a lot and he got me to play some games. He loves games. He taught me how to play backgammon, which was quite fun. Late Thursday night we played Farkle, which I used to call 5000 when I played as a kid with my older brother David. All night I did not just lose, I was crushed in humiliating defeat. Finally, I had had enough and Daren commented what poor luck I had. My retort was that I was saving my luck to get a good heart. We smiled and soon he took the cot in the corner and I lay in the dark wondering.

So much was going through my mind. All my life, as I lay in bed waiting to drift off to sleep, I would disengage the reins of my mind and let it run free. It would take me to glorious places as I imagined my future and developed my dreams. Often, I would find myself being interviewed by someone who would ask me some pointed question about anything, from physics to politics, racism to world peace. As I eloquently responded, I would continually reinforce my core values and beliefs. Ultimately, most of the responses I have made to such issues in my life have already been rehearsed in these late night pre-sleep self conversations. By the time I was 13, I already had a name for these: value discussions. I secretly wondered if everyone did this.

Generally, my mind never stops. In those quiet times of no distractions, my internal dialogue is incessant. Always before a big surgery, especially one that is relatively new for me, I will spend hours visualizing every step of the procedure in my mind. Anticipating any complications, I devise possible solutions. I don't actively do this. It has always been a part of my undistracted, unfettered existence. However, on that night I really could not imagine the future. There was a blank. I thought about Barbie. I refreshed my memory with the image she had texted me earlier that day of her on the beach in Mission Bay. She looked so good in her green bathing suit and her hat. Finally, with that image I fell asleep, completely unaware that this would be my last night with my heart of 49 years.

A family gathers around a bed in a hospital, miles away. They are with-out consolation. Suddenly, without warning, their son, their brother lay there

critically injured; too young to be gone from this world. The pain is indescribable. Tests are performed. Doctors and nurses quietly come in and out of the room. Between the tears, the sounds of machines hum in the background. His brain is gone, therefore he is gone; yet the rush of wind from the ventilator keeps oxygen moving through his lungs. The monitor above his bed beeps with each contraction of his still-beating heart.

In this darkest of all hours this grieving family makes a decision that will change the lives of strangers all over the west coast. Despite the loss of their son and brother, his organs will live on in others. Arrangements are made, the call goes out and then they are left to say goodbye.

It is incomprehensible how such a magnificent gift can and must occur from such a devastating loss. But it does and it did.

CHAPTER 27

Waking is like a sunrise. In the full darkness of unconscious sleep there begins a glimmer over the horizon. Within the abstraction of dreaming I become aware of the real world pulling me awake, the call of a morning bird, a full bladder, the constant whine of the fan overhead. Slowly the dream fades and then, as if the grade had suddenly steepened, the waking into consciousness accelerates. The dream and its memory disappear and reality rises as blinding as the new day sun in its full glory. Blinding now are the day's responsibilities that lie ahead. A normal person in a normal life pushes himself up into the routine: clean, feed, evacuate, dress, communicate, plan, travel, interact, work.

But for me, I wait. Daren takes off to get some food. I get up and go for a walk. I attempt a shower, but forget to notify the nurses monitoring my heart. Soon there is a knock on the bathroom door, "Are you all right?" "Yes, I am in the shower," I reply. And then I go back to bed. After lunch I call Barbie. She has a busy day with dinners and photographers and keeping all of the visiting family fed, comfortable and entertained. She prefers it when I am around to help.

Around 4:00 P.M. Dr. Weisshaar comes by to check on me with the fellow and then they leave. Bored, I pull out the bow-tie and try tying it again. Suddenly, the door opens. Dr. Weisshaar briskly walks in, this time with a big smile and says, "You will not need to practice tying that bow-tie anymore. You have a new heart."

Rebecca is sitting on the beach with my sister, Mindy, and her husband Thad. They have just spent the afternoon catching waves on Mission Bay on my old boogie board. Barbie and Caitlin are chauffeuring Samuel and Michelle around San Diego so that the photographer can get various tropical backgrounds in the wedding photos. She has left her phone with Rebecca. The discussion on the beach is about me and when I might get a heart. Just then Darlene and Harold join them. Soon, Darlene wonders at the wisdom of giving up the offered heart from the Mayo Clinic. Mindy responds by saying, "That was a good heart; we're waiting for a great heart." Suddenly, the cell phone rings. Rebecca answers, "Hi, dad. No, she is with Caitlin driving Sam and Michelle around town.... What? That's amazing!" She turns to the others, "Dad's got a heart. He's on his way to Stanford." Continuing the conversation with me, she adds, "Caitlin has her phone, you can reach mom through her."

Soon, I am talking to Barbie and tell her the news. It is too big to fully absorb in that moment. Immediately we talk logistics. I tell her that I will get her on the first flight to San Francisco once the reception is over on Saturday. We exchange words, attempting to convey our love for each other and then disconnect from the vapor of wireless. But the connection is still there. She is always with me, in my heart.

Daren and I are now scurrying around the room. We are shoving everything into plastic bags and the one travel bag that I brought. Anxiously, I get on the computer one last time to book Barbie a flight to San Francisco for the following day. She will arrive just before 4:00 P.M. I cancel the internet service for the Skype hook-up in the hotel ballroom so that we do not get dinged the $100.00 service charge. I only call one person, President Perez, my branch president. I think he would like to hear about this miracle.

Soon, the EMTs arrive. EKG leads are exchanged to make me portable. I long to feel the warmth on my face and bask in a 20 second sun-bathing moment as I leave the hospital and am placed in the ambulance. The only word that describes my emotion in this moment is giddiness. I am ten again and run out on Christmas morning to see my new Raleigh 3-speed bicycle. My exuberance is overflowing. During the 20 minute ambulance ride I talk incessantly. The EMT is from Rhode Island, so our common ground centers on catching waves on Misquamicut State Beach.

I am getting a new heart, a chance for a new life. I am so very happy.

Soon, the hallways of Stanford surround me with doors, bumps, elevators, and passing clinicians ignoring me. This is the patient's view of the university hospital. How many hours, days, months and years of my life were spent passing patients like me, unaware of their perspective, their fears, their hopes for a better life. It is now my turn.

I was deposited in a bed: a holding area of sorts. The room had six beds. Three were occupied. Soon Daren arrived. Good ol' Daren. When he originally agreed to spend the weekend with me, we had never imagined it would include this. Daren and I, however, both being Eagle Scouts, had already made a contingency plan. Not more than a half hour before getting the news, our conversation had turned to the question of what would happen if the heart came today. I explained to him the orientation that Barbie had been given the week before. I described how to get to Stanford and where to wait during surgery. So many emotions, so many thoughts, but mostly I felt anticipation. The one emotion that was completely absent was fear. I absolutely knew, without doubt, that everything was going to be fine. Ironically, as a surgeon, I did not really focus that much on the actual procedure. Only later did that occur to me.

Friday, August 15, 2008
Kevin Has A Heart!

Kevin just called and Stanford has a heart. He is being transferred by ambulance as I write. The surgery should take place in the next 5-12 hours. That's all

I know at this point. We are thrilled and overwhelmed once again. I will fly tomorrow night from San Diego right after the reception and be there by 8pm. Kevin should be in recovery at that point. We have been blessed beyond belief.

Thank you for all your prayers, love, support.

Barbie

CHAPTER 28

Surgery

The first time I laid knife to skin was on my 27th birthday. The morning had started horribly. I was an intern on the trauma service less than two months out of medical school. That morning a 2nd year resident had yelled at me for over 20 minutes about a patient who had died the night before on my watch. Early in the afternoon I got called to the O.R. Everyone else on the trauma team was busy, so I was needed to help the chief resident operate on an inmate from Folsom prison who had been stabbed. At that time, exploratory laparotomy was the standard approach to determine which internal organs might be injured. The chief handed me the number 10 blade scalpel and pointed to where I should begin cutting. At first I did not press hard enough and barely scratched the skin. His hand went over mine and pushed as I pulled. Soon there was an incision from the xyphoid process just below the ribs to just above the pubic bone. Just above his belly button he had a tattoo of a name. All I remember was cutting straight through the middle of the "H". Once inside we examined the liver, spleen, stomach and the entire bowel. We checked the retro-peritoneum to look for bleeding from the kidneys. We found no major injuries, and soon it was time to close the incision. Carefully I tried to re-approximate the "H" with my closure so that it did not end up crooked. I walked out of the room feeling for the first time that I was a surgeon.

Surgery is a unique profession. It is a combination of science and art, and a craft like no other. People give surgeons permission to cause major trauma and injury to their bodies in the hope that we will add quality or quantity to their lives. We take out things that are damaged, diseased or should not be there and then reconnect or reconstruct the anatomy to be as near normal as possible. Then the real magic occurs as the body begins the extraordinary process of healing itself. Sometimes we put new artificial things in; sometimes we even put in borrowed organs. For many surgeons, this daily routine can lose the sense of awe that underlies its true impact on thousands of lives throughout one's career. But that very compartmentalization is an essential part of surgery. The focus, the routine and the ordered environment allow for better outcomes. There is a necessary disconnect once the drapes go over the patient and anesthesia is administered. Gone is any empathetic revulsion at the exposure of human blood and organs that might occur in any other setting. The body before us is simply a field of anatomy in need of repair. Somehow we see the exposed tissue as separate from the individual person.

Becoming a surgeon takes years of training. I spent two years as a general surgery resident prior to beginning my four years of training in Urology. Finally, I left U.C. Davis to spend a year in St. Louis at Washington University to do a fellowship in minimally invasive urology and laparoscopic surgery.

I was privileged to work with outstanding mentors. When I arrived, Dr. Blaisdell was the chairman of surgery at U.C. Davis. A world renowned expert in trauma surgery, he had experience from M.A.S.H. units in the Korean War. One day, while a chief resident in Urology, I was called to the E.R. to see a patient who was bleeding after an operation. While there, the senior surgery resident asked me to look at some X-rays on a woman who had been in a car accident. I went to the area where she was and held the films up to the light. Immediately I noticed no contrast enhancement of the left kidney. Either she did not have a kidney or she had severely damaged the left renal artery. Initially she was stable, however, as we spoke at her bedside, she suddenly "crashed." Her blood pressure dropped and she became unresponsive.

A quick exam of her left abdomen revealed a rapidly expanding pulsitile mass. She had sheared off her left renal artery and was exsanguinating (bleeding to death) into her left retroperitoneum (the space where the kidneys live). We only had minutes. Since the chief surgical resident was off that day and the 4th year was covering, I was the senior surgeon at the moment. We got her to the O.R. in minutes and as I opened her up. I immediately saw the bright red mass pushing all of her organs to the right side. My classical teaching told me to enter at the midline to find the root of the renal artery as it came off the aorta. However, at that moment, Dr. Blaisdell walked in. It felt as if the cavalry had just arrived. In seconds he assessed the situation and asked my plan. Upon outlining my dogmatic approach he said, "might I suggest you reflect the left colon and approach laterally."

I knew this was not the classic teaching, but this was Dr. Blaisdell. He was the classic teacher. I did as instructed. When I incised into the retroperitoneum, more blood than I had ever seen came gushing out. With Dr. Blaisdell using sponge after sponge to clean out the clot while the senior resident had two suction devices going, we soon got to the kidney, which was completely smashed and fragmented. I scooped it out with a sponge and then saw the source of bleeding. Without words up to this point, I felt Dr. Blaisdell handing me a right-angle clamp. I placed the clamp on the source of bright red blood and the bleeding stopped. I took a deep breath and noticed there was still a lot of blood, however this blood was more purple. "Venous bleeding," I thought. Soon I had a clamp on the stump of the left renal vein and ovarian vein. Suddenly, the field was dry. This was when I instinctively turned to the anesthesiologist and asked, "How's she doing?" "She is stable," was the reply. Even before we started the operation, they had been resuscitating her with blood and fluids. Her blood pressure was stable.

Dr. Blaisdell, satisfied that the situation was stable, quietly interjected, "Good job," accompanied by a paternal pat on the shoulder. Then he was gone. We closed her up and transferred her to recovery.

I went by to see her a few days later. She looked up, smiling at me from her lunch. I introduced myself as Dr. Anderson, the urology chief resident, and asked how she was. She felt fine and said that they were going to discharge her the following day. She thanked me and I wished her well and left. Nowhere in the conversation did I mention the magnitude of her peril, nor the impact that the experience had had on me. I was not the same person after that surgery. She looked up from her bed as if nothing of import had occurred. But she knew. Silently, we both knew. The eyes can never lie.

Throughout my career, I have been privileged to interact with thousands of patients, always with the same goal: either improve the number of days they will live or improve the quality of those days; hopefully both. I have taught hundreds of medical students and residents, just as Dr. Blaisdell taught me. The weight of the overall impact upon humanity is immeasurable; however, I can never take the credit for that impact, since I am never alone in these endeavors. Teams of nurses, technicians, clerks, doctors and other professionals are always there to help.

After motherhood, I have always felt that teaching is the noblest profession. One thing that is impossible to teach is common sense. A good surgeon can think on his or her feet and immediately resolve a problem never before encountered.

I once had a patient who had been treated for a retroperitoneal cancer with chemotherapy and radiation. This was complicated by a permanently obstructed right ureter which had been managed with a small plastic tube (or stent) to drain her kidney to her bladder. It was necessary to replace the stent every three months to prevent incrustation with stones. Often, I would change the stent in the office to avoid the hassle of going to the operating room. It was simple: place a cystoscope in the bladder, pull the tip of the stent just outside the urethra, pass a wire through the stent into the kidney and then replace the stent over the wire. Ten minutes and I was done. I had already performed this relatively simple procedure a number of times on her. However, this time for some reason I felt that I should do the stent change in the O.R..

I began the usual process. I could see the wire on X-ray, coiled in the kidney. I pulled out the old stent. Then something very unusual occurred. Around the wire, emanating from the right ureteral orifice, was a rapid pulsation of bright red blood. Pulsating bright red blood always means arterial bleeding. Bleeding like this should not be coming out of the ureter. It could mean only one thing. There was a hole, or fistula, between the right iliac artery, as it split off the aorta, and the ureter. My brain raced to construct both cause and effect and then an immediate solution to the problem. First, control the bleeding. Since this was a closed endourological case and I was nowhere near the actual source of bleeding I needed a way to remotely stop an arterial hemorrhage. Arterial bleeding is very bad. The patient can bleed to death in a manner of minutes. The solution is to close the hole, or apply pressure to the leak that is higher than the systolic blood pressure.

My first asset was that I had a wire in the ureter passing beyond the level of the leak. I asked for a 10 cm. length ureteral dilating balloon. We use these high pressure balloons to stretch the ureter and dilate scarring. I figured the hole could not be much bigger than a few millimeters. If I could inflate the balloon next to the hole I could stop the bleeding. I could not see the bleeding on X-ray, but I knew the landmarks of where the ureter crossed the iliac artery. I proceeded to position the middle of the balloon at that point. I inflated it to three atmospheres of pressure. The bleeding stopped. Now we had time.

I called the vascular surgeon and asked if he could perform open surgery to repair and bypass the damaged artery. He thought for a minute and said that he had heard that the interventional radiologist was doing clinical trials on a new device that essentially consisted of a coated spring able to be inserted into the artery through a needle in the groin. The device would then self-expand on the inside of the vessel and possibly close the hole from the inside. We both went downstairs to the radiology department to see whether this new technique was a possible solution. The interventional radiologist was in his office. We presented our dilemma. He looked down at a flat box on his desk. He had just received it from a medical equipment company as part of a clinical trial.

This was years before heart stents and intra-luminal aneurysm stents had been FDA approved, and there just happened to be the exact device we needed sitting on his desk. He was game, so we brought the patient downstairs to the radiology department. The ureteral occlusion balloon was still in place and coming out of her urethra. She was awake enough that we could explain what had happened, and agreed to let us try this minimally invasive option prior to open surgery. I stood in the control room as the magic spring was inserted through her femoral artery and advanced up to the common iliac artery. The spring was then pushed out of its introducer sheath at the location of the leak; it was the moment of truth. I let down the pressure in the ureter balloon. The urine from her catheter immediately turned bright red. I inflated the balloon again. "What now?" I thought. We talked and decided that it might take a while to form a stable clot that would seal around the arterial stent and stop the leak. We waited 15 minutes. Again, blood drained from the bladder when I deflated the balloon. I re-inflated it. We had no choice but to wait some more. As I stood there, watching the clock, I prayed. Yes, sometimes surgeons pray. I realized that all of the events thus far had been unpredictable, yet fortuitous. I had chosen to change the stent in the OR instead of the clinic, thereby averting certain disaster. An experimental stent--of just the right size, no less--had happened to be upon the correct desk.

By now I had figured out the cause of the bleeding. The stent was moving up and down with every breath. Normally ureteral tissue is soft, supple and elastic and allows free movement. However, her previous chemotherapy and radiation had caused tissue scarring around the ureter right where it was kinked to pass over the artery. Hundreds of thousands of breaths moved the stent like a mini-hacksaw trying to cut through prison bars. The friction of the stent removal provided the final cut. Fortunately, it had happened not at home, not in clinic, but in the controlled environment of the Yale-New Haven hospital operating room.

It was time to let the balloon down. We waited 20 minutes this time. I saw the balloon pressure on the gauge drop to zero. All eyes were fixed on the clear plastic tube connected to the bladder catheter. It remained clear. A minute later it was still clear. At about two minutes we started to breathe. We smiled at each other incredulously. This procedure had never been done before in any of our collective memories. This is exactly how medical progress is made. The patient never bled again from her ureter.

I acutely knew all of the potential problems with any surgery or anesthetic. As I prepared to go in for the most important surgical case of my life, my own, I had not even one thought about the actual procedure, anesthesia or potential complications. I felt only absolute joy and hope. I was anxious to get started, yet had no anxiety. I knew without a doubt that I would arrive safe on the other side.

CHAPTER 29

Mortality Awareness event # 5

What is death? Some would define it as the moment when the heart stops pumping blood. Others might argue that death occurs when the brain no longer functions. Based on these acute observational approaches, I died that August night.

Merely 100 years ago, who could imagine that a man could live two hours without a heart inside his chest? As I lay there, functionally dead, anesthesia kept me in a completely unconscious state. All higher function was suspended. There was no dreaming, no memory, no perception of time, no thought, no sentience. "I do not think, therefore; am I?" Only a perceptible nanosecond before, I had been lying on an operating table looking up at Dr. Oaks, my anesthesiologist. She had been so friendly and positive as we spoke in the hallway. She had assured me that she would have me awake in time on Saturday to perform my floating head virtual visit to the wedding reception via Skype. Now I felt the buzz in the room of many people attending to their varied duties. Only Dr. Oaks focused on me. "The heart is on its way," she said. "I am going to put you to sleep so we can prepare you for its arrival." With that, she injected a milky white substance (Propofol or milk of amnesia, as we call it) into the PICC line, still in my right arm. The thought of the dangling end of the PICC line hanging out of the severed superior vena cava passed through my mind. The ceiling started moving to the left, and then there was nothing.

This memory has intentionally been left blank

Imagine twelve hours of your life disappearing in an instant. Where there is no memory, there is no time. We only perceive time because we have memory of the past. The world continued; I was absent.

During my absence, others were very busy. I asked for a copy of the operative report. Here it is in its glorious understated brevity.

Author Service	Author Type	Filed	Note	Time
Daniel Tang, MD (none)	Physician 08/16/20080928		08/15/2008	2227
Authorization info	Signed by Daniel Tang. MD at 08/16/2008 0928			

DATE OF OPERATION: 8/15/2008

PREOPERATIVE DIAGNOSIS: Restrictive cardiomyopathy due to AL amyloidosis

POSTOPERATIVE DIAGNOSIS: Restrictive cardiomyopathy due to AL amyloidosis

PROCEDURE: Orthotopic heart transplant

SURGEON: Philip E. Oyer, MD.

SECOND SURGEON: Daniel G. Tang, MD.

A suitable resident was not available for this case.

ANESTHESIA: General endotracheal anesthesia.

SPECIMENS: Explanted heart

Cardiopulmonary bypass time is 161 minutes. Cross-clamp time is 96 minutes. Ischemic time for the graft is 214 minutes. Lowest temperature 30 degrees Celsius.

INDICATIONS FOR PROCEDURE: Dr. Anderson is a 48 y/o urologist with a history of restrictive cardiomyopathy due to AL type amyloid with IgG kappa restriction. His disease appears to mainly involve his heart. After careful consideration, he was deemed an acceptable candidate for transplant (with plans for subsequent chemotherapy and stem cell transplant) by both the Mayo Clinic and here at Stanford. He was placed on both lists. A suitable donor was identified (XXXX XXX XXX) and he was transferred from

Kaiser on a dopamine gtt (@3 mcg/kg/min) for his transplant. The risks and benefits of the procedure were discussed with Mr. Anderson and his brother and informed consent was obtained.

PROCEDURE IN DETAIL: He was taken to the operating room. A time out verifying the correct patient, diagnosis, planned procedure and operative site was performed. The donor heart was visualized and found to be acceptable by the procurement team. General endotracheal anesthesia was induced and appropriate monitoring / access lines were placed. The patient was positioned supine and prepped and draped in the usual sterile fashion. Pre incision cefazolin was administered. A median sternotomy was performed; and a pericardial well was created. A large right pleural effusion (- 1L) was drained. The native heart was grossly dilated, markedly thickened and with impaired function. The great vessels were dissected free. Heparin was given and the aorta, SVC, and IVC were cannulated. Cardiopulmonary bypass was started. Once the procurement team arrived with the donor heart: the patient was cooled; the aorta was cross clamped; the well was flooded with carbon dioxide; and the native heart was excised. The atrial cuffs were trimmed for a bicaval anastomosis. The donor heart was rinsed, inspected, and trimmed for implantation. No structural defects were identified. The heart was protected with continuous topical and left atrial intracardiac cold saline irrigation. The left atrial anastomosis was performed with a running 4-0 Prolene. The IVC anastomosis was performed with 4-0 Prolene. The SVC anastomosis was performed with a running 5-0 Prolene. The aortic anastomosis was performed with a running 4-0 Prolene and the cross clamped removed. The heart spontaneously regained an accelerated junctional rhythm and subsequently sinus rhythm. The pulmonary artery anastomosis was performed with 4-0 Prolene. The remaining native posterior right atrial wall between the caval cuffs was oversewn. An atrial vent was placed in the right superior pulmonary vein. A needle was used to aspirate the aortic root. Deairing was confirmed by TEE. Following adequate reperfusion and rewarming, the patient was weaned from bypass. The heart demonstrated good function. Likely due to his history of chronic afterload reduction including ACE inhibitors, he demonstrated marked vasodilation requiring additional vasopressors. He was weaned from bypass on dopamine, epinephrine, isoproterenol and vasopressin gtts. The cannulas were removed. Protamine was given and good hemostasis was demonstrated. Induction methylpredisolone and dacluzimab were given. An angled posterior mediastinal and a straight anterior mediastinal 28 fr chest tube were placed. An additional angled 28 fr chest tube was placed in the right pleural space. The sternum was closed in the usual fashion. The patient was then transferred to the ICU in stable condition.

Instruments, needles, and sponge counts at the end of the case were correct. The attending surgeon, Dr. Oyer, was present for the entire procedure.

Electronically Signed by Daniel Tang, MD at 08/16/2008 0928

Imagine that you are a film editor. You are given five random strips of film, each spanning a time of 15 seconds to two minutes. During the first segment everything is dark. Suddenly you realize that you cannot breathe. Something is blocking your airway. You frantically thrash, trying to speak, but you cannot. You feel a hand on your shoulder.

The second segment also starts dark. Breathing is easy now. A voice says, "His bicarb is low."

Now you open your eyes. You are in a hospital bed. Your neck hurts. At the end of the bed you see your brother Daren and his wife, Rachelle. They are smiling. You try to smile back. There is a tube in your throat, making the effort awkward.

You lie there for a while now. You know you are in the ICU. The nurse is yelling at the man beyond the curtain, (because you cannot speak with a tube in your throat, medical personnel assume you are deaf, so they yell) "Mr. Smith, are you having any pain!? Mr. Smith, how would you *rate* your pain? On a scale of 1-10 what is your pain!?" You wish Mr. Smith would answer. This reminds you of a Brian Regan comedy routine from "I Walked on the Moon." You struggle to free your hands. The left hand emerges from the cover, and you give a thumbs up. The nurse is confused. She asks, "What is he doing?" The right hand is trapped beneath an arterial line and two I.V.s. Finally free, you hold up both hands with a definitive "Two Thumbs Up," an homage to the comparison of Roger Ebert's rating of movies to the absurdity of rating pain. "Four stars." "Two thumbs up!"

Daren and Rachelle get the inside joke and start to laugh. Appropriately, your first effort at communication after receiving a life-saving heart transplant is to make a joke, even before you can speak.

Splicing these disparate pieces of film would make it appear as if the entire sequence occurred over five to 10 minutes. From Daren's perspective, however, the incident took two hours. Fade in– Consciousness – clock starts. Fade out – unconsciousness – clock stops. No memory, no time. Even when we sleep at night, dreaming gives us the illusion of time passage, albeit altered.

Finally, I am awake. I am back with a full sense of reality and the import of what I have just been through. The power of that moment is overwhelming. Instinctively, my hand goes up to my heart to feel this new part of me. The nurse stops my hand, not sure that I will not disturb the wound. The wound; they *were* all correct at the heart transplant meeting. It really does not hurt that much. My only pain is in my right neck. I must have been positioned funny.

The time has come to remove the endotracheal tube. I am ready to breathe on my own. The nurse deflates the internal cuff and slides the tube out. I instinctively cough and get a bunch of junk out. She suctions the rest. It's like being born again. It is my new birthday, the first day of my new life with a new heart. A feeling of immense, overwhelming, infinite gratitude fills me. My only thought is to thank God for my life and breath. I ask Daren and Rachelle to come over to the bed. I ask in a low hoarse voice, "Can we say a prayer?" We then hold hands and I pray. All that I remember is thanking God for this great gift and asking a blessing on Samuel, Michelle and all of those at the wedding.

While I was sleeping, Samuel and Michelle got married. I was glad that if I could not be there, I was at least unconscious when it happened. It felt less lonely that way. Within 15 – 20 minutes my voice was enough recovered that I could speak to Barbie. I had rehearsed in my mind the first thing I would say to her, although I had never imagined it would be over the phone. I finally heard her voice and then I said, "I love you with my whole new heart."

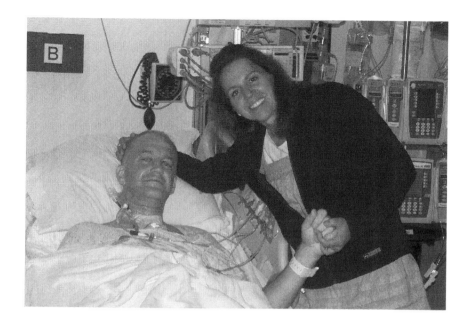

CHAPTER 30

Saturday, August 16, 2008
Kevin is well

I just spoke to Kevin. He feels great; he loves me with all his new heart! He's a bit groggy, but is happy this part is all over. The heart is a perfect match, the right size and it started pumping without needing to be shocked. I am going to see him in a few hours.

Sam and Michelle looked amazing. The temple ceremony was beautiful. They were supported by so many friends and family. More later...

Barbie

Sunday, August 17, 2008
A new Chapter

Kevin is amazing. I was so thrilled to see him last night and felt frustrated that I could only give him a gentle kiss and touch his head. I wanted to hug him forever. It was a joyous moment to be together again.

His progress is going well. He does not complain even though he has a lot he could complain about. I can see in his face that he is uncomfortable. He does tell me he is weak, tired, has pain in various places in his body and has discomfort in his chest. "Just a little", he says. Today he is less talkative than yesterday *coming out of anesthesia. The drugs allowed him to be funny in that groggy kind of way. Kevin has the will to recover quickly, but has limitations as he should at this point in recovery. He did sit in a chair today twice and is on a liquid diet, yet isn't hungry, but plenty thirsty.*

It seems redundant to keep saying that things always work out when they are in the Lord's hands, yet it's true. We have been astounded at how incredibly fast the new heart came after having the heart from Mayo turned down. This was a more perfect heart for Kevin and we are all close to home. He can see our girls and our families much easier. The best part is that he will be with Jeremy, Alexandria, Sam and Michelle in October at Rebecca's wedding! That will be a family reunion to remember. An anniversary to remember will be Sam and Michelle's. The day of their wedding is the day Kevin received his new heart.

His birthday is on Tues. this week. I asked him what he wanted; he responded he already got it.

More to come - I am sure you all will be thrilled to see his next blog(s). I know I will.

Bless you all,

Barbie

My time in the intensive care unit was a bit of a blur. Initially, I was on a number of potent drugs to stimulate the new heart. These 'drips' were similar to the dopamine I had received prior to the transplant to strengthen my old heart. My old heart; what a concept! It was initially strange to think of a stranger's heart beating in my chest. I felt the evidence of a new pump immediately. My toes were not freezing and I felt a pulse even in my scalp. I was finally perfused.

Barbie was at my side whenever they would let her in. It was a happy moment when she arrived from the San Diego. I couldn't get out of bed to hug her so I just held her hand. A half hour later the nurse informed her that she had to leave. It was change of shift and the nurse had to give report. Confused and despondent over being ushered out after so brief a reunion brought her to tears as she found an empty chair in the vacant hallway.

A little while later the same nurse exited the ICU and saw Barbie obviously troubled. In an attempt to justify herself she gave Barbie a perfunctory explanation of protocol that had required her expulsion. Through damp eyes Barbie silently looked up at her thinking, "you have no idea of what we have just been through! I was not even here for the heart transplant. How can you tell me to leave him now?!" The unuttered thoughts remained so as the nurse left her alone in the empty corridor. Soon, Barbie too left to go to the hotel room.

On Sunday I got out of bed into a chair, which was quite a challenge attached to so many tubes. I had two I.V.s and an arterial line in my right arm, one I.V. in the left arm, a central line in my right neck, an oxygen mask, two pericardial drains and one right chest tube. However, the tube that bothered me most was the Foley catheter draining my bladder. It did not hurt, but it was annoying. Every time I moved I had the sensation that I had to pee. I thought of the thousands of patients in whom I had placed catheters with their suspicious query to me, "Will this hurt?" And I would respond, "Not too much." After which they would then ask, "Have you ever had one?" Well, now I have. I asked the nurse a few times if they could remove it, but I knew the answer. The catheter usually stays as long as the patient remains in the intensive care unit so that the medical staff can closely watch the urine output. The first day I had a stiff neck from being immobile for so long in the O.R. The nurse asked if I had pain and I mentioned my neck. Soon morphine was roaming through my veins and the pain disappeared. This was the first and last narcotic I received during the rest of my hospitalization. They had carved my skin and sawed open my sternum, and yet it did not really hurt that much. I felt the ache in my chest when I moved, but it was not that bad. I was not overly surprised because I knew that nerves come around from the spine, but do not cross the midline in front. For that reason, midline incisions do not hurt as much as one would expect.

On Tuesday, my second birthday in one week arrived. Most of my tubes were removed and I was transferred to the regular floor. The nurses there brought me a cake, which tasted wonderful. The only tube remaining was the chest tube draining my right lung. Because I had had such a large pleural effusion prior to the transplant, the surgeons had placed this third tube to prevent re-accumulation of fluid in my lung. The hope, of course, was that the fluid was due to a bad sump-pump and not the amyloidosis. The constant presence of fluid draining from this tube weighed heavily on my mind. Would the leakage stop? I silently prayed that it would.

Barbie had asked what I wanted for my birthday and I told her that I had already received my desire in the gift of my new heart. But I had one more wish in my heart: another birthday. As Barbie and I talked about the wedding of Samuel and Michelle we decided to reunite in San Diego in one year, if possible, to celebrate the anniversary of their wedding and my heart transplant. That was my first long-term goal.

Through my window on the second floor, I watched as the sun dipped behind the hills. I felt such a peace. My prayers had been answered so miraculously. I could not bear the thought of leaving Barbie a widow. And now I had the hope of more years with her. How many, I did not know. This is the transformation that every person who passes through, and survives, a life threatening experience undergoes. Suddenly, the beauty of each moment becomes paramount. The number of days is less important than how you fill them.

I sat in the chair for a while, thinking about such things. Suddenly, I noticed Barbie sitting on the arm of the chair. She leaned forward and rested herself on my left shoulder. Quietly her hand went up my neck as she caressed my hair. I felt such infinite love for her. We sat there for a while in silence. I turned to look up at her and as our eyes met she smiled. She dipped her head towards me and we kissed. If there ever were a way to recreate the sensation of your first kiss, it would still not compare to what this felt like. The passion of that kiss, that caress, melted away all worry, all fear.

Time was suspended. There was no past. The future was but a vapor. There was only her. Her lips, her touch, her love healed me. It was one of the most passionate moments of my life. I felt eternity pass in that moment and God reaffirmed to me that I would have Barbie for an eternity. My new heart filled with hope as each beat carried both of us on our shared journey together. I was 49, momentarily pausing in the middle of infinity.

CHAPTER 31

Wednesday, August 20, 2008
Recovery

Kevin is healing well. He is walking - while holding my hand. He's a bit unsteady, but moving none the less. He's eating solids and things inside are moving, if you know what I mean! Kevin feels great and is itching to get to a computer to write a blog. I know he has been composing a number of them as he has been lying in bed.

We remain stunned to think that for a moment he did not have a heart and now he is alive because of someone else's. At this point we do not know much about the donor. Kevin can write a letter to the family and if they choose, they can respond. What an amazing creation God made that our bodies can accept an organ from another human being and the advances in medicine that allow it to be done. We've seen many miracles in this journey.

The plan as of now is that he could be discharged tomorrow or Monday. Heart transplant patients are only discharged Mon-Thur so that they can go directly to Santa Clara Kaiser for biopsies and tests right after discharge. Kevin and I will live in a hotel near the hospital for one month and then he can go home and recover for 2 more months. These last 2 months of recovery he will visit Santa Clara often for more biopsies and such, but can live at home. That means

Rebecca's wedding should very well be attended by her dad! The amyloidosis will be addressed some time close to the end of recovery.

We again are grateful and overwhelmed by this entire experience AND are much better together.

Barbie

On Friday Rebecca, Corey and Caitlin came to visit. Rebecca brought me a delicious chocolate cake for my birthday and Caitlin sang a song she had written while I was still waiting for a heart; hence the name of the song: "Waiting." She accompanied herself on her guitar. It was beautiful and we were all in tears. The nurses hovered near the door to hear what was happening as she sang of angels above and how she would give her heart for me.

"Waiting"
by
Caitlin Anderson

"I sit patiently, wondering about you.
Thinking about things you've gotten me through.
And I know that you will be all right.
In the end, it's worth the fight

I try waiting longer for you,
I try staying stronger for you.
And I would give you my heart,
Just so you could come home.

You have taught me more than I could explain.
You have loved me more than I could ever dream.
Your example has made me become more
than what I had settled for.
I try waiting longer for you,

I try staying stronger for you.
Your heart was so full of love,
they sent angels from above.

I try waiting longer for you,
I try staying stronger for you.
I try being braver, it's true.
I will always love you

I will always love you."

Saturday, August 23, 2008
What I have learned

Kevin is doing remarkably well. He spoke on the phone to many people yesterday and just hearing his voice puts everyone at ease since he sounds so good. The only thing he is waiting for now is getting the chest tube out so that he can shower; sponge baths only do so much. I believe they may be taking it out today.

What I have Learned

Being married to Kevin is easy. He is a 'take care of things' kind of guy. We, as in most marriages had our roles. There were responsibilities he took care of and others I took care of. Often times I would appear lazy and just expected Kevin (and knew he would) take care of things that I had no interest in. In my head I felt he was much better at it anyway. For the past two months I have had to take on many of his responsibilities; some I do not like and some I am uncomfortable doing. This experience has made me more observant & given me the realization that I can do more than I thought I could. I am more observant of my surroundings, discussions, maps, computers, learning about things

I never thought I could learn or needed to learn. It has changed the way I think. Everything now has importance to me. I have this feeling that everything I hear, I may need to know someday. So my challenge is to categorize it and store it somewhere in my brain for later use. Recalling it will be a challenge, but one worth trying. Life and knowledge have changed for me. They seem greater and like I said, have more importance.

Barbie

That evening, as I lay in bed in the darkness, so many thoughts and memories washed over me. I remembered the power of that hug that I felt from my friend Markell. I thought about the man who had just lost his life and saved mine. I anguished at what his family was experiencing. Words formed and I eventually wrote them down a week later.

Wednesday, August 27, 2008
A hug, A shared Heart

......August 15 was the day that two worlds were uniquely united, and at the "Coeur" of it all, a heart. This heart had already lived a lifetime in my donor. Each beat becoming the sum of his existence. Altogether they wove a tapestry of color and life that reflected all of his joys and sadness, his longings and toil. The heart was his witness and his strength, unfaultable in marking each moment, constant. But then, the unthinkable occurred, and as his life silently slipped away, his heart kept going, awaiting a new life. In that moment, my donor made the ultimate final gift, his heart to me.

My own heart has served me so well. I have experienced more joy and fulfillment in one lifetime than most men would have in three. But my heart was worn out, ravaged by disease and struggling daily to keep me going, and soon, it had marked its last beat.

While I lay there on the operating table, for at least an hour, I had no heart inside my chest. My survival was maintained only through machines and technology under the skilled hands of committed doctors and nurses. And then, his heart was placed inside me, and my life began again. I had a new heart, but it is not completely mine, nor will it ever be. For it is a shared heart. This shared heart has already lived a lifetime and must be remembered as such.

This must be why I have the strong desire to hug everyone. A hug, in such a simple act, can bring two hearts together, marking a brief moment of friendship. I feel like I should share my shared heart with others. I will honor the memory of my donor by offering his gift to others with a hug.

In doing this, I am really following the example of my cardiologist, Dr. Weisshaar. She hugs everyone, all of the time, and now I know why. Her life's work has consisted of bringing hearts and souls together, and what better way to symbolize that than an offering of a hug to all of her patients.

Two things that heartbeats and hugs have in common are that they are both strong symbols of the importance of being in the present. Past regrets and future concerns have no place in the moment of presence. What I have learned from all of this is to cherish the present.

My dream is that someday, if allowed, I may meet the family of my donor and through the simple act of a hug, reunite them with him one more time in the present.

In memory of my donor and his family.
Please say a prayer for them.

Kevin

CHAPTER 32

I was being given a lot of drugs, antirejection, antibiotic, antivirals and antifungals. I soon learned that I suffered a strange side–effect from high dose steroids. I was receiving very high doses of prednisone, which caused me to have hiccups. Now, hiccups and a healing chest incision do not cooperate well together. Each hiccup would shoot a pain through my wound. I tried everything to abate them, but to no avail. Then by accident, while eating a Milky Way candy bar, a chunk of un-chewed nougat and caramel got stuck in my throat. I let it sit there for about 30 seconds before I got water to wash it down. To my surprise, the hiccups disappeared for about five hours. Thereafter, whenever I got hiccups, I had Barbie go to the gift shop to find me sticky candy that I could get stuck in my throat. This technique continue to work intermittently, even as I began chemotherapy with dexamethasone. Finally, a year later Dr. Sardar prescribed Baclofen, a muscle relaxant, which has worked for my hiccups ever since.

Friday morning I had a surprise visit from Dr. Weisshaar and Dr. Nishime. They were at Stanford for the weekly heart transplant conference and stopped by to see how I was doing. I informed them that I felt great and that I was ready to leave the hospital as soon as they took my chest tube out. By now I knew that the earliest I would leave was Monday. I had decided early on to try to be a good patient and not second-guess or advise my doctors. But every day I would plead with the transplant fellow to remove my chest tube and every day he would say, "Not yet," because the drainage output from my lung was still high. I worried that the drainage would never stop, and then what? I could not help falling back on my own surgical experience with drains. As a urologist, I use drains all the time to prevent collections of blood, lymph or urine from impeding the healing process. I had found over the years that a drain on suction can paradoxically promote excess drainage. Sometimes when it is converted to passive gravity drainage, the leak heals. As I was lying in bed 24/7, my surgical logic overcame me and I set forth a plan. When the lights went out at night I would lean over the bed railing and shut off the suction to my pneumovac device so that it would only be on a water-seal. I thought that by doing this I could decrease my total fluid output overnight. When the transplant team came on rounds in the morning, maybe they would remove my chest tube. Sometime between when the nurse recorded my outputs and the doctors came by, I reconnected the suction to avert suspicion. My plan backfired, however, for as soon as I reconnected the suction, all of the leftover fluid drained. By now the wound in my abdomen where the ½ inch hose exited was quite inflamed and painful. I was allowed now to walk outside during the day, but I had to haul the fluid collection device attached to my chest tube with me. My sister Leslie visited from Seattle on Saturday with her adopted son, Finn. It was wonderful to see her. We walked outside to the fountain in front of the hospital. To be in direct sunlight was rejuvenating, even in my hospital gown, collection device in tow, with a pink Darth Vader mask to protect me from lurking fungi in the air.

Up to this point I had yet to meet my surgeon, Dr. Philip Oyer. I thought this was strange until he suddenly showed up on Saturday morning and remarked that he had left town just after my surgery. After a few pleasantries he asked at what point I had stopped operating. When I told him that it was only a month prior he was visibly shocked. He described how when he removed my heart it was so stiff that it did not even collapse on the tray as most hearts do. It felt like it was made of rubber and he wondered how I was still alive, let alone operating with a heart so damaged. Tenacity and prayer, I mused silently to myself.

The day had finally come. Monday we hoped to be discharged from the hospital. Just after 7:00 A.M. the surgical team came in for rounds. I tried to ascertain from the fellow's poker face what his morning review of my numbers indicated. No such luck. Finally he hesitantly said, "Well, I think we can get that tube out of you and get you out of here." I smiled in agreement. For years, first as a chief resident and then as an attending surgeon at Yale I would have patients that were improving from complicated surgery. Knowing that barring a complication they would likely recover, rather than give a set of specific orders I would just say, "De-tube and advance to discharge." Much of the systems in the body are based on plumbing. We put tubes in sick people to put stuff in and drain stuff out until the recovering patient can balance everything on their own. Removing tubes always correlates with a recovering patient.

This was my last tube and I wanted it out. About an hour later, the junior fellow came in to pull the tube. The site where the 1 cm drain entered my skin was quite inflamed by now. The entry site was in the abdominal wall just above and to the right of my navel. The hose then ran subcutaneously up to the chest wall where it then dove deeper into the space around my right lung. It was about 12 inches long. When they had placed it in the operating room they had sutured it in with a "purse-string" suture, which allows the person removing it to close the wound once the tube is out. First he unwrapped the long ends of the suture from around the tube. Then he slid the tube out as I hummed. The humming was intended to create a positive pressure in the chest so that I did not suck in air once the tube is out. I felt more like screaming than humming. It really hurt. But then he pulled the purse-string to close the bright red skin edges together and tied a knot. That hurt even more. However, it was worth it. I was free and independent. Everything I needed now to survive was inside me. All I needed to do now was take a few pills and heal.

Finally the moment came where they wheeled me out of the hospital to the curb where Barbie was waiting with the Prius. I had donned my HEPA mask to protect me from ubiquitous bacteria, molds and fungi that filled the unseen world around me. The mask actually made it difficult to breathe, since it required extra effort to pull air through the filter. I had to wear it outside (because of *aspergillus* and mold risks) and in public places (due to bacteria and virus risks). I considered the inside of the car clean and took off the mask as soon as I was inside.

The next phase of my recovery would take place in Santa Clara. We would remain near the heart transplant clinic at Kaiser for the next 5-6 weeks. Since we live over two hours away, they would not allow a daily commute. If there were to be an emergency, I needed to be close. Our discharge instructions required that we immediately go to the clinic to be evaluated, instructed and pick up my new medications.

However, we varied from these instructions slightly because I was so hungry for some real food. And I mean food that would put my new heart to the test. I wanted salt. We headed to a bakery in Sunnyvale called Specialties and I ordered what I had been craving for six months: a salami sandwich with extra pickles.

After this brief detour I entered the clinic, now as an outpatient. Everyone there -- the nurses, medical assistants, Janet, the social worker and the doctors -- beamed as they told me how great I looked. I felt fantastic. When Dr. Weisshaar came in the exam room to see us, She also asked how I felt. I responded that I felt wonderful. She said, chuckling, "Oh, that is the steroid euphoria." Slightly offended, I thought to myself, "No, this is really me. I truly feel great." She then turned to Barbie and gave her a warning. The steroids would likely make me moody and that she needed to be prepared. Again, I thought that her admonition was unnecessary. I determined that I was and would be in complete control of my emotions, as I had always been. I should have listened better to my doctor.

Dr. Weisshaar and me

We were given pages of instructions on "The Care and Management of Your New Heart." The new owners' guide explained what to look out for and when to call or come in. Additionally, was the list of medications and when I was to take each one. We went to the pharmacy to pick up a three month supply of my drugs. They filled 2 ½ grocery bags. Finally, after about two hours in the clinic we drove the three miles to our new home: the Marriott Residence Inn in Sunnyvale, California.

Monday, August 25, 2008
Rejection and Balance

The three-month supply of my new medications

It's great to be back. I am out of the hospital now and doing wonderfully. I wanted to explain a little about the next phase of my recovery.

I have always been averse to rejection, wanting to be accepted by all. My new heart feels the same way. While we were in Rochester, we met with the transplant surgeon, Dr. Daly. He did not mince words. He said that a heart transplant will change the rest of your life. It is not a question of whether your body will reject the organ, it is a matter of when. He stressed that I would need to take anti-rejection drugs forever. We accepted his guidance as a matter of course.

Rejection occurs because the body views the new organ as a foreign protein. Our immune system is designed to fight against foreign invaders that might make us ill or even kill us. These include organisms such as bacteria, viruses, and fungal infections as well as debris like a wood sliver. In each case the immune system recognizes the invasion and destroys it. Foreign protein from a transplanted organ (or allograft) causes the same response.

Two main systems of immune response exist in our bodies: cellular and humoral.

Cellular, as the name implies, is mediated through white blood cells, specifically lymphocytes called T-Cells and B-Cells. This is the type of pathway that most commonly causes transplant rejection, and as such, the therapy is directed to slow down or suppress the cellular response.

Humoral immune responses are directed by special- ized proteins called antibodies (or immunoglobulins). These antibodies can quickly recognize and make an antibody that will tag and attract killer cells to eat up the bad guy. This new antibody is then stored in mem- ory for up to a lifetime to prevent re-infection. This is why we only get chicken pox once.

Ironically, for me, amyloidosis is the ultimate manifestation of my warped sense of humoral. (That works on so many levels).

Currently, I have been started on many medica- tions that fall into three broad groups: Anti-rejection drugs, Anti-microbial drugs and body balancing drugs.

The anti-rejection drugs are cyclosporine, Cellcept and prednisone. These effectively suppress my immune system but there are costs. I am more susceptible to infections and the side-effects of the drugs mess up my physiology. Thus the need for the other two groups. The antimicrobials are Bactrim (antibiotic), Valcyte(antiviral) and Mycelex (antifungal). In addition, these drugs can causes imbalances such as high blood pressure, kidney problems, fluid imbalance, acid production, cholesterol elevations and mineral imbalances. All of the other drugs attempt to correct this.

This is why today, my first stop after discharge was to return to the transplant clinic at Kaiser in Santa Clara, to review all of my new medications. In addition, I must remain near the clinic for at least a month so that immediate intervention will be available at the first signs of rejection. This begins tomorrow with my first heart biopsy. They will continue weekly. In addition, I will receive biweekly I.V. infusions of Dacluzimab, another potent anti rejection drug for at least two months. They will monitor blood levels and chemistries frequently, as well as my general health.

It may seem like a lot, but I accept it gladly, if it insures a healthy heart that will last me a lifetime.

Kevin

Chapter 33

Friday, August 29, 2008
Another Goodbye

Today I am leaving for Utah to attend Sam & Michelle's reception there. Kevin's mother is driving down to stay with him while I am away. I leave at 1pm and will return Sunday morning. It will be another fast Utah trip. I'm excited to see Jeremy & Alexandria's new apartment as well as Sam & Michelle's. Saying goodbye to Kevin this time is not as hard as the last, though I do wish he were coming with me. He misses our children so much. I can tell this has not been easy for him to miss the wedding in San Diego and now the reception in Utah.

The Prednisone and Cyclosporine are taking a toll on his body. He does not sleep well so he is always tired. His body wants to sleep but his brain won't let him. He never feels like he slept well. He takes one or two naps during the day to try and catch up. Night time is the worst. Next Tuesday he starts to taper down on the Prednisone. Each week it will drop and then daily until they deem him clear to stop altogether. He's getting used to the mask and we keep bottles of Purell everywhere.

I have come to have great respect for caretakers; the ones who devote their time and energy to their loved ones. Especially those who care for individuals

*with chronic illnesses or disabilities that require years
of attention. They are the real heroes.
Know that Kevin is well, exhausted, but well.*

Barbie

In this, my new life as a heart transplant patient, I had to develop
the daily ritual of taking my medications. This would be a lifelong
effort. I searched out the indications, precautions and side effects
of each drug. At least seven of them caused diarrhea. Clearly, the
one with the most immediate impact was the steroid, Prednisone.
I have known for years of the miraculous benefits and devastating side effects of chronic glucosteroid use. People often lump
all steroids into the same category. However, glucocorticoids, or
prednisone, have nothing to do with the anabolic steroids used
and abused by body builders. I began at 100 mg a day, which is
20x the maintenance dose for the drug. This coupled with cyclosporine, Cellcept and bi weekly infusion of Daclizumab were
meant to suppress my immune system to prevent it from rejecting
my new heart.

Each drug brought its own unique alterations to my physiology. I assumed that by mere will and mental fortitude I would
be able to overcome and negate these side effects, but they took
their toll. Still, I was resolved to do everything in my power to
strengthen myself. I weighed about 173 lbs when I left the hospital.
There was very little fat and a significant amount of muscle atro-
phy. The new heart did an excellent job now at pumping fluid to
my grateful kidneys. The fluid in my right chest was mostly gone,
making me a little less short of breath. The edema surrounding my
gut, which had given me abdominal pain for the entire previous
year, was now gone. I would have had a wonderful appetite had it
not been for the nausea and anorexia caused by the prednisone.
The swelling in my legs was better, but not completely gone. My
blood tests revealed very little circulating protein in my blood. As
a medical student, we had hammered into us the importance of

positive protein balance in the post-surgical period to facilitate healing. Without a steady source of essential amino acids, skin cannot heal, muscle cannot repair and hypertrophy with exercise, and the immune system is left wanting.

The first week out of the hospital could be considered the honeymoon phase. I felt great that I was eating well and walking daily with Barbie around the neighborhood outside the hotel. I was amazed how far I could already walk without getting short of breath.

As the weekend approached, it was time for Barbie to leave me again to go to Utah for the reception there for Samuel and Michelle. Knowing that I could not be left alone in the hotel, I called my mom, hoping that she could come from Sacramento to stay with me. She said she would check her schedule to see if she was available.

Saturday started out OK, so my mom and I decided to drive to the beach in Santa Cruz. Whenever I am in need of rejuvenation, I am drawn to nature, usually either the ocean or the mountains. Both the sound of waves crashing on a beach and wind blowing through the trees has a particular healing effect upon me. This was the same beach where Barbie and I had gone on the day of my first biopsy. That was the day just two months ago when we had found out how truly sick my heart was. How much had passed in only two months. It seemed like an eternity. As we drove back I began to slide into a profound weakness. I slept most of the day and ate little. Sunday morning I had great desires to go to church. I so strongly felt the need to partake of the sacrament (communion) and pour out my gratitude to God. We found a chapel in Santa Clara. I did not have any church clothes to wear, and I do not remember the talks, but every time we sang a hymn I was overcome with emotion. I was especially touched by the sacrament hymn, "I Stand All Amazed." I could not contain my incredulity over how much my Father in Heaven loved me and had blessed me. I sobbed, not as quietly as I should have, with my mask buzzing as I failed miserably in my efforts at singing.

That afternoon I was so sick that I began to be scared. "What if something is really wrong with me?" I thought. I considered all of the possible disasters that could be going on. Was I bleeding internally? Was I in rejection? Did I have a bad infection? In desperation I called the doctor on call, Dr. Nishime. I described my symptoms, minimizing my fears as well as I could. She recommended I go in to get some lab tests. My mom dropped me off at the hospital door. As I walked down the hallway to the lab, it took all of my will and power to not fall down. I got the labs done and we drove back. I tried to sleep but to no avail. I anxiously waited for Barbie to return.

Saturday, August 30, 2008
Side-effects

I have had many patients who have not taken a prescribed medication because they read the package insert and saw potential side effects and completely missed the therapeutic benefit of the drug. In most cases, the list of side effects rarely occurs and they missed out on feeling better out of an unfounded fear.

However, when you are taking 14 medications of a very potent nature, you are bound to have side-effects. They are really affecting me now. I must continue to take my medication with the hope that as some are tapered-off, I will feel better.

I now have no appetite and everything tastes funny. Dr. Weisshaar warned me about the cyclosporine shakes, which have now begun. I began to have parasthesias today, (tingling in the fingers and feet) and feel general malaise and sick to my stomach. The edema and high blood pressure are also expected. I physically feel "washed out" and have little energy.

I am, however, recovering very well from my surgery. That was the easy part. I still have no pain.

I begin the prednisone taper tomorrow, not a day too soon. Hopefully, in two weeks, when I am down from 80 mg a day to 20 mg a day, I will feel better.

All of this is a small price to pay for the great future health that I know I will feel. There will, of course, still be bumps on that road.

Kevin

Monday was Labor Day which truly reflected any effort to get out of bed or even speak. I had two visitors scheduled to come, Dr. Chabra and my sister Lisa and her family from Fresno. Knowing what a terrible host I would be, I asked them not to come. I figured that they would not want to travel so far just to see me sleep.

Monday, September 1, 2008
A sick doctor

I probably feel sicker today than I have ever felt in my life. I know that it is the medication and that my body is trying to find a new balance. The side-effects continue to mount. The tingling in my feet has now spread to my legs and I just feel, overall, unwell. Wellness is something we take for granted and do not really notice until it flees us.

I have this constant gnawing in the pit of my stomach that I cannot really differentiate between hunger or abhorrence for food. The constant foul taste in my mouth makes all food unpalatable, and I find I have to force myself to eat. This concerns me as I really need the nutrition.

As I go through the twice daily ritual of taking my medication, I find myself staring at the sorted drugs on the table and my throat reflexively closes. I have to 'trick' my esophagus to accept the pills with some other food, like cookies or applesauce.

I really only feel good when I am lying down, which I have done a lot in the past few days. I catch naps during the day, but remain wide awake at night.

The drugs are now affecting my concentration, making even dialing a phone number a challenge. As I lie in bed awake my mind wanders to strange places. I was contemplating the myriad of forwarded emails that people seem to circulate listing pithy phrases and "feel good" scroll-downs and thinking how most of them are like a bite of a Butterfinger: momentary sweetness, but without substance. I began to compose my own banal list, but prudence stopped me; my mind, currently warped as it is would include such phrases as, "Sitting in a dark room is like a day without sunshine," or "Pictures of kittens are cute, until they become feral cats and attack you in your sleep."

When I finally do fall asleep, however, the effect causes vivid dreams. I dreamt that I was finally back to work in clinic and I was so far behind seeing patients that I was working late into the evening and the middle of the night. It was 4:00 A.M. and the hallway was pitch black so that I had to physically escort the patients to the front door. In the darkness I ran into Dr. Chiu, (he is my partner and tends to work late). I thought that was funny.

I share these only as examples of how being ill can affect us. There is this underlying anxiety that I will never feel better. Intellectually, I know that this is not true. I will get better. But in the moment, you cannot deny what you feel.

Above all, I know that I am not alone. Every person who has been ill knows what I am going through.

The important thing is that this teaches me to be more patient with my patients. Most of the time, what sick patients really need is a listening ear, a caring heart and understanding.

Boy, do I understand now.

I hope that the memory of this will serve to make me a better doctor.

Kevin

Monday, September 1, 2008

From Lincoln, to Rochester, to Santa Clara, to San Diego, to Stanford, to Sunnyvale, to Utah and back to Sunnyvale

I had been thinking about my weekend in San Diego and realized Sam & Michelle's wedding, at least on my part, had been overshadowed by Kevin: missing him and the news of the heart.

The moment the call came about Kevin's heart, I was in the car with Sam and Caitlin. I was taking Sam to meet Michelle for their pre-wedding photo shoot on the beach and had left my phone at the beach house. Sam's phone was in the back of my car, unreachable, and Caitlin fortunately had her phone. Kevin had called my phone, and Rebecca answered when he asked where I was. Rebecca explained and then he told her. She ran down the hall of the beach house and announced to my family and Kevin's family that a heart was available. As tears of joy entered the room, they joined together for a prayer to bless Kevin through the surgery and to bless the donors family. Harold, Kevin's oldest brother, offered the prayer. In the meantime, Kevin tried Sam's phone (unreachable) and then Caitlin's. She handed the phone to me. I heard him say something about a heart, but I could not really hear him and then in my sometimes inattentive way, I apologized for not having my phone and began to explain why. He stopped me mid-sentence and said, "They have a heart." I froze. A million things went through my head. I am not there, I am here. When will it start? How will I know he is well? What should I do? Can I do this? We hung up and I grabbed Caitlin's hand and we cried driving back to the beach house. We drove in silence. While I was happy about the heart for Kevin, I was not ready for it yet. In retrospect, everything happened as it should. While we were in the temple observing the marriage of Sam & Michelle, Kevin was in recovery, not thinking about being absent. While in the temple before the ceremony, I looked up and saw the chair empty that Kevin would have sat in, I started to cry, not so much that he wasn't there but with gratitude as to why he wasn't there. I was full of joy where tears just kept flowing. Jeremy, who would stand in for Kevin, came up to me and said, "Be strong for Sam." I pulled myself together and my mom came to sit next to me and held my hand. The rest of the day was beautiful. Sam and Michelle are so happy together. Our families and friends had a nice sit-down afternoon lunch hosted by the Morans. I was at ease because I handed off things I needed to do before I could leave to Leslie and my mom and sister, Kathie, grateful for their willingness to help. Mostly at ease because I would be with Kevin soon.

We both are looking forward to going back to Lincoln to see our home, our girls, and our dog.

Barbie

Thursday, September 4, 2008
My Dad

I have been thinking a lot about my Dad lately. My Mom came to stay with me last weekend while Barbie was in Utah and we had an opportunity to reminisce about him. My Dad died almost four years ago. When we moved back to California he was ill, but I thought we would have more time with him. It was only three months later when he passed away. My Dad died of Multiple Myeloma, which is interesting in that it is a cancer of the same cell-type that causes Amyloidosis. However, they are not related or of a heritable type.

California state law requires that all physicians take 12 hours of CME in end-of-life studies and palliative care. When I did my training, the course director asked all of us how we would like to die. Most people wanted a quick and painless death after a long and useful life. Unfortunately, only 10% die that way. When she asked, "Who would like to die of cancer?" I was the only person who raised his hand. She was puzzled and asked why. I was remembering my Dad and thought to myself, 'He died well' He was lucid and in control until the end. I explained this and she agreed. The rest of the class was consigned to die like most people do, after a long chronic illness takes its toll over many years. This may seem like a strange discussion, but it is the reality that we will all come to.

When I began work at Kaiser, I looked at my Dad's X-rays and was shocked to see how much the cancer had invaded his entire skeleton. I thought, "He must be in terrible pain." And yet, he never complained. Even then, his focus was not on himself. The center of his life was always on his family. He never spent one night in the hospital. He died quietly at home surrounded by his family. Two days prior, I spoke to him and promised him that we would take care of Mom. The last words he ever said to me were "Thank You."

My parents gave me two great gifts in my lifetime. First was a strong work ethic coupled with the value of personal responsibility. The second was that they trusted me to make my own decisions, which included the risk of failing. For a parent, this is a hard balance to reach.

In my years counseling with and observing parents, I have found that many fall into the two extremes of being too rigid or too lenient. They either micromanage their children's everyday activities, allowing them controlled successes, but without real risk, or they aim to be just their friend who would never impose on their personal freedom. Both approaches are fraught with problems and based in fear. The middle ground is harder to maintain. Give them guidelines to live by, supported by example, and then let them decide, without subtle threat or coercion.

This gift from my parents was so valuable to me, that even when I left home, I would not do anything to break their trust. No child feels freer than when they are trusted by their parents.

As I spoke to my Mom about this, I realized something I had not noticed before. My parents have nine children and all of us have chosen to be productive and honorable in our lives. What I find even more interesting is that this has carried on into the next generation. All of my parent's 34 grandchildren continue to follow this pattern. I think of Barbie's and my own children and how they have always chosen well. They have always brought us only joy.

It is no accident that I was born of noble parents. But with every true gift comes responsibility.

I have been given a "second lease" on life. The memory of my father reminds me that I must continue in this life, as before, and never do anything that would lose the trust of my parents; the most valuable gift I ever got from them.

Kevin

The days wore on. We were so ready to go home. For over two months Barbie had done everything for me. She shopped, she cooked, she drove me everywhere. I am not a good passenger. I am hard-wired to travel the shortest distance between two points. This does not just relate to geographical linearity but to everything, including time to finish a task and cost-to-value ratio. Barbie has accepted and put up with this for years. It was all that I could do to sit in the passenger seat of the car knowing that the route that she was taking would add an extra 52 seconds to our trip. I did my best to keep my mouth shut, but she always senses even what I am not saying. It was about this time when Barbie began to wonder what would happen now in our relationship. Would I soon begin to take over again as I became stronger and more independent? At the time, I was not fully aware of how much this weighed on her. She had truly enjoyed her independence from me always being in the driver's seat and did not want to lose it.

After having been married for so many years, we had moved into a certain understanding of what our roles were and the process of shared decision making. Suddenly, our habitual roles had been disrupted by my acute illness. Barbie, as the caregiver, took over. Ironically, it turned out to be much easier for her to adjust to the beginning of her role as the caregiver than to contemplate the end. At this point, I was still so focused on myself and trying to adjust physically and emotionally to my new world, that I did not fully grasp how difficult this was for Barbie. I knew at every moment how I felt. She could only guess, wondering if I was minimizing my discomfort, as I am prone to do. As she sat and listened to my responses to my doctors at our frequent visits, she often felt the need to interject and tell them how I was really doing, from her observation point. All of the attention was focused on me. Who was there for her in her silent suffering? I did the best I could.

There were a few evenings where the weight of it all became more than we could bear and all we could do was hold each other and cry. We said things to one another that we had never said before, as if maybe some complete catharsis of our souls would begin emotional and spiritual healing. Suddenly, those buttons marked as "Do not touch under any circumstance!" were exposed for the first time in decades. Now visible, they were pressed and activated by the weight of the moment. Those were difficult days.

The clinic schedule gradually lightened over the first month. Initially, I would go in 2-3 times a week. Soon I was going in just weekly for a heart biopsy and every other week for the Daclizumab infusion. They had told us 4-6 weeks before we could go home. When given any range, I always assume it will be the shortest distance. I find a way to make it happen.

The high dose steroids had a strange affect on my mind. and also caused insomnia, I would lie awake for hours and random images would flood my brain. One evening I began to visualize the killer T-cells from my bone marrow attacking my new heart as if it were an invading alien. Dozens of similes and metaphors began to form. I decided to write them down.

Wednesday, September 10, 2008
Legal Alien (just for fun)

I metaphoran alien recently and he entered into my life. I'll call him Jerome. At first I was anxious and then had a change of heart. He is, however, a legal alien. Unfortunately, once the IMS (Immune system) discovered him, they immediately set out to reject and deport him. Small squadrons of killer cells began to set upon him, but he was protected by his "Green Card." Actually, multiple green cards from different agencies: Gengraf, Cellcept, Prednisone and Daclizumab. These were all administered, by me, under one umbrella agency, not dissimilar to Homeland Security. Fortuitously, the agents of these killer cells were repelled back to their cavernous marrows, and with luck, will remain dormant, as sleeper cells.

He made his home in the heartland and began work immediately. He works fulltime, now, and specializes in fluid and energy distribution. He works with such regularity and precision that he is often compared to the ticking of a clock, earning him the nickname, 'Jerome, Jerome, the metronome'. (See Gattaca)

I hope to see him naturalized soon, and as a citizen, I can stand with him, hand over my heart, and pledge allegiance to this union. I sense that his tireless efforts will continue. I guess what I have learned is that we are all strangers on this borrowed land. Yet, as I serve to protect him and he labors to help me, alone we would remain alienated, but together we can stand free.

Kevin

Chapter 34

Wednesday, September 17, 2008
By his side

So now we are in recovery mode with the anxiety of moving forward to treat the amyloidosis. We did get an appointment with hematology at Stanford. Again, we are grateful for the fast moving process to treat him. I need him here for as long as possible; he calms my soul and comforts my worries.

I have been thinking about the adjustment we will have going home. We have been by each other's side during this entire process with the exception of two receptions. When we go home and back to a routine, we will not be together all day. I suppose we will adjust. I let him start driving yesterday; it was strange to hand him over the keys. It sort of felt like I was letting go of some of my freedom, but having been a passenger for two months, Kevin now has more patience for passengers and I for the driver. I have left him at the hospital or the hotel room to run some errands, but he has never left me. The moment we get home and he leaves to run an errand, I will feel the loss of his companionship. This may sound very strange to many of you, but my sensitivity level has heightened. I have taken care of him for so long now, I will worry when he is not with me, not a lot, but to some small degree. As he gains more independence,

I lose a little of him. But to leave on a happy note, the fact that I have been able to be with him is a blessing and has made me love him more.

Barbie

Wednesday, September 17, 2008
Going Home

We have waited for this day for so long. We left for Rochester, MN on July 15th and have not really been home since. We are so excited to finally be back with Rebecca and Caitlin and have our lives return to some semblance of normalcy. However, we do return with some trepidation. This time that Barbie and I have spent together has been extraordinary. We have been with each other all of the time, day and night. Some might think that this would drive us crazy and we would be craving our "own" space. But it has been just the opposite. This is because, after 26 years of marriage, during this experience, our roles have changed so drastically. I have been dependant on Barbie for everything and this will slowly begin to change.

But we do not want to go back to where we were. There have been some truly profound moments that have brought us to closeness reminiscent of courtship. On these occasions of quiet intimacy, the emotional range has vacillated from despair to exhilaration. These experiences have changed our relationship and each of us personally. The fear is that as we return home and to our responsibilities there that we will revert back to old habits. We don't want to lose what we have learned.

Barbie asked me the other day, "Will you still spend time with me?" I knew exactly what she meant.

Like so many married couples, our lives were often controlled by our responsibilities and our leisure time often was not passed in common interests. It was like we were dancing to different tunes.

The song has changed; and now we dance together. It will require a constant effort to maintain the harmony of that shared song to keep us in step with each other. We still have much to do. Soon we start treatment for amyloidosis; that is a big unknown. At some point we will both go back to work. But it is my commitment to Barbie to never lose what we have learned or fall back on complacent habits. I must always hear her song and avoid stepping on her toes.

We will find new ways to be together and make them habits in our lives. To do otherwise would diminish the magnitude and the memory of these powerful moments that we have mutually experienced.

Kevin

Wednesday, September 17, 2008
On our way

We just got the call from the clinic. My biopsy was NER (No evidence of rejection) and all the labs look great. We're leaving now and going home for good!!

Kevin

Part 4

REJECTION

CHAPTER 35

Even though we were home, it was still necessary to drive to Santa Clara weekly for the heart biopsies, which included the infusion of Daclizumab every other week. Fortunately, the year before we had bought the Prius, which did save on gas for the 300 mile roundtrip journey. Finally the day came to see the amyloidosis specialist at Stanford, Dr. Stanley Schrier. I did an internet search on him and found that he had been a previous president of the society of hematology and oncology and had extensively published in his specialty. I found an announcement of a celebration that had occurred sometime in the past recognizing his 50 years of service at Stanford. I did the math, trying to figure out how old that would make him. Let's just say he has been around a while. He is a professor emeritus and only works one day a week, on Tuesdays. He has the most experience in treating amyloidosis so it was natural for me to see him. I was warned that he tended to run late; of course as a patient, I was still required to arrive an hour early to get my labs drawn and check in. Up until now, all of my outpatient care had been through Kaiser, so it was difficult to adjust to the pace and discontinuity inherent in university systems.

Our appointment was at 2:10, and the warning turned out to be true. Finally, we were ushered back to where the medical assistant robotically weighed me and deposited me in a room. He told me to uncross my legs to get a blood pressure (I still do not know how crossed legs affect blood pressure.) He entered the data into the computer and asked, obviously with no interest in my answer, "Are you having any pain?" A little while later, the hematology fellow came in. As it turned out, she was the wife of the cardiologist, Dr. Ron Witteles, who had originally helped get me on the list at Stanford. Dr. Wesley Witteles was delightful. She took a full history and then examined me. She left and soon after returned with Dr. Schrier. Here was the quintessential old school professor. I had seen a dozen iterations of him during my career at Yale. Years of renown and recognition for his accomplishments allowed him a professional curtness that made pleasantries superfluous. He came straight to the point. "Stick out your tongue," he began. "Ah yes, notice that scalloping along the edges," he continued, motioning for Dr. Witteles to look. "Classic macroglossia seen in amyloidosis; the tongue is too big for the mouth and presses against the teeth." He continued the exam with the spleen check. For a doctor to feel an enlarged spleen requires the patient to take a very deep breath and hold it. This is repeated several times until the doctor is assured there is no splenomegaly.

I appreciated his physical exam skills in this era where it is fast becoming a lost art. Ultrasound and CT scans so easily replace the diagnostician's touch, feel and auscultation. When he was done, he sat down, looked at me, and spoke: "I think we need to treat you with Revlimid and high dose dexamethasone. You will start on 15 mg of Revlimid a day for 21 days and then take seven days off. You will need to take 40 mg of Decadron (dexamethasone) every week, even on the weeks off the Revlimid. If you tolerate the 15 mg dose, we may increase you to 25 mg." I asked for how many cycles I would need to do this and he responded that he did not know. "Let's just see how it goes," he told me. "I'll see you back in a month." He got up to go. I knew that he had changed his clinic that week to Monday because of the high holidays so I wished him a good Rosh Hashanah. He raised his hand dismissively and walked out. I liked him. No messing around; we had a plan. We could finally start attacking the disease that had been attacking me.

I began taking the Decadron and Revlimid on a Wednesday. The decision to take the drugs mid-week would later become fortuitous, as the side-effects would then always begin in earnest on Friday evenings, when I could hide at home for a few days. At this point, however, I was completely unaware of the side-effects.

I assumed, as I always do, that I would be just fine and fly through my therapy without ill effect. Of course, the literature recounted many instances of patients who had to abandon Revlimid due to complications. This would not be me. Through the first cycle I did well. I was scheduled to return to Stanford monthly to see Dr. Schrier. Given the distance, I always tried to set my monthly visits with him for the second Tuesday to coincide with my heart biopsy and the heart transplant support group in Santa Clara.

I truly looked forward with anticipation to the heart transplant support group. For years, many of my patients, newly diagnosed with cancer, would ask me about the availability of specific support groups for their diagnosis. I had never made an effort to find these on their behalf and usually answered that I was unaware of any. Personally, I thought that they were unnecessary. I pictured the patients just sitting around and commiserating about their shared plight. Only now did I realize how insensitive and stupid my attitude had been. Now I needed to be around people who shared my experience, and who could support me with their love and empathy. They are not called support groups without reason.

The group was facilitated by Janet Stevenson, the social worker for the heart transplant department, and Flavio Epstein, PhD. We would monthly gather just down the hall from the room where I had spent two weeks waiting for my heart. Now I would often wander to room 2200 and glance in at the new occupant, remembering my days there. For the staff, we patients were a rolling stream of new bodies, the next just as sick as the last. Only a few patients in the unit were actually waiting for hearts. We would then graduate and head north to begin a new life. Within hours, another person would take our place in that medical cell, heart failing, too sick to be at home.

Now, we graduates would sit around a table and take turns telling our stories. Some would come every month for years, each time telling the same story. Others would come for a few months and then move on. As they became stronger, their need to come would diminish. Occasionally we would get news that someone died. Often I did not recognize the name, but others would sigh in sadness. Janet knew them all. Each story was so very similar: progressive weakness, varying degrees of delay in diagnosis, complaint that one doctor ignored them while another doctor saved their life. I always cringed as they maligned their doctors. I wanted to yell, "Hey, we are not perfect! We are doing the best we can!" I personally knew that many of the symptoms that we shared fell into the category of what you might feel with a flu or what some people exaggerate to get a work release because they are lazy or malingering. The overwrought primary care doctor then has the task of separating the one patient with life threatening fatigue and malaise from the hundred who are just stressed and tired.

However, as I listened to these stories it became very clear what differentiated the hero doctors from the rest. First, they listened, or at least their patients perceived that they were being listened to. Second, they believed their patients and acted. They became more than doctors. They were advocates. Every chronically ill patient, and I mean one with a true and serious life-threatening illness, needs an advocate: the doctor that will not limit his or her responsibilities to only those symptoms and conditions that fall under his or her specialty. Rather, they will pick up the phone and open the door for the lost patient to the next step on their road to health. I have had many such advocates: Dr. Khurana, Dr. Weisshaar, Dr. Nishime, Dr. Parekh, Dr. Lacy, Dr. Edwards, Dr. Epstein and most of all, my long time friend and oncologist, Dr. Sardar. I see Dr. Sardar and Dr. Weisshaar as my guardian angels.

The other people I met at my support group were the caregivers. It was obvious that they needed support just as much as the patients. Sometimes it would be a spouse and sometimes a parent. Sometimes it would be a close friend. It is literally impossible to go through a heart transplant without a caregiver. This can be a challenge, since some caregivers must balance their need to take care of the patient with their responsibilities at work, school or with small children at home. At this point the extended caregiver network comes into play. In our case we had family. Rebecca and Barbie's mom helped with Caitlin. My partners in the urology department immediately assumed responsibility for my patients. Members of our church helped with rides, meals and general support. It was quickly evident to me that the support group was not just the people who sat around the table on the second Tuesday of the month. My support group extended to all facets of my life, and it was the same with the other heart patients there. It was clear that we could not do this alone. Mostly we went to the group to make sure everyone was still healthy and well. Seeing other patients who were still healthy after years gave me a much-needed glimpse into my own future. If Tom was still working 10 years after his transplant, then maybe I could too. We went for hope.

CHAPTER 36

Thursday, October 9, 2008
Impressions

I remember the first time I went to the Chicago Art Institute. I was captivated by the collection of art from the impressionist period. I find that I have always been drawn to art from this period. My favorite museum in Paris was the Musee d'Orsay which

housed a magnificent collection of pieces from this period: Manet, Monet, Pissaro, Degas, Renoir and many others. Someone once described impressionist art to me as the image one might notice in your peripheral vision as you were passing by a scene. It is a moment in time, more of a glance, out of focus. This is embodied in a painting by Manet (Gare Saint Lazare) in which a woman is sitting on a street bench as a train is passing; a mere glance by a passerby.

I realized that this reflected many moments in my life in the past. With so many duties and distractions, many moments passed by in a blur. Moments that should have been the focus of my attention. Sometimes I would sit at a basketball game or piano practice of my daughter and instead of focusing on them, I would be playing a game on my Palm organizer. I saw or heard the game or music, but I missed the essence. I had so many responsibilities, that even when I was with someone, I would feel anxious to move onto the next task or item on the schedule, not giving them my full attention. This was the impressionist period of my life.

This changed as I begin the period of illness whose symptoms can only be described as classical. The problem was that these symptoms individually were all common to other benign conditions and were easily dismissed as indigestion or de-conditioning, fatigue, poor appetite, difficulty swallowing, hoarseness, inability to walk up a flight of stairs, stomach upset etc… Taken together they were classical for amyloidosis. But who has ever heard or thought of amyloidosis? It would be like hearing a piece of music from the composer, Ernst Wilhelm Wolf; the style would remind one of the classical period, and it could easily be ascribed to Mozart or Haydn. So it was with me.

The diagnosis was finally made and my life then can only be described as surreal. Two different realities were juxtaposed; Kevin, the guy for whom everything always worked out, the lucky one, was now facing a fatal illness, incurable. It was difficult to grasp. Every day revealed a new detail which altered the path in many directions, Roseville, Sacramento, a pleural effusion, malnutrition, edema, a cardiac output with half the normal flow. How was this possible? How did I minimize my symptoms so much that I did not see it? Santa Clara, a biopsy is done; Amyloidosis, then to the Mayo Clinic for exhausting studies, back to Santa Clara, Dopamine, Lasix and confinement; Hard decisions and finally to Stanford for a heart. And so on. I realize that all of this may seem rather abstract, but it helped me to see what I had been missing.

The one true thing, the constant reality in all of this was Barbie. I never feared dying or pain or anything. The only fear was leaving Barbie alone. I relied on her, not only for emotional support, but for the first time in our marriage, for everything. She drove, she shopped, she lifted the heavy stuff. But, whenever we had a moment alone, we began to realize how strong our love really was. There were some tender moments so sweet, so powerful, that they changed us forever. Thus began my romantic period. Form and function folded into feelings. I see the color and emotion more clearly. And the recurring motif is gratitude.

Now when I go to hear Caitlin in her piano lesson, my Palm remains in my pocket; no games, no distractions. I want to focus on the music. I not only hear the notes, I can feel her essence expressed through the medium of the piano. If she makes a mistake, I do not notice it. The dynamics, the rhythm, the passion is all I hear now. And it is so beautiful. Things are so much more in focus now. I hope that I remain in this Romantic period and never again experience life as a passing glance.

Kevin
Friday, October 17, 2008
Changes

It has been two weeks since I have started the chemotherapy for the Amyloidosis. The Revlimid, which I take daily, does seem to have noticeable side effects. The high dose steroid does cause the usual insomnia and weird taste in food, but it also gives me intermittent hiccups. Of note, however, my heart biopsy on Tuesday did show moderate rejection (2R, on a scale of 0 through 3R.) A large percentage of patients will have this during the first six months. This is also treated with high dose steroids, so in addition to the Decadron I take weekly for the Amyloidosis, I am now on 100 mg of Prednisone daily, but with a rapid taper. They also stopped my Cyclosporine because even a supra-therapeutic dose was clearly not protecting me. I am now on Prograf, a different anti-rejection drug. I also got a call this evening that my Cellcept levels (another anti-rejection drug) were too high, so as of this evening, I drop the dose of that drug as well. There have been lots of changes this week.

I did have symptoms associated with the rejection: low blood pressure, a fast heart rate and severe weakness. Often when I stood up I would get very lightheaded. That has improved in the last two days since I have been on the high-dose steroids.....

Kevin

Thursday, October 23, 2008
Flexibility

I have not written in a long time. I had planned to write this morning with the title, "I miss my husband." For the past 1 1/2 weeks he has not felt well. Because of that he has been moody, fatigued and, over all, not himself. It has made life at home unpredictable. We had an amazing few weeks when we got home from Santa Clara where he felt great and was ready to go back to work, wanted to travel, and write. And then he started Revlimid and Decadron for the amyloid. Whether it is related or not we do not know for sure, but heart rejection began. That may be why he has felt so incredibly crummy.

My post this morning would have been before more news today from the transplant team. Sue Murray, our transplant coordinator called with results from Kevin's heart biopsy this week indicating that it showed the same rejection as last week. I was sad that the increases and changes in his medication had not helped, although his labs showed high levels of his cyclosporine. There is reason to believe that possibly Revlimid is causing rejection based on T-cells. Kevin will explain this much better than I ever could. What it means to me and us is that he may need to be off Revlimid until they know more or can figure out the cause of rejection and stop it. For how long, we don't know. A good thing is that the heart biopsy also showed no sign of Amyloid on his new heart. So far this heart is undamaged by the disease. That is great news!!

This afternoon, while I was busy with Rebecca and Caitlin doing girly things for the wedding, Kevin needed to go to Kaiser Roseville to receive an unexpected infusion of Solumedrol. Based on his rejection this week, he will need another infusion tomorrow and the day of the wedding, following the reception. Just when we thought we were moving along smoothly, this happens. It's another reminder that not everything in life goes as planned.

We are well. He will be at Rebecca's wedding. Our boys and their spouses will be here. And that is all we can ask for at this point.

As far as having my husband back, I think next week he should start feeling better. At this point, it is hard to know exactly how his body will react to drugs, when he will feel good and how much energy he will have at any given time. I am grateful that somewhere in my life I learned to be flexible.

Barbie

Friday, October 24, 2008
Trailblazing

For years I enjoyed hiking on the Appalachian Trail from New Jersey to Vermont. The trail in New England was almost entirely through forest and it felt like you were walking in one endless green tunnel. This made it very easy to get lost. To make the trail easily recognizable, the trees are marked with white rectangular blazes or trail markers. I can imagine how difficult it would be to navigate the trail without them. I also wonder what it might have been like for the first person to pioneer this path. I am sure that person fell into false and difficult trails and had to double back, losing precious time.

I feel that way right now. Since Stanford has not treated an amyloid patient after a transplant in many *years, it is unknown what the chemotherapy does to the new heart. Similarly, my doctors in Santa Clara are experts at protecting the transplant, but have not taken care of an amyloid patient after transplant either. They were all very concerned that my rejection did not resolve after two weeks of intensive intervention. Yesterday medical professionals from Santa Clara Kaiser, Stanford and the Mayo Clinic were all discussing my case together. The questions involved drug levels and drug interactions. Ultimately one pharmacist suggested that Revlimid might increase T-Cell activity and IL-2 levels, resulting in a direct toxic effect on my heart despite high levels of anti-rejection drug activity. This was unexpected, as the usual literature does not mention it. This trail blaze was missing.*

As a result, I have stopped the Revlimid for now and am again on high dose steroids in the form of an I.V. infusion of Solumedrol for 3 days. I imagine that within a week this will all resolve and I will be back on the correct path. I guess someone has to blaze the new trail. It will be more clear for the next person who follows.

Kevin

The adrenal glands make and release cortisone throughout the day, since we need it at a low level consistently. The amount of steroid that I was now taking for rejection was thousands of times higher than the normal level. This could have severe side effects. Solumedrol is the intravenous form of steroids. I was asked to take 1000 mg a day starting two days before Rebecca's wedding. This drug is so potent that most people need to be admitted to the hospital while they are getting the drug. One I.V. dose is equivalent to 16,000 mg of cortisone. The effects were immediate and paralyzing. It took a huge amount of mental effort just to get off the couch to get a glass of water. When the phone rang a few feet away from me, I would stare at it, willing myself to answer. Time felt like molasses. Finally, I would pick it up. "Hello?" I muttered. Some voice would ask, "Kevin, How are you?" "Doing well," I would always respond. Everything was hard. It was as if my mind were encased in cement and my body disconnected.

However, I could not stop; I had a promise to keep. Even before the heart transplant, once it became clear that I would miss Samuel and Michelle's wedding, I had promised Rebecca that I would be at hers; What I actually said was, "Rebecca, I promise that I will dance with you at your wedding." I meant to keep my word. Now I was in significant heart rejection for the second week in a row, and my promise would need to be fulfilled in three days.

CHAPTER 37

Rebecca had met Corey the summer after her first year at BYU. Their engagement became official on the day I learned that I might have amyloidosis, a month after Jeremy and Alexandria were married and Samuel and Michelle got engaged. With control of my future rapidly unraveling, all I could do was promise Rebecca that I would be there for her, and nothing would stop me. The marriage was on a Saturday. On the Thursday prior, as I was picking up the chair covers for the wedding in Rancho Cordova, my cell phone rang. It was Sue, the nurse from the transplant department. I always knew by the tone of their voices when they said "Hello," that it was bad news. "Your biopsy from yesterday is still 2R/3a," she said with great concern. "This is highly unusual." I had just finished the course of high dose prednisone and that morning I had taken my usual 40 mg dose of Decadron. But the drugs failed to reverse my heart rejection. I sat silent in my car eating a maple old-fashioned doughnut and waiting for my instructions. "Dr. Parekh wants you to get Solumedrol starting today through Saturday." I simply said yes and asked where I should go. She replied that she would find an infusion center in Sacramento where I could get it.

Unfortunately, for me to get this I.V. infusion that day for a non-chemotherapy drug did not fall into any nursing protocol, so I was initially told it could not be done. I was not going to drive five hours to Santa Clara so I pulled out my "ace in the hole." I called Dr. Sardar. Soon, I was sitting in the oncology clinic with an I.V. in my arm and an apocalyptic dose of steroids dripping into my vein. Penny, the nurse there, was amazing. She arranged for me to come in the following day to get my second dose. However, they were closed on Saturday, so she tried to get me an appointment Saturday morning in Sacramento for my third and final dose. She came back and said I could get it at 9:00 A.M. "I can't," I replied, "My daughter is getting married at 9:30, and I have made a promise that I cannot break." After some negotiating between her and Dr. Sardar, we finally decided that she would leave the I.V. in my arm with a saline lock. The pharmacy prepared me a bag of Solumedrol, which I took home with me on Friday. I would give the infusion to myself on Saturday after the reception. I had already missed one wedding; I was not going to miss another.

Wednesday October 29, 2008
A Dance with my Daughter

Life is measured in events. However, these events are rare compared with our day-to-day activities. But these are what we use to remember, mark and measure our life. These events can be seen as islands on the horizon in the ocean of time on which we spend most of our days. We float along in the glistening ripples and waves of daily activity, the forward movement almost imperceptible as we sleep, eat breakfast, answer emails, discuss the calendar, and talk and listen and do 95% of what our lives really are. These smaller moments are critical, but seem mundane. However, the big events are both behind us and ahead -- a reminder of what we have accomplished or hope to do. The islands in our ocean fade into past memory and appear anew on our horizons: birth, death, prom night, first football game, a major illness, a family vacation, a promotion, a new job, a new house. For parents, they are an inevitability. Someday, your children grow up and leave you. You prepare them for this their entire life, but it is always bittersweet.

As a father, you hope and pray that your daughter falls in love with a good man, a man better than you are, one who will respect and care for her, but as she dates, you give up hope. Then one day, she comes home with a sparkle in her eye. This is different. This young man is not like the rest. You meet him and he is what she needs and more. Suddenly, on the horizon, a distant peak of an island becomes visible for the very first time and you feel the currents pushing you toward that inevitable port. However, almost simultaneously, storm clouds begin to gather, obscuring the view and the way.

With two of our children getting married in the near future, it was difficult to know what to do.... To Sam I said, "I'll do my best to be there." It was not to be. But to Rebecca I promised, "I will dance with you at your wedding." I meant to do everything in my power to keep that promise. We arrived at the appointed date last Saturday. The beauty of the morning was only exceeded by the beauty of Rebecca. Her smile and unabashed joy kept us all afloat. The wedding was a dream come true. We all arrived, family and friends, at the reception where she floated around the room in her white dress with such grace and poise. Then the moment came. I danced with my daughter.

I took her in my arms, as I have done for 20 years, and carried her around the floor. She told me not to cry, but the emotion was overwhelming. We reminisced about how she used to stand on my feet when she was two as we danced around the family room. She loves to dance. I told her how much I loved her. I always will. But now begins her time to dance with another.

The dance with my daughter was done. The event now fades into past memories. The promise was kept. As I look back, this island paradise will remain in view for a very long time. The ocean seems a little bit more calm today and my vision seems to extend a few more miles than usual.

Kevin

Thursday, October 30, 2008
Mostly Dead

The Princess Bride is my favorite movie. In one scene, the man in black, aka Dread Pirate Roberts, is captured and thrown into the "pit of despair." Count Rugan, aka "the six-fingered man" and the Prince are conducting research on torture and have built a machine that can suck life out of your body. They start low and suck one year of life from the man in black, reducing him to a quivering, whimpering mess. But then in a fit of jealous rage, the Prince turns the machine to full power, killing the man in black. Well, not quite; it leaves him "mostly dead."

Mostly dead is what happens to you after five days on 100 mg of Prednisone, followed by one day of 40 mg of Decadron (200 mg prednisone equivalent) followed by three days of 1000 mg of I.V. solumedrol (Prednisone equivalent to an "uberdose") I felt wonderful at the wedding and reception though, where I was lifted by my daughter's beauty, exuberance and infectious smile. But once she and Corey were gone, so was my strength. I gave myself the last dose of solumedrol at home, in the I.V. left in me by the nurse.

The next three days, I could not move. It required huge mental effort just to get out of a chair. Speaking was a chore, and eating was impossible since everything tasted horrific. Note to self: Avoid high dose steroids in the future.

But then, with a finger wiggle and a head giggle, life began to return. Now, let's inventory our assets.

The heart biopsy last week showed no evidence of Amyloid deposits, and the heart biopsy this week shows marked improvement with the rejection now at a 1a. I will take a month off of chemotherapy to let my heart get better, and then, who knows? I am still on bolus Decadron weekly on the chance it may keep the amyloidosis at bay. My Kappa Light Chains (amyloid marker) remain low.

Many questions remain, however. Was it really the Revlimid that caused my strange rejection? Was it an occult infection, masked by steroids? Was it the economy or election season hysteria? I am sure my doctors must see me as two people since I am a paradox. Then again, I have always been unique. But I do not worry; if not plan B, then plan C and eventually on to plan 401K.

In the end, I am always aware of the sincere support of so many on my behalf, this makes the bad days bearable and the good days glorious. I have not written recently because, well, I was mostly dead. Miracle Max did offer me a cure, but it took a while to swallow, since the chocolate was still quite unpalatable. Today, chocolate tastes wonderful, and that says a mouthful.

Glad to be among the living.

Kevin

CHAPTER 38

Wednesday, November 5, 2008
Feeling Better

I am feeling great. I believe that I have mostly recovered from the high-dose steroids. A young man, a patient of mine, was recently admitted to the hospital. His grandmother commented to one of the nurses there on 3 South, named Windy (she is a great nurse, but, of course, so are all the nurses that I have met at Kaiser), how it was sad that Dr. Anderson had left his practice and had abandoned her grandson. Windy reassured her and showed her the website (Its mere existence being my own personal HIPPA waiver. In my case, personal knowledge of my medical condition actually has been helpful to others and continues to keep alive my desire to teach.) She was both moved and relieved that my absence was not of my own choice.

While getting labs, I dropped by to visit this young man and reassured him that I would always be his doctor. I am very concerned about him. Then it occurred to me, there must be other patients who feel the same way. If anyone knows any of these patients, please reassure them for me that I am still here. My goal is to return to work and I will remain their doctor as long as I can.

After visiting this young man, I stopped by the operating room to see Susan, a friend there, who had a gift for me. It was a bas-relief sculpture of the "Tree of Life." What a beautiful gift. This actually reflects a deep personal symbolism in my life that I alluded to previously, but is unknown to her. I thank her for it.

I looked at the board where all the cases were listed and had this desire to put on some scrubs and get back to work, but alas, I am an obedient and compliant patient and will abide by my doctor's orders and wait until she gives me the 'green light' to return to work. Right now she is saying February.

My next happiest day will be when I find myself with a ureteroscope in one hand and a 200 micron Holmium laser fiber in the other while blasting an elusive ureteral stone; what joy. Not like Bruce Willis in Armageddon, but like Michelangelo (I always tell my residents, "do not drill the stone. Sculpt it.)

To all of my patients, I will return and remain your physician as long as I can. This is my goal; this is my hope.

Kevin

Sunday, November 9. 2008
Coming attractions.

Timing is everything. I had the opportunity to attend the Northern California amyloidosis support group yesterday in Walnut Creek. With a rare disease, it is very reassuring to hear the experiences of others. What is more interesting is how much has changed in a few short years. There were nine people there with amyloidosis. Four of us were newly diagnosed. The other five had all had stem cell transplants about three to four years ago. For them, chemotherapy existed, but had limited application and a heart transplant was never offered. Of the four new patients, two had had a heart transplant (myself and Debbie, the Kaiser patient whom I met three days before my transplant.) and two were on drug therapy. Now there are choices which did not exist before. This is a very good thing, but can sometimes be confusing as well.

Last week when I went to see my cardiologist, Dr. Weisshaar, in Santa Clara, the pressing question was what to do next with me. Dr. Weisshaar called and spoke with Dr. Lacy, the oncologist who saw me at the Mayo Clinic. She confirmed that Revlimid could lead to heart rejection. She also added that waiting untreated for the Stem Cell Transplant sometimes might allow the amyloid to progress, since amyloid is quite unpredictable. As I heard this, they were like more pieces of a puzzle that began to reveal the underlying picture, which in this case was a plan to proceed. There are three drugs that are commonly used to treat amyloidosis: Revlimid, (which I probably will not take again) Velcade and Melphalan. The latter can suppress stem cells and is therefore not a great option if you plan on proceeding to transplant. This leaves Velcade. Initially, I was hoping just to be treated with medication and avoid a stem cell transplant, but I feel that a transplant is probably likely and, actually, I would accept that if it means a more permanent cure or control of the disease without having to continue to take steroids. I really do not like the idea of being on steroids for a long time.

I love the process of discovery, even if I am the one being used to reveal the right path. Like I tell Debbie, "I'd rather it be me than you." If what we learn from me makes it easier for her, it's worth it. Nothing makes you feel more alive than taking risks.

Can't wait to see what's next.

Kevin

(Debbie has continued to do well since her heart transplant.)

Monday, February 1, 2010
Against Traffic

Early one Saturday morning of my childhood, I woke up with a dilemma. I was completely out of ammo for my cap-gun. I started to formulate a plan. First I needed cash. I was only five years old so I didn't have a job yet. I knew, however, that my sister Elaine usually had a stash of cash in her piggy bank. I still was not totally clear on the concept of ownership, so repayment did not cross my mind. The nearest store to us was a Safeway located in downtown Novato on Highway 101. We lived in Ignacio, about five miles to the south. Soon I was out the door and on my tricycle. I didn't want to make the trip alone, so I went by my friend's house to pick him up. Willy Coates was only four at the time and at that tender age did not yet possess the sense to try to dissuade me from my Quixotic quest. We navigated through our neighborhood of Loma Verde and after about two miles made it to the freeway. I was moving a little slower than usual; Willy was small, but having him standing on the back of the trike did add extra weight, especially on Alameda de la Loma, which was a hilly street. Soon we were on the Frontage Road (appropriately named "Frontage Road") and passed a number of strip malls and a gas station. No one took notice, as this was 1964. In those days kids could play outside unsupervised without their parents being arrested. I had to make a critical decision: cross over the freeway to head north with the north-moving traffic or take the shortest distance between two points and just get on the off-ramp for the southbound lane. Actually, I did not even think about it. I have always taken the shortest route possible. I can only imagine what Willy and I looked like to the passing motorists. A five-year-old riding a little red tricycle with a four-year-old perched on the back (holding onto my shoulders for balance) moving forward on the shoulder, against traffic.

After about a half mile, we got to the intersection of Highway 37 as it comes across the top of the bay from Vallejo, and Highway 101. The overpass was actually just being built and still under construction. As we approached, a construction worker came up to us and asked what we were doing. I explained my dilemma and my quest. Somewhat confused and consternated, he suggested that we turn around and go home. I immediately saw the wisdom of his words and altered my course. We turned around and soon were off the freeway. Just as we passed a Laundromat, my neighbor Mrs. McNair came out to put a load of clothes in her trunk. She saw us and asked if we wanted a ride home. Soon the trike was in the trunk and we were safely unbuckled in the back seat breathing a cloud of second-hand smoke. I walked in the house and began my usual Saturday morning routine of watching cartoons for four hours. A few minutes later, my parents got up and went into the kitchen. I never said a word to them about my aborted adventure.

Last Saturday I was sitting in the hallway at the University of California, San Francisco School of Medicine, waiting for the amyloidosis support group to begin, when this memory came back to me, but with a new question. How is it that at the age of five I knew exactly how to get five miles from my house without asking anyone for directions? Is that typical for most five-year olds? I guess I have always had an uncanny sense of direction.

Amyloidosis is a very strange disease; it acts like a cancer but it is not. It is not just one disease either. It really represents more of a common final pathway, but even that path might lead to different organ involvement. This makes the amyloidosis support group a bit confusing because the main thing we have in common is the name of the disease. I have primary, the man next to me has senile cardiac, the woman across the room has a rare familial type. They are all treated differently.

To become an expert in amyloidosis requires knowing about at least two patients with the illness. We had a professor from UCSF come to the meeting and it became clear to me that no one really knows anything about this disease. That does not really bother me, but clearly everyone else is frustrated. Everyone wants the same thing: a good explanation and a plan in which they can have confidence. To get there you need a doctor who is your advocate. A good doctor is one that can tell you what they do not know and what cannot be done for your disease, and you graciously accept it because you trust him or her and know that he or she cares. I see the difficulty that my fellow patients have because they have not found their advocate. This may be because they confuse advocate with expert. There are very few experts in amyloidosis and the studies are based on small groups of patients. Most of our treatment plans are trial and error and every patient is unique.

And yet, I see great hope with this disease. In the last five years new options for monitoring and treating amyloidosis have prolonged lives. Doctors are no longer summarily sentencing us to death.

My journey with this disease has seen its successes and failures, miracles and reversals of fortune. But I

*have always had a sense that I was moving forward in
the right direction, even if it was against traffic. I have
trusted my doctors and accepted their plans even when
the outcome was an unknown. For me, having a plan
and moving forward is more important than having an
assurance that it is right. It requires a leap of faith.
In the end, the sum of all this forward movement has
resulted in great progress and improvement of my life.*

*My advice to my fellow amyloidosis patients is to be
grateful in your patience, but do not be passive or angry.
Get the information you need to make your decision then
move forward. If one door is closed because you are already
too sick, find another way. Even if your doctor is not an
expert, she or he still can help you to find your way.*

*Keep moving in the right direction, even against
traffic.*

Kevin

November 2008 was a month of confusion and contrast. It seemed that
nobody knew what to do with me. I had stopped the Revlimid only
to develop significant rejection yet a third time. I saw my heart transplant doctors at Santa Clara almost weekly and also saw Dr. Schrier at
Stanford. Anxious to have some normalcy in our lives, we had planned
a trip to Utah to spend the week with our children there. Worried that
my doctors would say no if I asked them if I could leave the state, I just
decided not to mention it.

Rebecca and Corey returned from their honeymoon in Palm
Desert a week after their wedding. They were acting unusually
morose for newlyweds, but the trip home from their honeymoon
had been complicated by flight delays. At the time, I attributed their
apparent funk to fatigue from travel. They had come over to the
house to open their gifts. I was not feeling well either, and decided to
leave to go shopping for food.

I slowly shopped that rainy night, holding on to the grocery cart for support. I had forgotten an umbrella so I walked as quickly as I could to the car and unloaded the bags into the back. Standing under the raised hatchback to stay dry, I tried to figure out how to dispose of the cart without getting wet. The carriage corral was nearby. I thought I could push the cart in that direction in the hope that inertia would take it to its proper destination and then friction would stop it. Unfortunately, I did not account for gravity. The sloped asphalt carried the cart across the parking lot. As it picked up speed I saw that it was heading for a black Mercedes. I ran into the rain to stop the runaway cart. I had not taken both feet off the ground at the same time in nearly a year. My inner ear, balance center, legs, and eyes had no idea how to coordinate such an effort. I realized belatedly that it requires a huge coordinating effort to run. The muscles to the knees and ankles must anticipate the landing, with the propriocepters telling the brain the position of each limb while the inner ear reports the body's orientation in relation to the center of the earth. I am not sure which nerve failed in my flight, but the next thing I knew I was lying on my back in the center of the Raley's parking lot. Streaming water soaked my back as I looked up at the black rain falling from the silent sky above. The absurdity of it all overcame me and I began to audibly laugh. (The Mercedes fared better than I did. The shopping cart never touched it.) I lay there for a second to assess the damage. I was fine, with nothing hurt except for my pride. Slowly I rolled onto my side, got my knee underneath my weight and pushed myself up. My clothing was soaked by the time I made it back into the car and drove home. It would be a while before I tried running again.

Barbie and I really needed to get away. The trip to Utah was going to be a welcome diversion from my full-time career as a patient. One evening I was driving to pick up Caitlin from piano lessons when the call came. It was Sue again. I was shocked to hear that I had rejection again. I so feared that we would not be able to leave for our trip. I wondered if we could sell three of the Coldplay tickets. It seemed so difficult to plan anything. We had already missed one of the three weddings this year and canceled a cruise in September. It seemed that

the degree to which I felt my life was no longer in jeopardy directly cor-
related with my willingness to commit dollars to a future event. Was
it worth buying $400 plane tickets for a trip two months from now? (I
had learned by this time that trip insurance does not cover pre-existing
conditions.) It seemed that my faith in my future well-being was limited
by my current uncertainty. I took my prednisone and hoped again to
be healed. I also asked my home teacher, a High Priest from my ward,
to give me a blessing of health. Frank Penney and Steve Hargadon
came over that evening. I do not remember the words of the blessing,
but I do remember feeling comforted.

Wednesday, November 12, 2008
Songs that make me cry

*I have noticed over the years that certain odors will
stir up a memory from the distant past. However, I
cannot always connect a location or an event with the
odor. It comes as more of a general feeling. I believe this
is because odors are perceived in our primitive brain,
which is not well connected to the memory center; in
other words, you get the zip code, but not the address.*

*Songs are different. An unexpected song comes on
the radio or iPod in random mode, and you are immediately taken to a specific place and time; and the emotion
of that moment washes over you uncontrollably. This
is only amplified if you are on steroids. Steroids bring
your emotions to just under the surface so that, as I tell
Barbie, they make me cry at toilet paper commercials.
That "quilty" softness gets me every time. So on days
like today, when I take 40 mg of Decadron, I feel it.*

*There are five songs that make me cry. (This quali-
fies me for a "High Fidelity" top five list.) The first,
(in chronological order) is "100 years" by Five for
Fighting. That was the day that I had made the decision to leave Yale and Connecticut to move to back to*

California. The second is "Viva la Vida" by Coldplay. Barbie and were driving home from Santa Clara having just been diagnosed with Amyloidosis and been told that I needed a heart transplant. The third is "Better Days" by The Goo Goo Dolls. That day I was alone in the hospital, as Barbie had to leave me to go to Sam and Michelle's wedding and we had to pass on the heart from the Mayo Clinic. The fourth was when Caitlin came to Stanford, just after my transplant, and sang the song "Waiting" that she wrote for my birthday. The fifth was tonight, while taking Caitlin to piano lessons and hearing Imogen Heap sing "Hide and Seek," knowing that tomorrow I have to go back on high dose steroids because my heart is once again in moderate 2R/3A rejection. And we don't know why.

Generally, with every side effect I get, I try to connect it with something that is temporary, reversible or fixable, be it drug reactions, low magnesium or diet and exertion. But this time, I am out of connections. I can only trust in my doctors and keep my faith in God and be patient. I go back on 100 mg of Prednisone tomorrow for three days with a rapid taper. Beyond that, I cannot predict. But do not pray for me. Pray for Barbie. She's the one who has to live with me.

We had planned on going to Utah to see Coldplay in concert and stay for Thanksgiving. It might end up being Boston Market in Roseville. (I actually love their turkey dinner; it's all the salt.) Seriously, though, I am actually feeling great, both physically and emotionally. I have the best doctors and the best family. I know everything will work out well. It always does. And there are so many songs yet to be written.

Happy Thanksgiving

The biopsy on Tuesday showed that the rejection is resolving. I am feeling much better and look forward to a wonderful Thanksgiving. I have so much to be thankful for.

Kevin

We had a wonderful time visiting our children at BYU in Utah, as well as my sister Elaine and her husband Mark. We had Thanksgiving at their house. Barbie's parents even joined us, since they only live a few miles from my sister. However, by the third day at 5000 feet, I began to feel the elevation change.

When we arrived home, I found a letter in the mail from the parents of the young man whose heart had saved and now preserved my life. It was hand-written and brief. In his mother's words I could sense that their grief was still acute. She wrote that she was grateful that Shane's heart could continue beating and that "his heart was strong and kind and loved very much." I was overwhelmed and touched at her kindness in sharing with me his name as well as his heart. I sensed that further communication would be premature and felt a need to ensure their privacy as they mourned his loss. I did however find his obituary. I felt constrained from searching any further as to the cause of his death. To this day, I know no more details. As I considered their suffering at his loss, the following words flooded my mind:

Thursday, December 4, 2008
Shane

A letter arrived the other day

From the parents of my donor

The pain in its penning twice mentioned.

Their mourning continues
At the loss of their son

So also their love remains strong

.

With mortal existence cut short

A vital part of him lives on

In me

His name was Shane.

Even in their pain his parents wish my happiness

A gift doubled in their charity

Such sacrifice inexpressible

My duty to them, to him

In each act of kindness I commit

May I shorten their mourning

Pain replaced by comfort

In time that they will again see

The beauty of the trees

The majesty of the clouds

And feel joy in the light of a new day.

Kevin

CHAPTER 39

My doctors made a decision to start Velcade. This drug was given intravenously; however, the infusion was only 2-3 cc and was given as a push directly into the vein so that it was quick. The most common side effect reported was that of neuropathy. Usually this meant numbness in the hands and feet, but it could affect nerves anywhere. I would get the injection weekly for four weeks then have one week off. They would know if it was working through a blood test measuring my kappa light chains. When I use the term "my kappa light chains," understand that those are the bad guys. The test measured the level of the bad proteins in my blood. If the treatment were working, the levels would go down. Soon I started to get levels and began looking for a pattern. However, what I found did not make sense. I had never had a level drawn at a Kaiser lab before my heart transplant.

The only one that I could find was from the Mayo Clinic and it was 66. My first level at Kaiser I had ordered on my own and it was 180. After a month on Revlimid, this dropped to 40. However at Stanford my level was 30 before I started treatment. There did not seem to be any pattern to the numbers. It was not until later, during a visit with Dr. Wesley Witteles, the fellow working with Dr. Schrier, that she informed me that different labs report the results differently. As I looked closer, I made an important discovery. Kaiser reports the results in mg/liter while the Mayo Clinic and Stanford report them in mg/dl. This is a 10-fold difference. Thus, a level of 66 at the Mayo clinic would be equivalent to 660 at Kaiser. Why had my doctors not seen this before? This was important. It was then I realized that the Revlimid had had a huge effect in reducing my disease risk. As I continued on Velcade, my number ranged from 180 – 160 mg/l. None of us knew if this would be enough to keep my amyloidosis from attacking my new heart, or the rest of my organs for that matter.

Wednesday, December 17, 2008
Be a Donor

Since my transplant many people have commented to me that they now might consider becoming an organ donor. When I ask why they have not so designated themselves in the past, the reasons vary widely. Clearly, there are some common misconceptions about organ donation, a few of which I will address here.

1: "I don't want my body mutilated." I find this very interesting, given the fact that, in California, if you suddenly die while not under the care of a physician (i.e. any accident), you are required to have an autopsy. Only the coroner can waive that. Prior to medical school, I was a Denier. In French that translates to "keeper of the morgue." It was after participating in my first autopsy that I determined I would forever be an organ donor. Transplant surgeons would be somewhat more delicate in harvesting my organs than would the coroner. When the autopsy was over, I put everything in a bag and put it back in the cavity and sewed up the body. I figured that organ donation would be less disruptive.

2: "For religious reasons, everything has to stay together for the resurrection." To that I always ask, "Which matter will be used in your resurrection: your 35-year-old matter or your 73-year-old matter?" Everything we eat, even the air we breathe changes the composition of our body every day. Physically, a large portion of the molecules in me today were not there

20 years ago. They were earth, oceans, clouds and other stuff. The matter does not matter. My guess is that God uses the 'blueprint' and rebuilds us with perfect materials. When we die, we decompose back to the earth from which we were created. There is nothing particularly sacred about those elements other than the memory of what they represented. All major religions both support and encourage organ donation.

3. "I don't want the doctor to let me die too soon, just to get my organs." This will never happen. As physicians, our primary responsibility is to save our patients. There is zero incentive for us to have transplant harvesting as any motivation to alter our care for any patient. This misconception can arise from a misunderstanding of when we die and is often exacerbated by how this process is depicted on TV medical dramas. We die when our brain dies, not when our heart stops. The heart does not need the brain to beat. Case in point: there are no nerves connecting my heart to my brain. It began beating spontaneously when my surgeon placed it in my chest and supplied it with oxygenated blood.

When the brain is damaged so severely that it is no longer viable, we die. However, if there is still a blood pressure and oxygen getting to the heart, it will continue beating for a time.

Of course, this is an extremely emotional time for the family, which only underscores the importance of having made the choice to be a donor prior to the moment of loss. I have 100% confidence in this process.

The true reason that we should be donors is because of how much good is generated by such an action. It not only saves the individual receiving the organ, but also affects thousands of lives of those who will be helped by that person's continued existence. Like a ripple in a pond, the gift continues to expand. Heart disease, kidney failure, diabetes, liver failure, lung disease and blindness can all be corrected. A friend of mine, a urologist from Connecticut, told me that both his kidneys were healthy and had served him well for 70 years. He felt he could live just fine on just one kidney. He became an anonymous live kidney donor. What fulfillment he must have felt. Being a designated organ donor can provide the same satisfaction, but without the pain.

It is simple to become a donor. Most DMV's allow you to designate your decision on your license. In California you can also sign-up online at the California Transplant Donor Network (CTDN). Once you have made this choice, you should let your family know your wishes to avoid later confusion.

Give Life; Be a Donor.

Kevin

The New Year began with great hopes. Soon, however, things began to unravel. New Year's Eve was strange. Rebecca came over by herself to spend the evening with us, as Corey was out with friends. He had begun to distance himself from us and we did not understand why.

Meanwhile, I began to experience some major side effects from the Velcade and Decadron. As the weeks wore on it became clear that I did not want to continue on these drugs forever. All along we had entertained the prospect of having a bone marrow transplant. The data on various treatments for amyloidosis was limited by the rarity of the disease. It is difficult to accrue sufficient numbers of patients to statistically prove with a reasonable degree of power which therapies were clearly superior. One study prospectively compared low dose chemotherapy alone to high dose chemotherapy with stem cell transplant rescue. The latter is where the high dose chemotherapy destroys and wipes out the entire bone marrow, including the colony of bad plasma cells producing the amyloid protein. The idea is to then repopulate the empty bone marrow with clean stem cells that will then dedifferentiate (become new blood cells) and recreate a new clean, and disease free bone marrow, *sans* bad guy cells. The study showed no statistical improvement of stem cell transplant when compared to low dose chemotherapy.

However, and this is always the great conundrum in medicine, most practitioners who took care of amyloidosis patients believed that, despite the findings of the study, a bone marrow transplant was still the preferred way to treat my disease. This is true in all facets of medicine and in life in general. We cannot escape our biases. Often, when science does not provide the answers, we go with intuition and experience. Unfortunately, sometimes the collective bias and intuition is wrong. But it is all that we have. As January wore on, motivated by my desires to distance myself from dexamethasone, I decided to join the camp of those having a stem cell transplant to once and for all rid me of the disease.

Thursday, January 8, 2009
Phase II

Recently, I finished my first course of chemotherapy with Dexamethasone (Decadron) and Velcade. Overall it went well, as I have mentioned, but as expected, three days of the week fatigue prevented me from accomplishing much.

Tuesday I had my routine heart biopsy (it is sad when a heart biopsy is seen as routine). It showed a good result with minimal rejection present. I also saw Dr. Schrier and Witteles at Stanford and he was concerned that my kappa light chains had significantly increased, despite the Velcade. Since the six-month anniversary of my heart transplant will be next month, he suggested that I go ahead and schedule the stem-cell transplant. That was actually what I wanted to hear. I would like to move forward with this. However, I had asked Dr. Weisshaar, my cardiologist if I could return to work in February, thinking that the stem-cell transplant would be far in the future. She reluctantly agreed, but wanted me to take a gradual approach, with Barbie as the judge to ensure that I would not overexert myself. But now I realize that I may have to delay my return until after the stem-cell transplant. I am a little sad about this, not just because I still feel a sense of responsibility to my patients and my colleagues, but in addition, psychologically I need to work to add some normality back to my life. However, my priorities are well placed and I will follow the counsel of my doctors. It is better to sacrifice now for something better in the future.

Barbie is going to start classes next week at Sierra College. She is taking organic chemistry and nutrition as prerequisites for dental hygiene school. So we will have a busy winter and spring this year. We remain constant in our hope.

Kevin

CHAPTER 40

Once the heart biopsy was done, the routine demanded a chest x-ray and then I was off to the clinic for my checkup. Was I taking all of my drugs as prescribed? How were my labs? How was I feeling? And a thousand other questions. I scheduled my appointment with Dr. Schrier at Stanford for that same day to avoid a separate trip to the Bay Area. Palo Alto was about 25 miles from Santa Clara.

Around noon, Barbie got a call from Rebecca. It was clear from the one side of the conversation I could hear that something was terribly wrong. It was about her and Corey. Finally, Barbie said that she would come home to be with her. As I had an appointment with Dr. Schrier at 3:00 P.M., we decided to meet Rebecca mid way, in Fairfield and Barbie would drive home with her and I would drive back to Stanford.

As we drove, Barbie explained that Corey had expressed his misgivings about getting married and had decided that it had been a mistake. He was not ready to give up his life with his friends. He was having doubts about having joined the church as well. We had seen his movement away from us, as well as the fact that he spent so much time at the gym and with his former friends, but this was a shock.

There is a park-and-ride off-ramp just east of Fairfield. A few minutes after we parked, Rebecca arrived. She ran over to Barbie and just cried inconsolably. It broke my heart to see her in such pain. It had only been two months since she and Corey had been married. What would they do now? After a while, Rebecca was composed enough to speak. On the way to meet us, she had called her Bishop and she and Corey had made an appointment to meet with him that evening for counseling. She was going to try to make it work. I hugged her and told her that I loved her. There we were, the three of us, standing next to I-80 with the sound of hundreds of cars whipping past, unaware as we faced such a heart-wrenching moment. The sound of the cars made it seem as if time itself were audible, pulling us forward into a new unknown. We clutched one another, trying to make friction to slow ourselves against the inexorable gravity of the future. Had we been in an actual physical accident, the passers-by would have slowed to see our plight. But there is no rubbernecking to witness a crash of the heart.

Soon, Barbie and Rebecca left together and I drove back to Stanford for my appointment. Dr. Schrier was running late. Today was a decision point. Should I proceed with an autologous stem cell transplant? Based on the poor response of my light chains to the Velcade, the feeling was that I should proceed to the next step. Dr. Schrier briefly discussed the reasons that he supported this and said that I would see Dr. Sally Arai, the specialist in bone marrow transplants for amyloidosis patients. When I asked him how cardiac amyloidosis patients did with this, he confessed that I was the first cardiac amyloidosis patient he had ever seen. All of the rest were kidney amyloidosis patients. This surprised me. He was the regional expert and I was his first. No one at Stanford had ever cared for a heart transplant patient with primary amyloidosis.

Finally, I asked the question that is forever on one's mind, but difficult to vocalize: "How long can I expect to live if the bone marrow transplant works?" He responded, "generally we see success for about four years and then the amyloidosis may begin to come back." He paused and then added, "You do understand that this disease is incurable?" I nodded yes and wishfully said, "I was hoping to live another 10 years."

"It sounds like someone is bargaining with God," he said with a slight frown.

Smiling right back, I replied, "we are actually on pretty good terms right now."

Dr. Schrier was taken aback a bit by my undaunted spirit. His hand went spontaneously up to give me a high-five for my statement of hope.

How hard should one hit an octogenarian's hand? Our hands met in the gesture of mutual celebration; he then stood up and walked out without another word.

It was a long and lonely drive home as I thought about everything: Rebecca suffering already in her relationship with her new husband, me with the decision to have a stem cell transplant, and Barbie having just started school.

Wednesday, January 21, 2009
Cakes - not of our choosing

It has been a while since I last wrote. I guess that even I, the eternal optimist, can feel discouraged sometimes. It has been a difficult two weeks for many reasons. As I mentioned, I was hoping to go back to work part time in February. Because of the impending stem-cell transplant, this probably will not happen. In fact, it might be quite a while before I get back. People have somewhat incredulously asked me, "Why are you in such a hurry to get back to the 'stress' of work?" Who I am has always been defined by my responsibilities to others, my partners, my patients, my friends and my family. Part of feeling "whole" again has its foundation in how I might serve others. I was really looking forward to that, as it will be both emotionally and psychologically healing. Even now, when I do a little administrative work in my role as chief of the department, I feel immensely normal. I hope for this as much as I hope to be successfully treated of my disease.

Second, I have finally admitted to myself that a stem-cell transplant will not be a 'piece of cake' unless that cake has liver pâté for frosting and sardines for candles. I know this will make me sick beyond what I have previously experienced. I know I will get through it; I do not worry about it, but it will be hard.

Third is the fact that I feel weaker than I did after my heart transplant. The drugs have taken their toll, (or the amyloidosis has). I feel fatigued all of the time and fight past it to function. I am dizzy all of the time, especially when I get up from sitting for more that 15 minutes. I feel bad for Barbie, because I am not always fun to be around, even though I try as hard as I can. I remember before my Dad died of multiple myeloma, he was on the same drugs that I take and he was often "grouchy," which annoyed us. But now I understand; it was not his fault.

Every patient who is chronically ill just wants to feel normal again. Often we must accept a new normal and come to terms with who we are, not who we were. Then again, I would rather feel a little bit ill half of the time than be a little bit dead all of the time. Ah yes, perspective.

How I feel does not diminish my gratitude by one iota. Nor has my hope waned. It is just that on some days the effort to self-motivation is the heaviest weight that I lift. I see six months from now a retrospective view that does not daily remember these difficult days, because they remain in the past. The more I can focus on others, the sooner that will come to pass. Until then, I have my fork ready to dig into liverwurst cake.

Kevin

CHAPTER 41

A week had passed since Rebecca met us in Fairfield. She and Corey tried to work things out. Then, suddenly, one evening the front door opened. It was Rebecca, hysterically crying. As she entered the house, she immediately collapsed in the hallway. It was hard to make out her words through the sobbing. Corey had told her that he had not only made a mistake in marrying her, but that he no longer believed in the church and wanted out. This was more than she could bear. She got in her car and came home. She never went back. A week later they filed for divorce. I helped her by taking her to the courthouse for a summary divorce since there was no property to speak of. Corey silently signed the papers. In my parting words to him I told him what he must do to repair the relationship: specifically, re-earn her trust. I liked Corey; he is a nice young man. Unfortunately he suffered from a symptom pervasive in his generation: the inability to commit. Months later I spoke with Corey and he shared that he felt that he was holding her back from her full potential, knowing that he could not fully support her in her faith. It was extremely painful for both of them.

Rebecca lived with us until she left to go back to BYU in April to finish her degree. As tragic as the situation was, we were glad to have her home.

In the months after the heart transplant, Barbie and I had a lot of time together. One would think that once you passed such an event of life preserving magnitude that all would be perfect ever after. We had both changed, yet we were still who we had always been. Barbie struggled as I became even more independent. Not only had she spent time in complete charge of everything, she also knew of the frailty of our daily existence. She feared that my intellectual independence and emotional absolute optimism would outstretch my practical physical wellness or lack thereof. I was prone to minimize, so she often did not know how I really felt or whether my very bad days might have necessitated more than patience and waiting. Should I report pains and fatigue to my doctors? Were the anorexia and diarrhea serious or just a drug reaction? She was used to my stolid momentum; a resolute posture in the face of any crisis. As a surgeon, I felt that if immediate death was not proximate, there was no need to worry. It would all work out; it always did. This perceived unpredictability weighed heavily upon her. Every morning I woke up and got out of bed and by the time I walked to my sink, I knew what kind of day it was going to be for me; Barbie could only guess.

There were many unknowns about our future together on all levels of our relationship. Would I go back to work, and if I did, for how long? Would we see our grandchildren together? Would we ever enjoy sexual intimacy together again?

For years prior to my illness, I had suffered from impotence. As a urologist, I am an expert in the area of male sexuality. I felt the daily irony as I helped hundreds of men deal with this difficult subject, which I always approached as a "couples" issue. Unbeknownst to my patients, I used my personal experience to better understand and treat them. With the progression of my disease, things only got worse.

I had learned that many men tried to convince their wives that is was not their fault, and assured them that they still found them attractive. Unfortunately, many of the women involved could not accept this reassurance, and blamed themselves for their husband's poor performance in bed rather than blaming his diabetes, high blood pressure and beta-blockers. The most frustrating thing about sexual dysfunction is even though it may be possible to intellectually grasp this at its most organic and physiologic level, the emotional loss and pain associated with the uncertainty of achieving uninhibited intimacy is inescapable. The mind cannot relax sufficiently, leading to the dreaded and deadly performance anxiety. The end result is conditional lowering of libido resulting in subtle efforts to purposely throw off the schedule of the day to avoid the inevitable failure. All the while, the wife suffers silently, resolved that this part of our marriage is in its twilight, so as not to get her hopes up, only to be dashed yet again. Emotional fortresses, founded on denial, are built in this corner, while otherwise life appears to go on as normal. It was hard for me to talk about it with Barbie, so I just imagined that the problem was not there. To lose intimacy in a marriage is akin to removing one of the colors from the rainbow.

As my heart failed, even the urologic interventions that I had prescribed to myself no longer worked. However, this coincided with our anxiety about my health in general, such that the issue was pushed below the radar. We still loved each other completely. Our sexual intimacy would be just one more casualty of disease. I had heard this story a thousand times from my patients. Now it was our story.

During the heart transplant surgery, the surgeons close the chest by first using interrupted wires to pull and secure the cut edges of the bony sternum together. It takes months for the bone to fuse back together. Immediately post-op, I was instructed not to do anything that would put lateral pressure on the sternum, which is hard since even the act of getting out of bed requires chest muscles. Sex was out of the question.

Everything else filled our lives: doctor visits, heart biopsies, drug reactions, medications, remodeling our house, returning to a new ward at church, Rebecca's wedding, my recurrent rejection and chronic fatigue. However, in the midst of all of this tumult, there were some wonderfully beautiful days where I felt well. The kind of well that feels like suddenly coming out of a prolonged thunderstorm and seeing the sky for the first time in 50 years. The kind of well that reminds you that you had forgotten what it feels like to feel normal.

At the end of one such day, Barbie and I went to bed both feeling happy and began to cuddle. Soon I realized that a heart transplant has multiple benefits with regard to better perfusion. As we shared that most intimate of moments that define and reflect the magnitude of our emotional love through physical love, we left behind all cares or concerns. There was no outside world. There was no amyloidosis or illness. There was only the two of us, together still. Neither of us expected that the new anatomy would improve the old physiology to such a degree. In sex and love, the ultimate experience requires letting go; of fears, of anxiety or of doubt. It is the most profound demonstration of trust. In this moment we felt something that had been lost to us for a long time and then was suddenly and unexpectedly found. As we lay together, I felt her tears on my cheek. What we thought was lost to us was given back. All of the colors were back in the rainbow. Nothing was said, nor could it be. The utterance of any words would have been insufferably insufficient and only serve to sooner bring us back to the world of cares. However, in my whole new heart, I knew and shared the emotion of our re-unified existence.

CHAPTER 42

The question of my life expectancy was a sensitive subject. Regardless of the answer, it was obvious to both of us that there would likely be a prolonged period of time where Barbie would be alone. Without focusing on the widow aspect of that, we talked much about the practical necessities of such a contingency. It made sense for Barbie to have a career that would not only support her financially, but afford her the opportunity to be involved in something she truly enjoyed. Two years prior, she had begun to work as a dental assistant. She found that she enjoyed dentistry and patient interaction. Months before I was diagnosed she had already expressed an interest in becoming a dental hygienist. Now it seemed even more relevant considering the current state of things. She was, however, quite apprehensive. She would first need to take a number of prerequisites, all in the basic sciences. This scared her. She was an artist, a musician, a vocalist. In her previous life she had sung cabaret in Midtown Manhattan. Generally, when I would digress into my numerous side-tracks on every possible scientific topic from string theory to global economics, she would tune me out. Now she would have to not only study, but excel in chemistry, anatomy, physiology and microbiology, to name just a few. She looked to me for an out, but I would not give her one. I would repeat my mantra, "You can do it. You can do it." Without saying it, I knew that she had to do it.

A more pressing concern was the looming prospect of the stem cell transplant. We did not know the if and when at this point. She feared that if the transplant occurred while she was in school, she would not be able to support me. I again assured her that it would all work out. There would be others to step in if she could not be there. It was clear, however, that this would be a huge sacrifice on her part. Finally, and the most difficult of all, this could be a four year commitment of her time. No one could predict what my health might be like in four years when she was done. She worried about the lost opportunities that we might have if she was gone all day and studying all night when she got home. These might be the best years that we would have together and we would miss out on travel, vacation, time with our children and who knew what else. In the end, she made her decision. However, the choice of her first class back in college after more than 10 years would not be hers. She was forced to sign up for the only pre-requisite available that semester. The worst possible first class; Organic and Biochemistry.

January 28, 2009
The Most Noble Profession

I consider medicine a very noble profession. At its core is the commitment to both extend and improve the lives of others. But, it is for the endeavor to fill those lives with meaning that I reserve the designation of the most noble profession: that of being a teacher. I have always seen myself as a teacher first. I absolutely love to teach. When I was in sixth grade I went to the third grade classes to assist with reading. I continued with peer teaching through junior high and high school. At church, I began teaching the Priests at age sixteen (the age that we become Priests), and have continued as a teacher at church since that time.

I had the privilege of dedicating two years of my life teaching the Gospel of Jesus Christ in Argentina, and the lessons that I learned there still serve me today. Argentina es lo mejor lugar para ser misionero.

When I returned to college, I had a professor named Dr. Bradshaw. He taught Cellular and Developmental Biology. He had a unique style of teaching. Rather than present to us a laundry list of facts that we would regurgitate onto the test and then summarily forget, he taught us how to analyze data. The test would consist of an experiment that we had not previously seen. He had given us the tools to understand the process and would then ask, "These are the data; what do they mean?" What a concept: asking a student to think.

In his first lecture, he likened each of us to a sponge. He even had a slide showing a sponge with head, feet and arms. "All of us are students and teachers throughout our lives", he said. "As we learn we are filling the sponge, and when we teach, we are wringing it out." How that rang true. I will always be both a student and a teacher.

When it came time to choose my path in medicine, I was influenced by an observation of one my professors during my residency at UC Davis. I was a little disillusioned about academic medicine, as it seemed so focused on publishing and getting grants. Dr. Stone reminded me, "Kevin, academics is about teaching." I had the great privilege of being on the faculty at Yale University School of Medicine for 11 years and taught specific lectures in all four years of the medical school curriculum. The greatest "rush" that I would get as a teacher was when halfway through a lecture, such as male infertility, the hands would start to go up and the questions would begin. Then I knew that I had made a connection and they were thinking. I cannot tell you how much I miss that.

Teaching did not stop when I came to Kaiser. I still get to work with residents, and of course I teach my patients; but that also is now temporarily gone. However, I can still teach.

Becoming a patient has taught me some truly

valuable lessons. I will be able to share these experiences with others. Today, while getting my chemotherapy, I was sitting next to an elderly woman. As she heard me banter with the nurse, she commented, "How do you stay so positive?" She is fighting a tough battle with brain cancer. I asked her, "What are your goals?" She responded that she recently became a grandmother and wanted to have time with her grandchild. I reminded her that her goal can keep her focused on winning those extra days.

Friday I will meet with the Bone Marrow team at Stanford. Stem cell transplant for amyloidosis in heart transplant patients is rare. So rare that Dr. Lacy at the Mayo Clinic suggested that I return to Minnesota for the treatment. It is trickier after a heart transplant because the anti-rejection drugs can make the infection risk even higher. Stanford, however, has begun a new multidisciplinary amyloidosis treatment center and they need to build a program that will also give them the expertise to treat patients like me. I will be their first BMT after heart transplant. I figured that as they treat me I can be their teacher. They will learn from their communications with the Mayo Clinic. They will learn from my bad days, they will learn from my complications, and hopefully they will learn from my successful completion of the treatment.

And thus, I can still be a teacher.

I have been given so much in my life. I can never fully recompense, no matter how much I serve in return, but I am always happy to try.

Kevin

Part 5

STEM CELL TRANSPLANT

CHAPTER 43

The time had come. The decision was made to proceed with the autologous stem cell transplant. If I had not been sure about it before, I was convinced on Friday the 30th of January. I had two appointments at Stanford that day. Fridays were generally hard for me, because two days after the high dose Decadron and Velcade I always became very weak and fatigued. I first had an appointment with Dr. Sally Arai. She is a specialist in bone marrow transplant. Additionally, she is a member of the multi-disciplinary team recently developed at Stanford to treat amyloido-sis. She would see me through the entire process. She was petite and demure and somewhat reserved, but very nice. We went through the usual doctor-patient formalities. I asked my questions and we left. I thought that I had an appointment with Dr. Ron Witteles in cardiology, but when we arrived, there was no schedule for me to be seen. At this point, I was really sick and not very patient. I informed them that I would wait, and wait we did. They let me into an exam room and I collapsed on the bed. I felt like 'my insides wanted to be on my outsides'. Finally he came and we spoke about the upcoming transplant and then we drove home.

I knew how sick I was, because I let Barbie drive. I wished I could vomit, but I could not. I had not eaten. We stopped at Subway in Cordelia, hoping that I could at least sip on the broth from chicken noodle soup. The young man behind the counter blandly said, "we're out." Did he not understand how sick I was? Could he not just go open another can? I got a 7-Up and went back to the car for the ride home. Oh, how I wanted the stem cell transplant to work so that I would never have to take Decadron and Velcade ever again.

Monday, February 2, 2009
Groundhog Day

Today I saw my shadow, which means, like Bill Murray, I will need to stick around until I get it right. I am always struck by how different each day can be. I get the chemotherapy ... every Wednesday. By Friday I feel like death and all his friends are visiting. It consists of that very uncomfortable feeling where, on the one hand you are hoping for reverse peristalsis (euphemism for vomiting) and simultaneously holding on to avoid the mess. At least it is predictable. I know that no matter how bad I feel on Friday, I will survive and Saturday will see my appetite return. By Monday I am ready for anything. I know that in life we must have opposition in all things, but I am often struck by its immediacy.

When I was in Junior High School, I dreaded P.E. This was because whenever teams were chosen, I was always the last one standing on the sidelines (the irony of being 6' 2" and unable to dribble). What a difference now. With all of this new-found coordination among all of these teams, I've been elevated to a first round draft pick. I guess I'll be playing for Stanford.

The game plan begins, after the preliminary workup, with four to five days of stem cell stimulation with a hormone called G-CSF (granulocyte colony stimulating factor). A Hickman catheter (semi-permanent IV) will be placed into my right subclavian vein and after five days the stem cells will be harvested in a process called apheresis. My blood will then be run through a machine which magically pulls out the stem-cells and puts everything else back (just like my daughters picking their favorites from a box of See's Candy). These cells will then be frozen. A few days later, I will get a drug called Melphalan which will kill my bone marrow, including the plasma cells responsible for my amyloidosis. Two days later, the stem cells will be re-infused to "reboot the hard-drive" to a clean, unaffected state. It will take some time, however, for my red blood cells (RBCs), white blood cells (WBCs) and platelets to return to normal. During this two- to four-week period I will be anemic, prone to infections and bleeding. This will also be compounded by the fact that I am on immunosuppressive drugs for my heart. Bring it on!

But that is all tomorrow. Today was beautiful; California, in the dead of winter. It is 70 degrees outside and I went for a bike ride. I rode five miles on highway 193 into downtown Lincoln. I felt great. But my atrophied chicken-bone legs were yelling up to my brain, "What the heck is going on here?" Meanwhile my heart was querying, "Are we exercising? No one tells me anything, always out of the loop." My adrenals just rolled over and went back to sleep..

..

Kevin

Wednesday, February 4, 2009
Marrow to my bones

I received the schedule for the stem cell transplant. I begin stem cell stimulation on February 23 and the apheresis or harvesting will take place on February 28th. I will then have a week off (fortunately the same week that Caitlin is off from school) and receive the conditioning with Melphalan on March 10th and 11th. March 13th is the day that my new bone marrow will be born, which is fitting, as that is Samuel and Jeremy's birthday. The pattern must continue since the anniversary of my new heart is the day Samuel and Michelle got married.

Today was my last dose of Velcade and Decadron (and I hope last means last). I also had a bone marrow biopsy by Dr. Sardar, with Laura, his MA, assisting. This one was even less painful than the last two because "Phil's good." Tomorrow I will do a skeletal survey, which does not refer to the mapping of a cemetery. All of this is in preparation for the transplant.

Preparation for all of this began a very long time ago. When Joseph Smith, the founding prophet of my church, received a revelation from God in 1833 called "The Word of Wisdom," it instructed his followers on issues of health, both spiritual and physical. I have followed this guidance all of my life. I have never smoked, I have never tasted alcohol or drunk coffee. I have tried to eat in a healthy manner. At the end of this revelation, the following promise is given:

Doctrine and Covenants: Section 89

18. And all saints who remember to keep and do these sayings, walking in obedience to the commandments, shall receive health in their navel and marrow to their bones;

19. And shall find wisdom and great treasures of knowledge, even hidden treasures;

20. And shall run and not be weary, and shall walk and not faint.

21. And I, the Lord, give unto them a promise, that the destroying angel shall pass by them, as the children of Israel, and not slay them. Amen

With my new heart I can walk and not faint; now all I am waiting for is the healthy marrow in my bones.

Kevin
Friday, February 6, 2009
Where Have I Been?

I know it has been forever since I have written. For my own personal reasons I have kept most of my feelings to myself. My sister-in law, Darlene, told me once that when things get really hard to write a letter to myself and then destroy it. I wrote privately for awhile, but I have not destroyed them yet. I feel that my private writings will help me later somehow. I wrote privately for myself mainly because I was embarrassed and tired of complaining openly to the blogging world.

I am going to be open now about what has been happening here from my perspective.

I'll start with Rebecca first. Just after Christmas Rebecca's new husband, Corey, decided that Mormon life and married life was not for him. It was only a few weeks later that we moved Rebecca home and realized the marriage was over. We will never know exactly what happened in his heart, but we do know that Rebecca did all she could to try and save the marriage. Corey has made a decision and in his heart I believe he feels he is doing right for Rebecca. For the few weeks of early January we watched Rebecca torn; she was still in love with him and hoped he would change his mind, while at other moments she was angry at what he had done to her. As time went by her heart healed and she wished as we do for him to find happiness in his life. Some days I miss him, but mostly I just wonder why. She is strong now and happy and will be heading back to BYU for Spring term to continue her degree in Advertising. We have loved having her back home with us. She brings laughter and playfulness to our home. Caitlin is also enjoying having her sister around.

Now, about Kevin. He is my love and will always be. Does this mean I am good at being a sensitive and loving caregiver? No. I am good some of the time and at other times my selfishness comes through and I am tired of him being sick. I miss the easier life we seemed to have before, but am grateful for the outcome of every trial that has come our way this year. Without the love and knowledge of God, I would not be so calm. I look forward to him going back to work. Not because I want him out of the house, but because it will be good for him and will give us both the sense of normalcy again. I am truly scared of what is ahead with the SCT, more so than the heart transplant. My fears have little to do with it being successful, but my ability to care for him in all that is required. I must sterilize his water. Make everything from scratch. Keep him away from public places. Drive him everywhere. He will be on a Microbial diet because of his immunosuppressive drugs. This means he also cannot have fresh fruits, vegetables, deli meats, open breads, yogurt and many other specifics. He is not allowed in the kitchen or allowed to clean in any way. And all this will be in a hotel again in Stanford. I know, it sounds like I am complaining again. Sorry. I am just stating facts. With Rebecca home until March, she will be able to help out at home with Caitlin. Once she heads back, we'll figure things out again.

Now about me. I have started taking prerequisites for Dental Hygiene school. I am taking Organic Chemistry and Nutrition. It has been a good distraction, but also extremely time-consuming. I have classes all day M&W. I know that when the SCT process starts in a couple of weeks it will be hard to keep up with classes and if I fail, I fail and can repeat them. If I need to drop, I will drop them. We are grateful and will call upon family and friends who have offered to help when he needs 24hr. care in the hotel and I am in class. Some may wonder why I would even think to start these classes now and not wait until things were easier. As Kevin puts it, "things may never get that much easier," and honestly we both felt it was the right thing to do. He knows me and I know myself better than anyone.

My way of coping now in my life is to work through today and plan for tomorrow, not the "future" tomorrow, but just the next day tomorrow.

I am happy, healthy, love learning about carbons, (REALLY...) and, I might add, tired. But because of my faith in God, I know that only he can carry my burden and make it light.

Barbie

C H A P T E R 4 4

Be Patient
Day -22 Health Score 87

I had decided to do daily entries on the days that I am receiving treatment and preparing for the stem cell transplant. I believe you get a more honest sense of what is happening if it is not filtered through the "retrospectoscope." Day 0 is March 13th, the day I get the transplant. I feel it might help someone going through the same process to know what to expect. The health score is how I am feeling on any given day (physically, emotionally etc...) This is quite subjective. The scale is from 1 - 100 with 1 being dead and 100 signifying perfect health. For instance, if I were severely nauseated and unable to eat, but could still get around, drive and function, that would be 50-60

If I were in bed, unmotivated to do anything, with no energy; that would be 40-50. (However, one must subtract 8 points for unbridled optimism). If I were able to boogie board, bicycle 100 km, backpack 8 miles or do a ureteroscopic Holmium laser lithotripsy, that would put me at 100. So 87 is pretty good.

The day began well as I drove down Sierra College Blvd on my way to Stanford. As I looked eastward over the town of Loomis, the sun was just coming over the Sierras, the broken clouds being illuminated with a myriad of colors: multiple shades of grey, blue, peach and pink. The cherry blossoms added a corresponding cloud of pink from below. It felt like a glorious spring morning right after rain. Californians take spring for granted. A spring day can occur here any time of the year. In Connecticut, spring does not arrive until May, making it highly anticipated. The trees and ground-cover are bare in New England from November through April. The green is replaced by gray, black and brown. People flock to New England to see the colors of fall; which are spectacular. But few outsiders realize that the colors of spring are equally vibrant and diverse; and much more appreciated. They signify the new life aris-ing after months of dreariness. Becoming well, after months (or years) of illness is similar to the feeling that spring gives: a new beginning, a new hope.

Then I arrived at Stanford and became the patient. First I went to the BMT unit on E1 in the main hos-pital to sign all of my consents. Informed consent is the process where all of the possible bad things that can happen are explained in detail. Everyone signs, assuming it will not happen to them. And then some patients are shocked and angry when bad things do occur. Complications do not bother me as long as I know that they are expected and I can overcome them. I repeat my mantra to myself: "prepare for the worst, hope for the best." With BMT, nausea, fatigue, hair loss and painful mouth sores are common. The most feared complication is infection, which can be fatal. Many precautions are taken to prevent infections.

I then went to a class for training on the care of the Hickman Catheter that will be placed on Monday. My appointment was for 2:00 PM. At 3:00 I asked the receptionist what the delay was and he said that they were very busy and that no rooms were available. At 3:15 the assistant took me in the back hallway to get my vital signs (for a class?) and had me watch a video. I asked if she was going to put me in a room and she said it was being cleaned. The nurse came to begin teaching at 3:45. I asked if we were going to a room for teaching and she informed me (with some irony, I thought) that someone else had taken the room. I share this because I know that thousands of patients experience this every day. Some days things do not go as planned; that's why we are called patients.

When some serious surgical mishap is investigated, often the root cause is a series of simultaneous mistakes. The system is built with enough backup to handle two maybe three simultaneous mistakes, but on the rare occasion that four or five occur, there is a bad outcome. The opposite can also occur. Four or five fortuitous events can simultaneously occur, causing an equally rare but beneficial outcome. This has already happened to me, resulting in my receiving a healthy new heart. I can appreciate and be grateful for this set of fortuitous events, because I know that the odds were stacked against me. Therefore, I will be patient and not complain about minor bumps in the road. Getting angry only hurts oneself. All concern left me as I drove home to witness an equally beautiful California sunset and was reminded that every new day is a new day to get it right.

Kevin

Friday, February 20, 2009
Moving Forward
Day -20 Health Score 86

Today I met with Dr. Arai one final time before starting stem cell stimulation. This was to review all of the results from the re-staging process. Everything looks fine, so we will proceed on Monday. I also saw a specialist from infectious disease who will assist in the effort to avoid or treat infections. They take everything seriously. I mentioned the mild congestion that I have, which is common this time of year. As a result, I had a nasal swab to rule out a viral upper respiratory infection. I am not complaining. I fully support their vigilance.

Kevin

CHAPTER 45

Monday, February 23, 2009
Straight for the jugular
Day -18 Health Score 83

*Every institution has its own style. University
hospitals move at a certain pace because of their size
and hierarchical complexity. Private hospitals tend
to market their flexibility and efficiency. Kaiser has
superior integration and collegiality. The VA moves by
the weight of its own inertia, carrying a gravitational
field relative to the behemoth that it is. The Mayo
Clinic is unique in its ability to fast track a diagnostic
work up while greeting you with a sport coat, tie and
smile at every visit. What is not unique is the caliber
of physicians and nurses at each of these institutions.
There are great doctors everywhere (just as those with
poor bedside manners are equally well distributed).
One should not judge the quality of medical care by the
length of the wait or whether the front desk just sees
you as just another warm body.*

We waited a lot today. But that's OK.

*I picked up my mom at 4:00 a.m. to drive to
Stanford.*

*I received my first Neupogen shot this morning and
then went to the ATP (Ambulatory Treatment and
Procedures). Once I finally arrived in the fluoroscopy
room, the nurse asked what style of music I wanted.*

He programmed Coldplay into Pandora.com. Then he gave me some wonderful chemicals: Fentanyl and Versed. I felt just fine as they tunneled the 12 French Hickman catheter over my right clavicle and into the internal jugular vein. The doctor had a little trouble getting into the inferior vena cava due to the distortion of the anatomy where my donated heart is connected to my native IVC. But the 0.035 inch angled glide wire with the "magic" Terumo tip once again saved the day. (That Terumo tip is the same tool I rely on to get past obstructed stones in the ureter.) Also, I am so happy when MD's buffer their lidocaine with sodium bicarb. It does not burn so much. Now I have this catheter hanging out of me for the next few months (resulting in my banishment from the hot tub).

I am staying at yet another Residence Inn here in Mountain View. They have experience with BMT patients and their strict precautions. Overall, today went fine; I am just left with a sore, stiff neck. (No longer hard-hearted, now just stiff-necked.)

Kevin

Tuesday, February 24, 2009
Study and sleep and, oh yes, eat.

Tomorrow is my second Organic Chemistry exam. I have been crazily studying all day except for the time I spent with Kevin for lunch, a surprise since I did not think he would be done so soon today. I feel ready -- we'll see. I felt a little sad when he left Monday morning and I could not go with him to his first day of the treatment process. Fortunately, his mom was available to be with him since the sedation would prevent him from driving. He is alone now but I will join him tomorrow after my exam. It's not until the afternoon so I will get there as soon as I can.

As much as I could do without all the necessary studying, I really am enjoying all that I am learning in O-Chem. The class is so time-consuming that my Nutrition class seems so easy. I do count down toward the weeks when my time can be more focused on Kevin, my children (even married ones) and my house (it's getting a little disorganized). Oh, well. A few piles never hurt anyone, right?

Barbie

Thursday, February 26, 2009
Sequoia
Day -15 Health Score 85

The Sequoia is the largest tree in the world. California is home to a number of Sequoia groves. Most of the remaining groves are in the Sierras. For years, uncontrolled deforestation annihilated most of the coastal groves. However, a few remain. I grew up in Marin County, just north of San Francisco. There is a grove of Sequoia nestled into the north slope of Mt. Tamalpais not far from Stinson Beach. Muir Woods is named after the naturalist John Muir, and aptly so. He spent his life working to preserve the natural beauties of California. As a child and young adult, I would return again and again to the majesty of Muir Woods; trees, 2000 years old, wider than a Chevy Suburban, lined the needle strewn path. It seemed as if these gargantuan sentinels had quietly observed as two millennia of human history passed beneath them.

I have previously mentioned my affinity for trees. I have always avoided cutting them down (I refer to the *ones in our yard). However, at times, this is necessary. They become diseased, overgrown, or present a danger to the house or power lines. But I have probably planted more than I have hewn. However, the deciding factor on the location of the lot where we chose to build our house was the view of the natural oaks present there. In Connecticut, I had grown accustomed to the view of the forest from the kitchen window every morning as I ate my Lucky Charms.*

Today, feeling the need to escape the hotel again, Barbie and I headed for Big Basin State Park. Prior to today, I had never heard of it. Like Muir Woods, it is a grove of old world Sequoia, hidden and spared. It is in the Santa Cruz mountain range, just west of Saratoga. One again I stood in awe of the immensity and longevity of these symbols of life. Sequoia are adapted to thrive through adversity. Storms make their roots stronger; fire is an essential part of their life cycle. Fire clears the underbrush while also allowing more light to reach their branches. Many Sequoia survive multiple fires in their lifetime. The scars of the fire remain, but they continue to grow. Aren't we the same? Challenges in our lives unclutter and unencumber us from the banalities of daily living while enlightening us with greater clarity and acceptance of those things that really do matter. The memories remain, but not the pain.

Fire also promotes new growth of Sequoia offspring. It is common to see a circle or ring of Sequoia around an empty space where a giant Sequoia used to stand and is now dead. Its death allows new trees to grow in its place. They forever circle the spot, and almost enshrine it, in quiet reverence to their fallen progenitor. The metaphor reminds me that some must die to allow others to live.

I know that my heart donor's family has planted a Sequoia tree to honor his memory. Soon I will go and visit that tree to reverence the life he gave so that I could live.

Kevin

Apheresis
Day -14 Health Score 82

Today I underwent my first apheresis. This is a process during which my stem cells are removed from my blood and then frozen. They will be given back to me on March 13 after my bone marrow has been wiped out. The goal is to harvest at least 2,000,000 cells. I am not sure exactly how the machine does this, but I imagine it is like when you put your loose change into a coin sorter; as it spins the coins drop according to their size. Whole blood is pumped out of me through one of the ports of my Hickman catheter. The machine then runs it through a centrifuge, which separates the cells by size and collects just the stem cells. The remaining blood is then returned through the other port. Because I have amyloidosis, it is their protocol to also monitor my heart because of potential fluid shifts that would stress the heart (although with a heart transplant, that risk is low).

As the nurse began today, I sensed that they were having some trouble with the machine. The one nurse kept saying, "The interface is labile." This sounded more like something you would hear on Star Trek as Scotty calls up to the bridge exclaiming, "Captain, we can't hold on much longer; the interface is labile!!" I assume is was nothing, as the next four hours of collection were uneventful. Soon they will let us know the count to see if another collection tomorrow is necessary.

Kevin

Friday, February 27, 2009
Collection day

I arrived Wednesday night around 8:30 pm. Kevin and I were glad to see each other, but walking into another Residence Inn brought back a flood of memories. Not all the good memories came back; those ones are always with me. But the ones you put way back in your mind; the ones you prefer to forget. Yesterday was a harder day for me. To be in the hotel again and think about what is to come. I felt much better after giving myself a little time to process the next few months. I enjoyed our walk in the Sequoia and today while waiting for Kevin's room we walked around the Stanford campus. They have a beautiful collection of Rodin in an outside courtyard and a gorgeous campus. Around 2 p.m. the room was ready and after some time, Kevin was hooked up and ready for collection.

While he read and napped I worked on my term paper for organic chemistry. It seems appropriate that my topic is "Amyloidosis - the misfolded protein with heart involvement." It's kind of strange for Kevin and me to discuss it as a disease not related to us personally. And then we stop and are aware again of the closeness of it all. I arrived in the hotel room tonight and will be here again tomorrow night. Just as I was leaving Kevin's room, the nurse came in and stated that not enough stem cells were collected so they will be collecting again tomorrow. Hopefully we will be able to leave Sunday morning.

My bedtime reading tonight: Autologous Blood and Marrow Transplant Guidebook.

Barbie

Day 2
Day-13 Health Score 80

The collection yesterday harvested about 1.1 million stem cells. Their goal is five million. I was on the machine again today for four hours and will have another collection tomorrow; hopefully the last. It did give me a chance to re-read one of my favorite books, The Ministry of Fear *by Graham Greene. It is a great psychological thriller. Graham Greene also wrote the screenplay for* The Third Man, *a must see post-World War II thriller with Joseph Cotton and Orson Welles.*

I am always impressed by writers who have the narrative ability to paint a scene or a mood that makes the reader feel like he or she is actually there. Reading Greene's work, I can really feel the surreal grittiness of war-torn London during the Blitzkrieg with the same uncertainty that the author must have felt with no knowledge of how the war would end. Writing a story, not knowing how it will end, lends it a certain air of authenticity.

It will be good to go home tomorrow.

Kevin

Monday, March 2, 2009
Paroled for good behavior
Day - 11 Health Score 78 (physically) 86
(emotionally happy to be home)

Today my blood went out for another spin. When it got back, I noticed that the stems had been trimmed.

Each consecutive day of apheresis, my body provided fewer and fewer cells for harvesting. 1.1 million on day one, 0.95 million on day two and 500,000 on day three. I wondered, "what can I do to improve this situation?" Then I remembered a young patient I once had. She was a seven-year-old girl with an obstructing kidney stone. I performed ureteroscopy and fragmented the stone with a laser and removed what I thought, were all of the fragments. I recall being impressed with how stoic she was about the whole experience, complaining much less than most of my adult patients. Two weeks later, however, her pain returned, and a retained fragment was seen in the ureter on X-ray evaluation. I explained to her mother and her that we would need to re-operate if the stone did not pass. It was clear that this upset the girl, but she held back the tears, trying to be strong. A few days later I got a call from the mom requesting that the surgery be cancelled. She related that her daughter informed her that she was going outside to jump on the trampoline to make the stone pass. Her mother felt conflicted, not wanting to crush the indefatigable confidence that only seven-year-old logic can assert, but without also promoting false hope.

Twenty minutes later her daughter came in the house and, heading to the bathroom, exclaimed, "I passed the stone." Not knowing what to expect, the mother was completely shocked when three minutes later her excited daughter came out with a tiny brown stone pinched in her fingers.

I thought, "I have been lying in bed here for three days; my stem cells are just lying asleep in my bone marrow. I need to wake them up." So I designed a very biased, non-randomized, non-controlled study with an 'N' of one. I would ride the stationary bike for 30 minutes and go for a walk through the hospital for 20 minutes, thereby increasing blood-flow through my long bones and washing out the stem cells.

Results: My count today was 700,000 cells, proving that theory was correct. However, the difference was statistically insignificant with a p-value of 1.5 liters.

This was immediately accepted and published in Bogus-Science.blog between the articles, "Show me a food that isn't organic" by Hart E. Appetite and "Bottled water is a bargain and better for you than tap water" by Major U. S. Scam.

I escaped the hospital with the help of my mom and brother, David, and am happily reunited with the beautiful women in my life. It's good to be home.

Kevin

CHAPTER 46

I always tried to maintain a positive attitude when I was around others, especially Barbie. However, the emotions could not always be contained. Whenever I was anxious, I was drawn to nature. Standing below the wide expanse of sky with its ever changing hues, listening to the crash of wave on the beach, meandering through trees; all allowed me to escape personal concerns or fears. Fear. Was I afraid? Up to this point I had always felt that everything was going to be all right. But I knew that the stem cell transplant held greater risks for me than anything else up to that point. In August of 2008, only one month after I had met Dr. Lacy while at the Mayo Clinic, her group had published a paper on the Mayo Clinic experience with performing stem cell transplants after heart transplant. During my career I have been on editorial boards and served as a reviewer for numerous journals. Never had I read an article that had such clinical relevance for me personally. This was me: stem cell transplant after heart transplant.

The facts were shocking. Out of 110 patients who needed a heart transplant to save their life, only 11 were candidates. Reading between the lines, I easily surmised what had happened to the other 99: they had died. Of these 11 patients who then went on to get a stem cell transplant (SCT), two died of complications related to the transplant, specifically from infections. The team at the Mayo Clinic had observed more complications with the standard dose of Melphalan at 100 mg/m2 and thereby suggested using only 70 mg/m2 in heart transplant patients, postulating that their pre-conditioning with anti-rejection drugs made them more prone to complications. I discussed this paper with Dr. Arai. She had read it and said that they would likely follow this protocol and only use 70 mg/m2 on me to limit my potential complications. I knew that the risk alone for any patient to die from a SCT was between one and 10%. One percent of patients would not engraft, leading to an empty bone marrow and eventual death.

I placed myself at the beginning of my journey back in June. I had had no idea of my odds at that time. I had read on the internet that I had an 18-month expectation of survival. What I did not know at the time was that the degree of my heart damage in that moment was a level three. This I learned much later in an article by Dr. Lacy's colleague, Dr. Gertz, which had me actually at a six-month expectation of survival. Cardiac risk level three patients were too sick to get a stem cell transplant. The only option for survival was a new heart.

In my head I started crunching the numbers: 9% chance of getting a heart multiplied by a 20 to 30% mortality from the stem cell transplant. If I had been told last June that the odds of surviving to see June 2009 were less than 5%, would I have done anything different?

I kept my fears silent. I never liked to even admit that I felt fear. That would undermine my hope, our hope. I certainly was not overcome by this sense of dread, but there were private moments.

The rain hit the windshield of the car as I sat there alone waiting for Caitlin to finish her day at Lincoln High. The radio was on as I sat alone with my thoughts. What would happen if I died from the transplant? I was already immuno-suppressed. An infection would kill me. Music from Coldplay filled the air in the car. The syncopated piano and drums resolved into the lyrics of "Death and All His Friends."

"So come over, just be patient and don't worry.

I don't want to follow death and all his friends."

I was overcome with grief and began to weep uncontrollably. The rain on the windshield and the tears in my eyes made everything blurry. I could not clearly distinguish anything before me. All shapes were distorted; reality had no clear edges.

I needed to compose myself, as I could see Caitlin hurrying across the street in the rain in the rear view mirror. I had to be strong for her. I had to be strong for Barbie. I would bury the fear. It could not defeat me. I knew that I could die; it did not matter. We had made the decision and would live with it. Hopefully.

Friday, March 6, 2009
Preparing, mentally, to go.

I have noticed Kevin has not written since he got home Monday night. It has been great to have him home. We have been soaking it up knowing that he will be gone for some time starting next Monday. I am not sure what health number he would have given for the past few days, but Tuesday he was a little tired; he did not have a lot of energy. Wednesday and Thursday were really good days for him. He seemed to feel stronger and was in good spirits. Today he felt washed out, tired, weaker, a bit fatigued. It could be that his chemistry levels are all messed up from the stem cell collection or side effects from his medication. Do not really know. He may have some labs taken tomorrow to figure out what may be going on. We will cherish the next two days at home together. I love being home. It's my sanctuary from all the commotion of the world. I will miss sleeping in my own bed with my own pillow every night. I cannot imagine how Kevin is feeling right now knowing he will be away from home for five or more weeks.

Heading to bed now.

Barbie

CHAPTER 47

Monday, March 9, 2009
Back at Stanford
Day -4 Health Score 81

I hitched a ride with my friend, Josh, down to Stanford today. I did not want to drive and leave my own car here for a month. Because I was somewhat fatigued last week, I got some labs done on Saturday and my hematocrit is 30%. I am anemic. I am sure that they will probably transfuse me this week. Today I met with Dr. Arai to determine if I can get the poison tomorrow. Since I have a mild dry cough, she did a viral swab of my nose again. I guess if that's OK, we will proceed.

The nurse coordinator, Zoe, went over the process in detail and it does not sound fun. She said I will be admitted for two to three weeks and probably will not be able to leave my room for two weeks. She spoke of nausea (lots of it) pain, fatigue and mouth sores. Bring it on.

Tomorrow should be interesting.

Kevin

Tuesday, March 10, 2009
I am not alone
Day - 3 Health Score 80

I was admitted today to start what they call "conditioning." Which is a euphemism for "poisoning." Melphalan truly is a poison. The goal is to kill my bone marrow without killing me. I received the first dose today, which is 70 mg/m2. The pre-medication was my favorite drug, Decadron. They also gave me 32mg of Zofran, an anti nausea drug.

As I lay in bed during the chemo infusion, I offered up a silent prayer. I heard the nurse enter the room to check on me. She asked how I was doing and I said that I was lost in thought. As I said this, I was trying to suppress my emotions. She responded, "Are you sure you are OK, because you are making a face?" I responded quietly, "It's the face of gratitude." She immediately understood and gently touched my arm. No other words were spoken.

I am physically alone here today, and yet I feel surrounded by the faith and support of so many people. Friends and family often ask what they can do for Barbie and me and our family. What they do not realize is that in the act alone of asking with sincerity, they have already done so much to show that they care.

Kevin

Wednesday, March 11, 2009
Visitors
Day - 2 Health Score 83 (despite the hiccups)

I kept waiting for some side effect from the Melphalan. None came. If anything, I feel a little better today (the upside of steroids) and the only side effects I have noticed have been insomnia (easily corrected with Ativan) and hiccups. Even my sore throat and cough have gone away (my nasal swab, yuck, was negative for any viruses.) I rode the exercise bike for 15 minutes and walked the hallways for 15 minutes. I have to get out while I can. In a few days I will be confined to my room. My labs are good today and my hematocrit went up to 29%, hence, no transfusion.

I also spent a good portion of the morning on the phone with my Assistant Chief, Dr. Chabra, trying to hammer out departmental issues. The physical therapist comes by to make sure I am out of bed and exercising and the dietitian comes to reinforce the virtues of the low microbial diet, (salt, yes; pepper, no)

I also started writing my autobiography today. I have struggled for some time on the question of who is the audience and what style and structure I should employ. I am not a huge fan of the linear narrative, or in other words, recording memories in a purely chronological litany. Rather, I see life and time not as completely linear. The decision I make right now is not often based on the experience I had 10 minutes ago or yesterday, but rather from something I learned 15 years ago, or a value I developed when I was nine. The structure, then, necessarily must reflect how I became who I am. The risk of failure in writing such a tome is high. But I will give it a try.

Kevin

Thursday, March 12, 2009
One more day
Day - 1 Health Score 77

I am a little more fatigued today. My Hematocrit is 26 - 27%. But the good news is that my creatinine dropped to 1.4 from 1.6 (normal kidney function); that is reassuring. Still no nausea or pain of any kind. So I am ready for the stem-cell slushy tomorrow. They infuse them rapidly right out of the freezer.

It's been nice to have Barbie, Rebecca and Caitlin here today. They will leave soon for San Francisco to see Wicked.

If these hiccups do not subside soon, I will claim psychosis and take the Thorazine (a drug for psychotics also treats hiccups).

I had a visit today from Tony from the amyloidosis support group. He went through this five years ago and is doing great. He was very encouraging.

Kevin

CHAPTER 48

Friday, March 13, 2009
Closeout Cell, All things must go in
Day 0 Health Score 75

Today I received my stem cells back. There were five bags to infuse. I was premedicated with 100 mg of hydrocortisol (equivalent to 20 mg of prednisone) and Benadryl. This helps to diminish any allergic reaction to the DMSO preservative with the cells. The first and second bags were infused over ten minutes each. I only felt a little heat in the back of my neck. When they infused the third bag, the flushing extended through my head and chest and within a minute, I had a nasty ache in my stomach. Within seconds I was returning my lunch to its tray (no major loss). I immediately felt better. They gave me some Ativan to calm me down and the last two bags went in without further incident.

The hard drive has been formatted and those malicious viruses and Trojan horses should be eradicated. Now the fun begins: rebooting the system. My white count and platelets will drop and I will need blood transfusions. The mouth sores should start next week. They assure me that once the white cell count comes back, I will feel better. I am confident that I will be better.

My gratitude remains insufficient for all the love and support that I feel from all of you. It carries me daily.

Kevin

Saturday, March 14, 2009
The day after Christmas
Day +1 Health Score 79

My nurse, Gayla, kept reminding me that this experience should be like the day after Christmas: anticlimactic. Today could be well described as that. I actually feel much better now that the hiccups have subsided. I have had the opportunity to help Barbie with her Organic Chemistry, which I really enjoy. She is grasping the concepts so fast, but she will never admit that. I have never seen a student so dedicated.

The chaos and uncertainty that we so long feared with her in school and me here has been resolved through the kindness and generosity of so many people. Through our friends, the Hargadons, Barbie has a place to stay while I am in the hospital. While she is in school from Monday to Wednesday, friends and family will be here to keep me company and keep her updated on my progress. Truly these are answers to prayers.

I remain in great spirits. My bad plasma cell clones are dead and dying, while Captain Stem Cell is coming to save the day. I expect next week to be tough, but that's OK. I am learning so much through all of this.

I guess I smell bad today, it's the DMSO preservative for the cells, Barbie keeps feeding me breath mints. What would I do without her?

Kevin

Sunday, March 15, 2009
Ministering
Day +2 Health Score 77

Today has been a quiet day. I sat and looked at Barbie's empty chair after she left. I was sleeping most of the morning while she was here and now I am awake. That's not fair. But it is always nicer when she is around. Nothing much has changed for me yet. My white blood cell count is only now beginning to drop, but it is still in the normal range and my hematocrit went up to 29% after the transfusion.

I sit and think a lot. I did a little writing today. However, I fear that I write like I think, which mostly consists of random associations and patterns that make sense only in the context of my memories, but would likely be incoherent to anyone else. I hope in time I will be able to bring some order to my contextual chaos.

I was pleased to be visited this morning by some elders from my church who came by to give me the Sacrament. They were from a local ward (congregation) near here. The gentleman was a bit forward, however. He came in my room and said he saw my name on a list of LDS patients and without so much as asking my name began to proceed. I felt the need to at least tell him who I was and why I was here. Notwithstanding, I truly felt the Spirit and was so very grateful for their dedication in coming to help me, a stranger.

It brought to my mind the difference between administering and ministering. To administer in one's duty, to fulfill one's responsibility, is an important part in serving any group or individual. Certain people are quite adept at administration because they are efficient, organized and focused. However, to minister is vital as well. There are times when a suffering soul only needs to be heard. Such people need a listening ear not only for the concerns they voice, but also for their unuttered fears. This type of ministering is not uniquely relegated to the ecclesiastical realm, but is necessary in all professions. How often have I administered the diagnosis or treatment to my patient with an efficient and focused approach, ignoring the suffering person's greater need for clarity and understanding? Ministering cannot be rushed, but always requires intense listening. It is impossible to minister to someone you do not care about. Ministering occurs between individuals, not between groups.

I am so grateful for the lessons that I continue to learn from this experience. I hope, from this, to be a better doctor to my patients. That I will not fall back on old habits and always remember whom I serve.

Kevin

Monday, March 16, 2009
'Guy' Stuff
Day + 3 Health Score 73

The day passed quickly, as I had the company of a friend of mine from church, Neal Hinson. He drove the 2 1/2 hours from Lincoln to Stanford just so I would not be alone today while Barbie was in school. Neal is a Captain in the Air Force and flies U-2 spy planes out of Beale Air Force Base. It was fascinating to learn of his experiences as one who flies so high and so alone. We both commented on the similarities between pilots and surgeons. In a moment of crisis, all of your experience, training, intuition and common sense combine with a heightened perception and awareness as you first control the situation, second make a plan, and third fix the problem. I remember that this would occur to me, while I was performing surgery. I would often enter an almost trancelike state, shutting out all external input. I did not sense time or body aches. I was completely focused until the job is done. And then, all at once, I would look at the clock, finding that what seemed like five minutes had actually been an hour, and your back was starting to hurt.

The personalities that seek these jobs are clearly similar. It is strange that we might both be in awe of what the other guy does, whereas for us, it is just a day's work.

*The mouth sores began today. But I can still swallow. This was good because Neal brought "guy" food (Cheetos and Hostess Donettes) and "guy" movies (*The Right Stuff *and* Master and Commander*) to pass the time. It was good.*

What a true friend.

Kevin

CHAPTER 49

O n Monday I got a call from Maria Boatman. She said that Ty, their seven-year-old and youngest son, had blood in his urine. This is unusual for a boy his age. We talked about stones versus infections, but I said he needed at least an ultrasound to look at his kidneys. I told her about my partner, Dr. Andrew Huang, a pediatric urologist, and said that I would contact him. I then called Andy and he said that he had already heard about the case and suggested a CT scan. Two hours later he called me back. Ty had a large Wilm's tumor involving his right kidney. These cancers are rare and potentially deadly. It would have to come out. He informed me that Dr. Du Bois, the pediatric surgeon, was already planning the surgery for the next day.

Later that day I spoke to Maria and Don again. I tried to be positive for them. It was hard to speak, as the mouth sores caused such pain when I moved any muscle in my throat. I thought of how it felt to receive such news about oneself. It was hard, but I knew I could handle it. Yet, I could not imagine how it felt to get such a shocking revelation about your child. I reached back into my memory regarding everything that I had learned about Wilm's tumors as a resident. I knew that it was treatable and responded to chemotherapy, surgery and radiation. So much depended on the stage and grade of the cancer, both facts that I did not have. I tried to be as hopeful as I could. Don, a dentist, asked the fact-based questions that I would have asked, but then Maria asked, "how do you think I will be able to handle this?" I knew what she was asking. My immediate thought was, "you don't have a choice." I responded that I knew that she would do everything that she could; she was strong and would be there for her son. I reassured her that she had the best doctors (having personally operated with both of them.) I did what I always do: I gave her hope. In my heart, I truly believed that Ty would be OK; I prayed that my tone and my concern would convey that, even if my words fell flat.

When adversity comes, we often do not have the luxury of time to prepare. We are expected to be strong. Yet we are fragile. I knew what she was in for, but nothing that I could say at that moment would really make sense in the present context.

Tuesday, March 17, 2009
Day + 4 Health Score 68

Sometimes I may lie in bed for hours, awake, and with my mind racing with random thoughts and remembrances. Occasionally some will push to the surface. They are not action plans, but mere reflections.

I guess I would call the following a poem in a minor key because it has no tonic.

Fear

To what end do we profit in fear of the inevitable?
Only to paralyze us into inaction to neither
submission nor reaction

To what end do we profit from fear of the avoidable?
Deluding our actions into lives uncontrollable.

To what end do we profit from fear of the unknown?
Our light extinguished in failure to discover,
Whether it be a painful truth or a hidden jewel to uncover.

The only profit in fear is to those who feign to sell us complacency
That all pain is avoidable, that risk is unnecessary and that for a price we can be insulated.

Thus delaying our preparations in hope; that will free us to grow.

(For Tyler)

I am tired today. The throat pain is worse and eating is a struggle. I know it is temporary and will try to focus on other things.

Kevin

CHAPTER 50

Essay on Fear

Fear is the greatest plague to ever afflict humanity. This statement might seem to border on hyperbole; nevertheless, it is true. All life on earth, in order to survive, must defend itself. Fear and pain are essential to our existence to the degree that they warn us to flee or avoid those things that could permanently destroy us. Unfortunately, humankind, the most advanced form of life on the planet, has also developed the ability to expand, augment and explode fear far beyond its useful and protective limits. Ultimately, fear paralyzes us, resulting either in inaction or in bad action.

What is the greatest of all human needs? Many would answer love, which is true. However, love itself has in its essence a combination of respect and losing control; or giving control of one's life to another person. Before we love, we essentially look to control the environment around us from the moment of our first breath. The newborn uses all of its energy to cry and thereby attract large strangers to keep it warm and fed and to protect it from the environment. This need to control the environment stays with us throughout our lives. However, as we grow, we find more effective and less annoying ways to do so. We quickly learn, as social animals, techniques to get others to do what we want, as they also do this to us. Through rewards and punishments we find ever more effective ways to increase our control of the world and its inhabitants.

If we take a purely physical view of human survival, it is control that allows us not to starve, not to freeze to death, and not to be killed by others. Socially, however, we learn also to control others for more selfish reasons than mere survival. It is not enough to just get sufficient calories to survive. Rather we find that through abundance we can eat well, live well, and be held in regard and respect. We develop forms of social, emotional and intellectual control beyond the purely physical forms of control to which most others forms of life are limited. This complex, symbol-based set of rules that we employ is inherently fraught with ambiguity, leading to uncertainty of what the decisions of others who have control over us might bring. Couple this with the additional peril that nature might inflict upon us and the fragile psyche can be prone to fears, whether imagined or real.

Others people who wish to control us sometimes employ imagined fear to limit or influence our behavior to their advantage. People are by nature selfish and dishonest. If all mankind were completely generous and honest, there would be no need for politicians and lawyers. Part of our need for control is also the great desire to be treated fairly. This is a subset of our need for respect. Being treated unfairly engenders huge personal discordance and often anger. Ultimately one may convince oneself, or be convinced by another that retribution is deserved, which may come as a legal action or through a physical or psychological act. Numerous are the methods in which we inflict this punishment upon others: ostracism, gossip, *ad hominem* attacks, guilt and shame.

Fear then becomes more than an anxiety over physical injury or death; in includes loss of social standing, loss of personal relationships, loss of income, loss of security and loss of respect. Currently, in our society, fear affects the decisions made by many people who surround us every day. These types of fear fall into various categories. First, fear of litigiousness, which is especially prevalent in medical contexts. In every institution in which I have worked I have heard almost every day someone make reference to a decision or action, usually supported by some policy or procedure, which is an attempt to keep them from being sued. Ultimately, this stifles thinking. We practice to the lowest common denominator and are prevented from adapting to the immediate needs of the individual. Whether it is a law such as HIPPA or ADA, we stop doing what is right for fear of doing something wrong. Then in an effort to not approach the hard line cliff of the letter of the law, we create new, even more restrictive policies to prevent anyone from even getting within a mile of the cliff to the point that employees spend so much time documenting, labeling and reporting that the individual needing help is invisible and lost.

Second would be the fear of terror. This might range from the act of a political anarchist to the abduction and abuse of a child. Our role as parents is to protect and teach our children so they will be prepared when they leave us to make responsible decisions on their own. We assume that the world around us is full of bad people who want to harm us. These fears are often out of proportion with reality and lead us to overprotection. This attitude may be even more dangerous than any real or imagined threat outside of our door. I often hear of the good old days when we all played outside without any concern for our safety. The random social interaction of play in the community exposed us to all sorts of opportunities to make decisions without the control or guidance of our parents. We dealt with bullies. We planned and built tree-forts. We wandered through nature and discovered life as we imagined ourselves explorers and heroes.

Many say that today's world is more dangerous, full of pedophiles and murderers. I doubt that. But whether it is true or not, we have coddled and overprotected a generation that is now ill-equipped to make the critical decisions that would allow them to function independently. They enter the workforce only to find that work is hard and they have a boss who expects them to show up on time and perform. This is new to them. Neither their parents nor teachers had ever required so much of them, so they quit. They have been given a false sense of entitlement such that they believe that merely because they are breathing, society owes them. These problems are also exacerbated by the third fear which is prevalent today: fear of failure.

This is one of the saddest of the fears. Many people will not attempt an action or make a decision because of concern that they might fail. They remain motionless. Life without risk is merely existence. Momentary pleasures are all that occur in the absence of true and lasting fulfillment. The only true failure is to never have tried. It is true that we gain confidence from our successes and each success then allows us to move on to greater risks and ultimately greater success. Yet failure is also a teacher, allowing us to gain wisdom that we could not gain in any other manner, even through our successes. True, we can learn much from observation of the failure of others without having to personally suffer the same pain, but the character and memory of the wisdom gained may be more acute and long-lasting from our own personal failures. Even worse is the generational fear of failure prevalent in our culture, resulting from parents carefully programming their offspring as young as three to participate in activities intended to cultivate intellectual and sports prowess which in their design do not allow for failure. Before children can feel the pain of their mistakes, the parents intervene and deflect the taking of personal responsibility by the child. We pay for it so they do not have to. This is the most dangerous thing we can do for them.

So much of fear is based on loss of control. However at a certain point we mature. Experience teaches us in whom we can trust. As we trust, our actions can earn us respect, first from ourselves and then from others.

Often, the final fear that may be manifest is the fear of pain, illness and death. These are inevitable and unavoidable. As sentient beings we are capable of contemplating our existence. Coupled with this, then, is the ability to contemplate the *absence* of existence. To imagine the end of being is incomprehensible, and psychologically terrifying for many. This fear, not so much of death itself, but rather the void of emptiness, has plagued humans since the beginning of perceived time. Time itself is part of the problem. There is something inherent in our conscious existence that gives us the illusion of time. We fix time; we sub-divide it and measure it. We move and act in time. When we quantify time it becomes finite to us. There is a beginning and an end. We do not remember the beginning and we fear the end. In the science of physics and theoretical mathematics, time has no direction. There is no past or future.

However, in our universe time always moves in one direction, from past to future. At least this is how we feel it. Yet, this perception of time is learned, not innate. When we were young, there was only present. Time moved extremely slowly. The time between age three to four felt like an eternity because we could not anticipate four based upon past memory. The illusion of time is a function of memory. What then fills the present is therefore dependant on how we view the past and what we expect of the future. Is death our only future? What if death is not the end? How does faith affect fear?

Regardless of our ultimate destiny, fear steals from us that which has the most value to us: the present. The optimist takes the memories of the past, successes and failures, all cruelty and kindness, and from it gains wisdom -- the wisdom that will strengthen future choices. The pessimist has no such insight. Past, present and future for the optimist, the person of faith, is manifest as wisdom, joy and hope. Whereas for the pessimist, the man of fear, it is regret, despair and dread.

I am the eternal optimist. I have very few regrets. I am full of hope. I am not afraid of either death or dying. My only fear is leaving Barbie alone. I have not and will not let fear prevent me from doing the right thing. I will poison my body if it means more present moments of joy with Barbie. I believe that after I die I will continue to exist and be reunited with my eternal love. That is my faith; that is my hope.

CHAPTER 51

Mortality Awareness event # 6
Wednesday, March 18, 2009
Hard Day
Day+ 5 Health Score 61

Morning is difficult. My throat swells overnight and it is like someone has closed the drawbridge; nothing passes. Talking hurts and swallowing really hurts. I was able to drink a can of Ensure. I hope this can keep me off I.V. nutrition (TPN). It's hard to get out of bed, but the best remedy for all of the above is a hot shower. That was revitalizing. Since my white cell count is now 0.5 K I am officially 'neutropenic' and confined to my room until further notice.

Steve Hargadon came and visited me last night and brought me Haagen Daz mango sorbet. It was so good. He had called me while he was travelling here and asked if my hair had started falling out. I told him that it started falling out 15 years ago, but that I would finish the job this week.

Kevin

For the most part, we ignore our bodies. How many muscles, joints and bones do you use to walk, to talk, eat or swallow? When you are in pain each movement, contraction or stretch becomes acutely real and distressing. To merely swallow requires cheek, throat and neck muscles. As these contract, they move and distort the inner lining of your mouth and throat. Imagine that each swallow of a sip of water, a small cough or sigh cause searing pain in the back of your mouth and throat. You tend not to talk or move much. I lay in bed most of the day, trying not to move. By afternoon the pain was severe. I was given a slurry to swish in my mouth and then swallow. It numbed things for about 10 minutes and the pain returned. For the most part, I usually tolerate pain knowing that it will pass. Up till now I had had many moments of temporary discomfort: shots, swabs, biopsies and tube placements. I am still puzzled at why I waited for so long to ask for pain medications; probably because I had never asked before. Finally, after suffering all morning and afternoon, that "duh" moment arrived. I felt a little stupid for not asking earlier.

I pushed the red button with the nurse symbol on it. A voice crackled through the intercom. "Yes?" It anonymously queried. "Can I get something for pain?" I whispered hoarsely. A few minutes later, my nurse entered with a small syringe. "What is that?" I asked. "Dilaudid, 2mg," she responded. I had been ordering I.V. narcotics for decades, but had not ever volitionally asked for one. Quickly, she attached the syringe to my I.V. and pushed, turned around and without a word, left the room. This was completely routine for her. 15 seconds later it hit my brain and I finally understood why people go to such great lengths to get this stuff. I felt wonderful almost as fast as I felt no pain. "Why did I wait so long?" I thought to myself. Within minutes, I fell asleep. I was awoken by Barbie arriving from school. Wednesday was her last day for the week. She would leave from Roseville and drive the distance to be with me each week. It was wonderful to see her.

Because of the marked fluid shifts that occur with bone marrow transplants, Dr. Arai was trying to keep me on the dry side to prevent fluid buildup and edema. In addition to running my I.V. fluids at a very low rate, I had also been given a diuretic (Lasix) that day. This was part of their routine protocol. I had no appetite and had not really eaten anything since the Cheetos on Monday and a few spoonfuls of sorbet the night before. I dozed off and on while Barbie sat near my bed and studied her biochemistry. Finally, it was time to say goodnight. She came over to my bed, gently kissed me and left. And thus began the worst night of my life.

I first woke up about 1:00 A.M. with the feeling that my tongue was fused to the roof of my mouth. I literally had to pull on my tongue to peel it off. I fumbled in the dark for my water cup and took a sip to wet my mouth. This process repeated over and over almost every 20 minutes. I felt as if all the water had been drained from my body. After about two hours of this the nurse's aide came in to check my vital signs. I remember that I had a fever. I asked her to contact the doctor on call to see if they could at least increase my I.V. rate. I knew I was at a low rate and that the Lasix had dried me out, or so I thought. A while later, she returned and said that the fellow would evaluate me in the morning. I thought of how many times I had given the same answer to a nurse who had woken me at 3:00 A.M. I relied on their assessment. I wondered what she had told him. I had never felt so thirsty in my life. The water was there next to me, but it seemed to just evaporate on my tongue and quenched nothing. Suddenly, I had the incredibly strong urge to void. I grabbed my urinal and stuck it under the covers. I felt almost nothing come out. This was followed by an even stronger sensation to void, bordering on painful. I immediately knew what this was. I was passing a kidney stone.

My sub-specialty within urology is stones. I had also previously passed three stones myself. I knew from both clinical and personal experience that half of the human population is wired in such a way that the sensory nerves from the lower ureter are shared with the bladder. The brain perceives irritation from a distal stone as an unyielding pressure to empty ones bladder. The thought that I might have a stone passing in this moment terrified me because I knew I was in no position to tolerate the surgery necessary to free me of a stone. As I anguished over this new development, fatigue set in and I finally fell asleep.

Suddenly, I awoke with the most excruciating pain I have ever known. The bladder issue had since disappeared. This was something different. It was as if every nerve ending in my body had exploded simultaneously. Every muscle contracted involuntarily. My body sense became distorted to the point that I had no idea where my limbs were in space. If I had not already been lying down, I would have fallen. My pain receptors, propioceptors, pressure, heat and cold receptors all were firing at once. I closed my eyes tightly and prayed that this would end. What may have been only 30 seconds seemed an eternity. Finally, the sensations ebbed away as does a crashing wave upon the sand. I lay there, my eyes wet, breathing rapidly as the true sense of my body and proportion returned. My limbs soon felt as if they were the appropriate distance from my head again. Completely exhausted, I again fell into unconsciousness.

When I opened my eyes it was light outside. Somehow, with the darkness gone, I felt a little better. The night was finally over. Soon my doctors would come and give me fluids. But how long would I have to wait? No, I had to take matters into my own hands. I was severely dehydrated. I called out to the desk. "Can I have some Gatorade?" I asked. I.V. fluid replacement is often a combination of electrolytes and sugar: D5 0.5 NS with 20 KCl at 125 cc/hr. I had ordered this a thousand times -- 5% Dextrose solution with half the concentration of normal saline with 20 meq per liter of potassium chloride added. I figured Gatorade would get me close to that even if I could not get a doctor's order for it.

The bottle of redness arrived. I studied the label to check the volume. 591 cc; that would get me started. I drank it, knowing how it would hurt to swallow and was pleasantly surprised to learn that the throat pain had significantly diminished. Finally, I drained the bottle. I felt a little better.

The prior week, the physical therapist had given me a list of exercises that I was to do every day to keep me moving and my muscles in shape. These consisted of giant green rubber bands that I would step on and then pull up like a biceps curl. I scooted my body around the bed rail and swung my feet to the floor. I was already out of breath. The chair next to my bed was about three feet away. I pushed off from the bed so my momentum would carry me to the chair. As I caught the handles, I swiveled my body to land my butt on the seat. I tried to pull the elastic band once and could not do it. "What am I doing?" I thought. "This is crazy." I clearly was not thinking straight. I tried to get out of the chair and back to bed, but my strength failed me. Instinctively, I put my right index and middle finger on my left wrist to palpate my pulse. I could barely feel it. I began to become alarmed. I needed to get help. The call box was on the bed, just out of reach. Holding onto the chair, I leaned forward just enough to catch the cord leading up to it with my finger. I pushed the button and a voice answered.

"I need someone to come and check my blood pressure." I flatly said.

The box in my hand responded. "They are on rounds right now, someone will be there in an hour."

Frustrated, I got straight to the point. "I think I am hypotensive."

This must be a strange thing to hear from a patient's room. Generally "hypotensive" is not something most patients would say, and even if they did, something must be really wrong for them to say it. After a few-second pause came the response: "someone will be right there." And someone was.

I slumped back in the chair and waited. Soon a nurse and an aid were there helping me back into bed. I was able to stand enough to make the transfer with their help. The cuff was placed on my arm. I looked at the display as it finished and reported my pressure to be 60/38. I was indeed hypotensive.

I made sure that the flurry of activity that followed included a call to the bone marrow transplant fellow. Within a short time he entered the room. He confirmed that, indeed, I had low blood pressure and that he would give me some I.V. fluids. I would start with 500 cc of NS. "You've got to be kidding," I thought. I just *drank* more than that. I suggested that a liter bolus of fluid might be more in line and he acquiesced. For the rest of the day he periodically checked my blood pressure and then gave me more fluids to try to increase it. After pouring four liters of fluid into my veins (or so we thought) they had the great success of getting my pressure up to a magnificent 85/60.

Consider that one liter of water weighs 2.2 lbs. Rapidly infusing four liters of fluid increases your weight nearly ten pounds. Since my pressure had barely risen, the fluid could not have remained in my vessels. It had leaked out into the tissue between my capillaries and my cells. This is what we call the "third space."

In the midst of all this, Barbie arrived. By now I was in bed and being resuscitated with fluids. I reassured her that all was fine and simply told her that I had had a hard night. She could always see through my optimistic minimizing. My nurse that day was wonderful. Whenever I woke up, I always found her in my room. I felt a little guilty that I was keeping her from her other patients. But it also felt good to know that she was not going to leave me in my time of true need.

One of those needs became quite embarrassing to me. The ulcers that chemotherapy causes in the mouth are the only ones that the patient feels. However, the entire gut, from mouth to anus is affected. This causes the sudden and urgent need to visit the toilet. In one such episode I voiced my need to get out of bed. Barbie and the nurse helped me. It was not easy, as I was attached to an I.V. pole which had to be unplugged. This all takes time. Finally, I made it to the toilet and sat down. As I stood up, I was shocked to see that I had not made it in time and my entire right leg was soiled. This is hard to see as an adult. Given the situation, I should not really have cared, but I felt ashamed to walk out of the bathroom and ask Barbie for help in cleaning me up. What lesson did I need to learn here? Where is the line between being humbled and being humiliated? It is clearly in how we perceive it. I stood there with my pants down, and Barbie and the nurse cleaned me up and helped me back to bed. I felt so useless. All that I had ever been was finally destroyed in that moment. I was completely broken. I had deluded myself if to think I had control over my existence. Rather, I learned that we should surround ourselves with people who care enough to catch us when we fall.

After that, we figured out strategies to avoid such major accidents again. There are many ways in which a wife or husband shows love to a spouse.

The word got out that I was not doing well. Dr. Arai was there early to see me. One concern was my transplanted heart. Could the low blood pressure be a sign of rejection? It did not seem likely, as there were no white cells floating around to attack my heart. However, just to be certain, they called Dr. Witteles and he ordered an echocardiogram. The ultrasound tech came to my bedside with a gown and mask as all visitors did, and pushed the probe against my chest.

I knew that I was in trouble. My urine output had dropped off, my blood pressure was still low, I had a fever; I suspected that I might be in septic shock. If my new heart was also in trouble, there might not be any turning back.

And then Dr. Witteles walked in. He stood near my bed and said that the echocardiogram had confirmed that my transplanted heart was doing just fine. There were no wall motion abnormalities, no pericardial effusions, no decrease in ejection fraction. In sum, my heart was strong and working well. Once again, just as had happened so many times before, in my darkest moment the kind words, touch or embrace of another served to give me new hope. Somehow, when he said that, I knew that everything would be okay. My shared heart would save me a second time. I felt a great peace after he left. The nurse came in to inform me that I would be getting a blood transfusion because my hematocrit was 23%. "That is pretty low," I thought.

CHAPTER 52

Friday, March 20, 2009
Fighting off infection

When I arrived this morning Kevin was asleep and on oxygen. It turns out he does have pneumonia, but they caught it early and started him on high doses of antibiotics that specifically target the lungs so all should be well soon. He is still not eating, just a little Ensure now and again.

I had a breakdown in the car this morning. I guess I should rephrase that. My car did not break down, I did. Eventually your body just says, enough. I cried it out while driving. This has been a long road and I think I am tired. The car seems to be a safe place for me to cry; some may disagree. I am alert and careful, I promise. Everywhere else I want to be strong and together. Mostly I am. It's just hard to see Kevin suffering so and to be far from home. I miss my girls and I wish I could there to see Ty and his family. Tyler is seven and the son of our good friends. He was just diagnosed with Wilm's tumor, type 4. Tyler had a long day of surgery and will have an even longer road ahead with chemo and radiation. We are praying for the family.

Kevin is optimistic still and fighting this as he knows how. He sits up in a chair to help the lungs open and take deeper breaths. He has not said much today except, "People volunteer to do this?" He is right, but in his case, as in many others, there ARE no other options.

Barbie

Friday, March 20, 2009
Waiting for engraftment
Day + 7 health Score 59

My breathing is improved today. But I think I have pneumonia. They caught it fast and have me on Zosyn and Amphotercin-B. I have not yet "turned the corner" meaning that I am not diuresing (making urine.) It takes a lot of energy to get out of bed, but I was up in a chair for an hour today. The doctors and nurses are very vigilant and taking great care of me.

Kevin

There have been times in my career (fortunately few) when I would round on my patients in the morning and find as I entered the room that the bed was empty. Most of the time it was simply a room change. However, there were those rare occasions when the empty bed meant something else: that the patient had died during the night. Because of this inescapable possibility, the empty bed anxiety is always there. That anxiety is what Barbie may have felt on Friday morning.

After a difficult day on Thursday, my doctors finally decided to put me on pressors. Fluids alone had not succeeded in stabilizing my blood pressure. My vessels were a sieve. The liquid just leaked out. Pressors are drugs that tighten the blood vessels and kick the heart, both of which push the blood pressure up. During my residency I had seen these drugs used as a last ditch effort to save a dying patient, many times with positive results. However, there were other times when the body's capacity to recover never returned. Drugs such as dopamine, epinephrine, and Levafed were used. In the less politically correct eighties, I had heard the cynical intern's dark humor when they told us students that instead of Levafed, the patient was on "leave-em-dead." These memories had haunted me beginning six months earlier when I first saw Dr. Weisshaar; she had seen how bad my heart was and suggested immediate hospital admission and placement on dopamine. These drugs are powerful and usually reserved for the sickest of patients.

Late Thursday night, after Barbie had left, my doctors decided to put me on Dopamine in an attempt to raise my blood pressure. Long-standing low pressures are dangerous, especially to the kidneys. However, my room was not close enough to the antennas required for continuous telemetry. The bone marrow unit had two rooms in the back that shared a wall with the cardiac unit, so the telemetry monitors could work. Given the propensity for these drugs to cause arrhythmias, the patient must be monitored while receiving them. So I switched rooms just before midnight. Barbie's last words before she left were to let her know if anything changed. But it was late, and I did not want to wake her. The next morning when she found my room empty, I can only imagine her panic. My excuses seemed weak when she finally found me and I realized her fears. My rationality was irrational. When you are delirious, you do not realize that you are not thinking straight.

After they moved me they put me on oxygen. Initially it was with nasal prongs, but that did not help at all and just dried out my nose. Then they put an ill-fitting plastic mask on my face. It was uncomfortable and I still felt short of breath. Finally, in the middle of the night they called in the respiratory therapist, who fitted me with a snug re-breather mask that delivered a more effective concentration of oxygen. Two nights before I had been thirsting for water; now I was thirsting for air. This new mask felt like drawing a long cool drink from a crystal clear spring. Soon I was sleeping comfortably. I awoke to a beeping sound; or I should say a new beeping sound, since there was always some level of beeping going on. I turned to look at the oxygen saturation monitor and noticed that the percent of O2 in my blood was 84%. For a moment, my mind wandered back to New Haven.

During my time at Yale, I was the education coordinator for the Section of Urology. As such, I arranged for the medical students to receive a number of lectures from university faculty and community urologists. Additionally, I gave a lecture to the students every Tuesday. One lecture that I gave for almost 10 years was on ventilator management. The students were always shocked that a urologist would teach about pulmonary physiology. However, when I asked them if anyone had ever given them a lecture on how to manage a patient on a ventilator, the resounding answer was "no." So a lecture by me was better than no lecture at all.

My desire to teach about ventilator management was multi-factorial. First, I am a pragmatist. I like to teach stuff that is useful in the everyday practice of medicine. In medical school, we had four different lectures that taught us about Kuru, a rare infectious disease that is contracted by eating the brains of one's ancestors. We knew we would never see a case. But never was there a lecture on ventilators. This became painfully obvious when I was a new intern on the trauma service at U.C. Davis. I was rounding with Dr. Holcroft, a brilliant surgeon, after my first call night as a doctor. I had pre-rounded on all 42 patients on the trauma unit and kept notes for rounds. We started on the ninth floor and worked our way down. On the eighth floor I was terrified to learn that I had left my notes on the floor above. Too embarrassed to say anything, I tried to wing it all the way down to the trauma ICU. It was an unmitigated disaster and was only made worse at the end of rounds when Dr. Holcroft quietly ripped me apart for my poor preparation.

I drove home after having been awake for 40 hours straight on only my second day as an intern. I saw Barbie and could not speak. I burst into tears and went to our bedroom and crashed for six hours. I thought that my career as a doctor was over. However, the next day I got up and went back to the hospital to try again. A few days later, Dr. Holcroft decided to teach us how to manage ventilators. In twenty minutes, he explained it with such an elegant simplicity that I used that new knowledge for the rest of my life. So valuable was that lesson that I felt the need to teach it to every Yale medical student who rotated through our service. I remember a young internal medicine resident at Yale who, seeing me in the elevator, thanked me for that lecture, saying that it had helped him with more than one question on his board examination.

Essentially, the lesson reduced the ventilator to a box with four knobs, two of which controlled ventilation or CO_2, (tidal volume and rate) and two knobs that controlled oxygenation or O_2 (FIO_2 or the percent of O_2, and PEEP, positive end expiratory pressure.). There were a number of medical conditions that could make oxygenation worse and require adjustments to the ventilator. On that night I had two of those conditions: pneumonia and pulmonary edema.

As I lay there, looking at the monitor measuring my own oxygenation, all of these teachings reflexively passed through whatever neurons in my brain were functioning at 2:00 a.m. I had always taught that if the O_2 saturation drops below 90%, one should address it by turning the appropriate knob. What knob could I turn? I could not reach the O_2 meter on the wall. I decided to increase my respiratory rate. Even though this knob affects CO_2 levels more that O_2, I started breathing faster. I watched the monitor with anticipation. After about 30 seconds the oxygen level crept up to 91%. Satisfied, and out of breath, I rolled over and went back to sleep. I am sure that within minutes I dropped back down again, but at least I had silenced the alarm.

The next morning a transporter showed up with a wheelchair and took me for a CT scan of my chest to determine if I had pneumonia. I was surprised that they transported me without oxygen. I lay on the machine, and then came the moment of the actual scan when I was instructed to hold my breath. There are two lighted smiley faces on the machine. The one with "puffed cheeks" lights indicating "No Breathing" and then a countdown timer indicating how long this will be. 13 seconds, 12, 11, 10 …. I was already dying for a breath, but I held on. To breathe now would mess up the study and expose me to more radiation if it were repeated. 5,4... I felt as if my lungs would explode. How was it possible that I could not hold my breath for 13 seconds? Finally, the happy face with an open mouth lit and a robotic voice said, "breathe!" I gasped for air as would a drowning man finally freed from the gray, cold clutches of impending doom.

I was soon back in my room. A while later, Dr. Arai and a cadre of followers including fellows, residents and medical students entered the room. They remained bunched just inside the door as if they were ready for a quick escape. Dr. Arai's diminutive form stood in the center, flanked by the taller team. I recognized the look of anxiety on her face. She was clearly worried. I felt a mirrored response in myself. I could recall too well looking anxiously from the door at my own patients who were on the cusp of disaster. Having done all that I could, I prayed that they would somehow "turn the corner" and heal themselves. As physicians, there is a limit to what we can do. A physician cannot always predict which way a critically ill patient will go; either a return to health or descent into death. I knew that look, and I saw it in her eyes.

However, with all of my experience, with all of my knowledge, I did not in that moment share her concern. This time I was not the doctor. I was the patient. I knew something, no, I felt something inside me that she could not see. I felt a peace that seemed to fill me with hope. I knew that I was going to be OK. I even remember reassuring her. She said that it looked on the CT as if I had bilateral pneumonia. I tried to talk her out of that diagnosis, saying that maybe it was just scarring from the pleural effusions that I had had prior to the heart transplant. She gently rebuffed my rebuttal and I knew that she was right.

To prove her point, it was required of me to produce an acceptable sputum sample for culture in order to determine the bacterial source of my pneumonia. This would prove to be quite difficult. My mouth sores had just healed. The sample had to come from deep within my lungs. I had to cough a deep cough in an attempt to "hock a loogie." Finally, I produced a thick tan-green inspisated sample. The lab tech rejected it with the disheartening words, "not good enough. It's just saliva."

I tried again. Trying to coordinate thoracic muscles to expel lung contents and not stomach contents proved to be difficult, as I have a sensitive gag reflex. Soon my stomach contents returned, only for me to realize that it was the mango sorbet from Tuesday. The positive pressure from retching also caused a bleed in my left eye so that the white part was now red. It looked horrible. The petulant lab tech still rejected my efforts. The plan was then to do a bronchoscopy to forcibly retrieve sputum from my lungs, and this procedure was scheduled for the next day. At this point there was debate as to whether I should be moved to the intensive care unit. However, the concern over the potential infectious risk of going to such a "dirty place" counteracted that suggestion.

Saturday, March 21, 2009
Balance
Day + 8 Health Score 62

When I was in High School Chemistry, we spent a lot of time discussing the importance of equilibrium, homeostasis or balance. And that was just for chemical reactions. Later I learned of the critical nature of balance in all living systems. Essentially, all illness reflects being in a state in which you are out of balance. All efforts in medicine are to restore that balance at all levels: chemical, cellular, organ and organ systems, psychological/emotional and spiritual. It is the goal of caregivers to re-achieve that lost balance. However, sometimes to achieve that goal, the physician must temporarily cause the patient to be in greater imbalance. It could be surgery to restore normal anatomy, insulin to balance blood sugar or administering poisons such as radiation or chemotherapy to destroy cancers. All of these maneuvers require the same thing to succeed: the body's ability to heal itself. Without this, I would be out of a job. However, some therapies are so drastic that for a time they wipe out this capacity for self-healing. Stem Cell Transplant is in that category. For three weeks the doctors try to keep the body in a fragile balance, until the patient regains the strength to do it on his or her own. I am slowly progressing to that goal.

The CT scan of my chest yesterday showed that I have bilateral pneumonia. They already had me on very powerful antibiotics and anti fungals, so that by last night I was already improving. Currently, I am not on any supplemental oxygen. My blood pressure stabilized and they stopped the dopamine. I slept great and am now back to eating. There are still many issues left to resolve, but I am hoping to achieve greater balance every day.

Kevin

CHAPTER 53

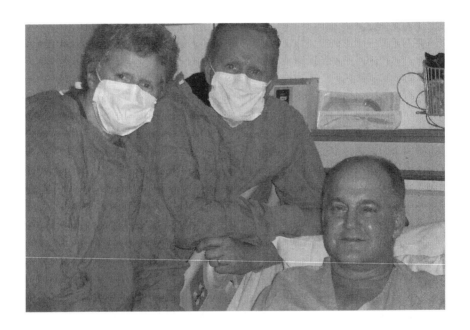

My sister, Leslie, and my brother, Daren

By Saturday, my urine output had not returned. At one point the bone marrow transplant fellow came by to inform me that they would place a Foley catheter in my bladder to check my urine output. This incensed me. The other lecture I used to give to the students at Yale discussed the use of catheters. I was emphatic that a catheter never be placed for the sole purpose of checking urine output on a patient who could void on his or her own and was not in the ICU. I surely caught the fellow off guard with my response: "I will provide you with every drop of urine that hits my bladder, and if anyone is going to place a catheter in me, it will be me." He left without further argument.

I was very concerned. I was not making any urine at all. I was acutely aware that a major complication of septic shock is a kidney injury called acute tubular necrosis. This would be manifest by little or no urine output and an elevation in a blood test called creatinine. My fears were realized when my creatinine rose to 2.8. Normally, I was around 1.1-1.3. This worried me. If the kidneys did not heal themselves, and quickly, I would likely need dialysis to carry me over. In the back of my mind was always the concern that my kidneys already had low level damage from the amyloidosis and limited recoverability.

High dose chemotherapy kills rapidly dividing cells. This included the lining of the gut. Around midday I hobbled to the toilet and was shocked to see a dark burgundy color in the bowl. On top of everything else, I was now bleeding from my gut. My doctors could not take my word for it, so they tested the stuff for blood.

Sunday, March 22, 2009
Spoke too soon

Kevin is still the eternal optimist and yesterday I was as well. We waited all day for him to "turn the corner," but he never did. His guts and kidneys aren't working as they should yet and his lungs are still a problem. He received two units of platelets last night and two units of blood this morning. He is weak, short of breath, and still retaining fluid. His creatinine is high, which is not good and could present problems for his kidneys. We hope for a better outcome today. Leslie, Kevin's sister is with him now. She, being a physician's assistant, will be my eyes and ears while I am home for a few days. She said her job is to make sure the nurses do not fall behind in his care. With the exception of yesterday (during the day) he has had great nurses.

I just arrived home, wrote this blog and am leaving now to attend Caitlin's piano recital. I am utterly exhausted, but am holding on.

Barbie

Sunday, March 22, 2009
Michelin Man
Day + 9 Health Score 49

I feel great, never felt better in my life. Sorry, I should not use sarcasm here.....

Today I feel very weak. I have a GI bleed (gut), and massive swelling. It takes all the effort and motivation I can muster just to get out of bed. I have not eaten in days. But you needn't worry about me. I will get better. I am quite tenacious. I may be only halfway up the cliffs of insanity, but I have a clear view of the top.

This I know. I derive extreme comfort in the hundreds of gestures of support given to me and my family. But, above all, I could not survive this without Barbie. For she is the reason that I continue on this path, for Barbie, my Princess Bride.

Kevin

The bleeding from my gut really worried Dr. Arai. Up to now, every complication that I had had, she had seen before. This was new. Given that I was her first heart transplant patient, and therefore her first patient who had been on immuno-suppressants prior to the bone marrow transplant, she looked for advice from the doctor who had done this before: Dr. Lacy from the Mayo Clinic. Dr. Lacy had seen this before in patients like me. My body, having been on corticosteroids for such a long time, had difficulty in mounting a stress response to such an insult. My adrenal glands were on perpetual strike. The suggestion was to give me steroids, and lots of them. The result was immediate and positive. Within 24 hours I began to turn the proverbial corner.

Additional support came from my sister, Leslie. She had flown down from Seattle to be with me when Barbie left on Sunday to go back to Lincoln. Leslie is a physician's assistant and specializes in bone marrow transplants. I was very happy to have her there to make sure nothing was missed.

Finally, it came time to repeat the CT scan to see if the pneumonia was improving. The ride showed up at my door and I was wheeled to the radiology department. This time I found that holding my breath for 13 seconds was not so difficult, and within minutes I was off the table. But there was a detour to the ultrasound department. I am not sure why an abdominal ultrasound was ordered, maybe because of the GI bleed. The room for the ultrasound seemed very cluttered and I was placed on a gurney with a curtain on one side and medical equipment stored all around me. I felt like I was in a broom closet. The ultrasound technician quickly got down to business.

To her I was just another patient. I could have been a man on his lunch break coming from work. The fact that I was hypotensive, with pneumonia and a GI bleed -- if she was aware of it at all -- did not seem to faze her. The exam began. She pushed the ultrasound probe down firmly on my abdomen and then said, "hold your breath." She then moved the probe to a new location; "Hold your breath." After she did this for the 20th time, it was becoming very difficult for me to hold my breath. I began to tire and sometimes take a breath while she was snapping a picture. Her impatience with me was obvious. I wanted to scream, "I am not well! This is hard for me!" I had always assumed that an ultrasound is the least painful, least obtrusive of all diagnostic tests. But I was in pain.

Finally, she had fulfilled the criteria of the protocol for the study, with no deviation relative to the needs of the individual lying before her. As she was leaving to go discuss the case with some unseen manager I asked, "is there a restroom nearby?" Still looking at the machine she answered, "it's around the corner in the main corridor," and walked behind the curtain. The constant pressure had stirred up something in my bleeding bowels. The urgency was overwhelming. I finally was able to roll myself off the gurney. I grabbed my I.V. pole for support with one hand and tried to close the gap in my gown with the other. I made it to the hallway and looked for the restroom sign. I felt like the astronauts in *The Right Stuff* running with their enema bags in search of a toilet. Soon I saw the door and prayed that it was not locked and that I wouldn't leak. It was open. Everything takes longer when you are handicapped by I.V.'s, tied gowns and feeling like crap. But I made it.

Soon I was back on the gurney in the closet. I waited. The ultrasound tech never returned. Finally a transporter came to fetch me and deliver me to my room. He was very nice. I needed nice at that point.

CHAPTER 54

Monday, March 23, 2009
The Bald Identity
Day + 10 Health Score 66

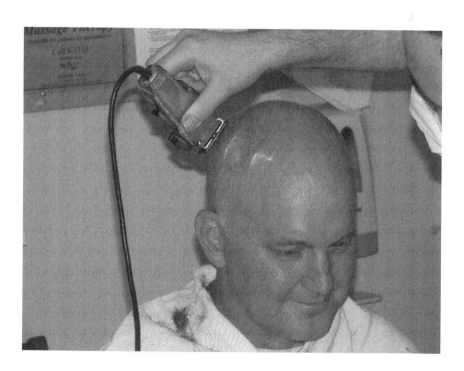

Today was definitely better than yesterday. Let me explain; "no there is no time, let me sum up."

My kidney function is improving and they are working overtime.

I woke up hungry for the first time in a week. I attacked the can of Strawberry Ensure that had been sitting on my table for three days.

I felt strong enough to get out of bed on my own and proceeded to take the first of two long, hot showers. As I washed my face, I noticed hair on my washcloth and wondered how it got there, immediately realizing that it was coming from my head. Then returning to bed I discovered the telltale "pelo on the pillow." It was time for action. I was able to schedule an emergency hair appointment with my stylist, Evan. And as we all know, even with a menacing asteroid hurtling toward the earth, you never cancel a hair appointment!

My physical therapist came by and had me walk 12 laps around my room and then 15 minutes on the bicycle.

By then, my sister, Leslie, had returned with a pint of Ben and Jerry's Phish Food; my favorite ice cream. It was heavenly.

How could I go from my lowest point ever to such improvement in one day? Prayers are answered in many ways. My doctor, Dr. Arai, was very concerned with some of my atypical complications. She had read a paper written by my other doctor, Dr. Lacy at the Mayo Clinic, describing these unusual symptoms in amyloidosis patients. She called Dr. Lacy and discovered that steroids, specifically Solumedrol (one of my least favorite drugs) had produced improvement in both the lung and gut bleeding complications. One dose was all it took. What value there is in the combined wisdom of so many people.

Since my lungs showed so much improvement on my CT today, the pulmonologists have cancelled the bronchoscopy scheduled for tomorrow. All that's left to wait for is for my new bone marrow to wake up and start making white cells...........You will never believe what just happened. I stopped writing for a moment to speak to my doctors and I spoke with Sam and Michelle, since they called to see how I was doing. The nurse then came in and casually said, "I just got your labs back and they've improved." I was not prepared for what she said next: "your white count is 0.4." I was stunned. That means I am engrafted. The stem cell transplant was a success. You cannot imagine my relief. I felt like I should add 10 points to my health score and call it 76. Now all that is left is to continue getting healthy. Why am I so blessed? Why am I so loved? This is a gift that I can never repay.

Thank you to you all from the bottom of my strong, shared heart.

Kevin

So much was changing so fast. My silent fear that I would be the one percent that did not engraft evaporated instantaneously. My frozen stem cells had found their way back home and there was now a fire in the hearth. This warmed my soul. Kidney function had returned. As promised, I saved every drop of urine that my kidneys filtered. It was difficult to un-entangle myself each time my bladder filled, (which was every 20-30 minutes) so I figured a way to use the urinal under the covers without making a mess. I was shocked to realize how much my bladder could actually hold. I would then hang the full bottles on my I.V. stand so that the nurses could chart my output. However, I was filling them up so fast that they could not keep up. Soon three full bottles with clear yellow liquid, each measuring 1200 cc, proudly announced my "turning the corner." I knew I was healing. The worst was behind me. As quickly as I had put on 25 lbs of water, I lost it. I was up at 5:00 a.m. each morning with anticipation to be weighed and note the drop commensurate with my diuresis. Balance was returning.

Tuesday, March 24, 2009
Systems Note
Day + 11 Health Score 72

I am a little tired today, as they have stopped the steroids and my body is using all of its energy to rebuild a new bone marrow and heal all of the other damaged tissues. But despite that I feel wonderful. I had a visit from my Home Teacher from church who drove all the way from Lincoln and while he was here found Coldplay tickets for their concert in Marysville for July 14. What a treat to look forward to.

When doctors write a simple note on an uncomplicated patient, they use the SOAP note format.
S: Subjective
O: Objective
A: Assessment
P: Plan
A patient in an ICU setting has more than one system that may be failing, so they do a systems note, assessing each system individually. These generally include: CNS/mental status, cardiovascular, pulmonary, gastrointestinal (GI and nutrition) Genitourinary (kidney function) Hepatic, Infection, Immunologic and blood.
If three or more systems fail simultaneously, it may be difficult for the patient to recover.
Last week my systems review was as follows: Infection: on Thursday I went into septic shock with a blood pressure of 60/35. My fever was 101.6 and I stopped making urine. I was resuscitated with 5 liters

of fluids and 1 liter of blood. This only brought my blood pressure to 80/60 and still no urine output. (30 cc/hr). Finally, I was put on 5 mcg of Dopamine which raised my pressure to 95/60. Pulmonary: The next day a chest CT revealed bilateral basilar pneumonias. I was started on aggressive antibiotics and my fever decreased and breathing improved within 12 hours. Vascular: The infection caused my peripheral vessels to collapse and become leaky allowing all of the intravenous fluid to leak out and cause massive edema. Kidneys: The combination of dehydration and toxic drug effects caused my kidneys to fail and my creatinine went from a normal of 1.1 to 2.6 in 5 days (it is now down to 1.6) This made it difficult to get rid of the extra fluid. Mental status: I only had some mild delirium which lasted two days and only when I nodded off and would gesture and speak audibly to people in my dream. Gastrointestinal: The combined toxic effect of Melphalan and edema on my gut made for a complete inability to eat. This, in addition to painful mouth sores meant no nutrition for 6 days.

Fortunately the mouth sores last only two days and ended before the sepsis began. Immunologic: On vacation for the duration. I had zero white cells to help fight off the infection. That was the whole point of the transplant, and they were not back yet. nor were my platelets to prevent bleeding, but transfusions of platelets and blood saved me in this category. Two systems were left. Hepatic: my liver remained healthy managing to metabolize all of the new drugs in my system. But my heart was the star. Cardiac; Early on I worried that all of this stress would put my heart into rejection; but an echocardiogram revealed that my heart was working above normal physiologic levels. It alone was keeping me going. It was perfusing my kidneys so that they could heal. It was maintaining my blood pressure even when they turned off the dopamine, but most critically, it was keeping my lungs free of excess fluid allowing me to breath. And possibly preventing the most dreaded of complications: Adult respiratory distress syndrome or ARDS. Which by itself can have a 50% mortality rate.

As my cardiologist told me, "Your heart is doing a great job." I had to think, "My heart?" It is actually my "shared" heart. And this is now the second time that it has saved my life.

Kevin

Wednesday, March 25, 2009
Another day

There are two things wonderful people ask me: "How are you doing with all this?" and "Can I do anything for you?" The kindness of the "ask" in itself lifts me. When asked how I'm doing I usually say that I'm fine. And for the most part that has been true. When they ask me what they can do for me I say, "No, I'm good." The truth is I need more sleep and need to be cloned.

This past week took a toll on my ability to think clearly. I went out of the house with two different colored shoes, missed a hair appointment, and I left the garage door open all night. But those things aren't so bad, right? The problem is that it is now affecting my school work. I have completed the wrong assignment twice, cannot concentrate on studying for my test today, and have lost my motivation, and have been waking up at 4 a.m. for no apparent reason and can't fall back to sleep. I am completely exhausted and just want to lie down. Today is another long day of classes, *my test and then I drive to be with Kevin. I'll be fine because I was given a blessing by my Bishop that I will find strength that I did not know I had.*

I am so thrilled that Kevin has pulled through (his white blood cells are GROWING) and so amazed at how quickly he turned from the sickest I have ever seen someone. I am ever so grateful to the kindness of friends who have adopted our girls when I am away, have brought in meals, cookies, flowers, and messages of support. We will never forget this experience and will be forever humbled by the love we have felt from so many and the comfort we have felt from our Savior.

Barbie

CHAPTER 55

The healing process moves at its own pace and will not be hurried. So many Americans do not have the patience to be sick. They blame their doctors if they are not well in time to travel to a business meeting or golf tournament. Our cells are not aware of our agenda. That does not mean that we cannot help the process along. First we must not hinder or impede the healing. The triad of healing is not a secret to anyone. It is so simple that many will dismiss it altogether. Eat well, exercise and have a positive attitude. To heal we must supply all of our cells, our organs and tissues the materials necessary to do their job. Solution? Energy, in the form of calories. This is no time to diet. Protein is the scaffolding, wood and cement to rebuild tissue. My goal was to get as much protein as possible. "Got milk?" I would have two cups of milk with each meal. At 11 grams of protein per cup, that was 66 grams per day. I had not eaten for a week, so I had a lot of catching up to do.

Exercise sends messages to the body to do specific repairs in certain areas. Tissues are better perfused when we are upright and moving. Clots cannot form. Skin gets a breather from having too much pressure in one spot. Every part of the body gets to participate when a person is moving. The feedback to the brain sends off a cascade of messages to the body to activate critical pathways, hormones and metabolism that more efficiently utilize the resources the gut and lungs are providing.

Finally, the mind must do its part. Anxiety, fear, anger and frustration only serve to activate stress pathways that over the long run slow down healing. I have found it critical to have a goal and a plan to pull oneself out of the pit of self-pity. For many this is so difficult. I have a patient who was so depressed after his wife died that he just gave up. He wanted to die. He refused treatment critical to prolonging his life, complaining, "What's the point? Just let me die." The only solution that I could offer him was what I had also learned:

"To save your life, you must first lose it."

The only way to be truly happy is to lose oneself in the service of others. I suggested ways in which even he, physically limited as he was, could engage and help others. It was his only hope.

Now, for nearly two weeks I had been inwardly focused. Finally I had a little energy and it was time to do my job.

I was moved to a double occupancy room once my white blood cell count had risen sufficiently to protect me from my neighbor's microbes. Through the curtain of ultimate privacy, I could hear the plight of my roommates. Each day brought a new one. Most of these men were elderly and fighting different forms of cancer. On the second day I heard only Spanish as the patient's family visited with him. He did not speak much, but I could sense that he was scared. Early in the evening the family left. A while later, a nurse came in and went through a lengthy explanation of what would happen the following day when he received his chemotherapy infusion. As is common with many non-English speakers in a hospital setting like this, he did not admit to her that he spoke no English. I have seen many patients politely nodding at the appropriate non-verbal cues as if they understood. Finally she finished and left.

I got up, threw on a second gown to cover my back and went around the curtain to his bed. "¿Entendió todo lo que la enfermera le dijo?" I asked. With an inquisitive look, he responded, "no." I then explained in Spanish all of the instructions that she had given him. He asked some questions that I was able to answer and then he thanked me.

I could only imagine how difficult it must be to be alone and critically ill and then, in addition, not be able to speak the language well. It must have been a frightfully lonely experience for him. Later, his regular nurse came in and I called her over to my bed and explained that I would be happy to serve a translator for him for whatever she needed to say to him. It felt good to be useful.

Thursday, March 26, 2009
Everything's better

When I arrived last night, Kevin looked great. He is still a bit weak, so I guess I should not expect a marathon anytime soon. I was so happy to see him that everything felt right. (Just like you said, Cindy.) My test was not a big deal and I was in the car driving by 2:45 p.m. I usually don't get on the road until 6 p.m., so it was nice to get here earlier than normal. I slept great last night in the apartment. Kevin has slept for about six hrs since I have been here today. When he woke up, he wanted Ben & Jerry's Phish Food. That is a great sign.

Barbie

CHAPTER 56

It was still dark outside. There is an intangible moment when the mind transitions between dreaming and the haze of waking. External sounds register in the auditory canal and brush the brain, but are barely processed. Somewhere between the dream and the haze, a kernel of a story entered my brain. Just as the sun lightens the morning sky before it escapes the eastern horizon, the thoughts expanded, slowly at first and then with an intensity commensurate to a sunrise. I could not control or alter my thoughts. The story engulfed me as I lay in the dark room. The sounds of the hospital remained only background noise. Normally dreams fade fast, since they are necessarily disconnected from both our short and long term memories. Otherwise, our brains would be overrun with the random and chaotic visuals filling the void of the submerged emotions that are truly the essence of a dream. To remember a dream then becomes an active process. We replay the fast-fading reflection from our sub-consciousness in the waking mind and re-imprint it into cortical memory.

What was happening to me now as I awakened was different from the intentional process of recalling a normal dream. I could not stop it. The story ideas ebbed and flowed and sprouted like seedlings in time-lapse photography. For the rest of the day I could scarcely think about anything else. When the outward distractions were turned off, even for a few minutes, my mind took me back to construct the life of a person whom I had never met or even heard of. His name was Arthur. For the next few days, the story kept me company and filled my waking thoughts. I wondered if this was how novelists wrote books of fiction. Did they try to come up with an idea, or did the story find them?

I have written many scientific articles and book chapters related to my subspecialty in urology. I was, however, not a writer; especially not a writer of fiction. I tried to let the ideas fade, but they filled the quiet corners of my mind.

Just after lunch, I got a call from a friend of mine, Jerry Haar. He was a Hamm radio operator and was on the radio with Capt. Neal Hinson, USAF, the U-2 spy-plane pilot. Neal was flying somewhere above 80,000 feet. (The exact altitude was classified) Through the phone I could hear Neal's voice from his cockpit. This was surreal. Neal said, "Kevin, go outside and look up." As I hurried down the hallway past the cafeteria, Barbie suddenly appeared at my side. From the hallway bathroom, she had recognized my distinctive footsteps among the scores of people walking by. I told her that Neal had something special for us. I wondered how we could possibly see a U-2 plane flying at that altitude. We walked outside, trying not to bump into people as we craned our heads skyward to see something.

The sky was cloudless and a deep azure. We saw nothing. And then, directly overhead, a wisp of white appeared. It began to take on a shape; a semi-circle, a smile. And then we smiled. At that altitude, while Neal created a con-trail, a fellow pilot who was flying hundreds of miles away could see the sign that Neal was leaving for me. Neal was flying in a circle. He had just finished the smile and was going to do the eyes to complete the smiley face when his fellow intrepid high altitude observer asked him what he was doing. Neal simply stated, "a morale mission." He decided not to finish the face. But the intended effect was complete. Mission accomplished. Barbie and I just stood there looking up, with the biggest grins on our faces. The other passersby occasionally looked up inquisitively. But no one saw what we saw or knew what we knew. This message was just for us.

Saturday, March 28, 2009
Freedom
Day + 15 Health Score 77

I was finally released from the hospital today, and what a glorious day it is. It is beautiful in Palo Alto. A family here, the Brand family, has been gracious in opening their home to us. It is only two miles from the hospital. We are staying in the guest house with a back yard reminiscent of the Garden of Eden and a Koi pond just outside. Barbie has already stayed here off and on for two weeks. I continue to be overwhelmed by the kindness of so many good people. I cannot imagine a more serene place to recover.

The real work begins now for Barbie. I have strict diet restrictions; I can only eat packaged processed junk food. My water has to be boiled daily. I will continue to go into the ITA (Infusion Treatment Area) daily for labs and treatments as needed.

I am still quite fatigued, I am still recovering from the pneumonia, but I feel a little stronger every day. But every day from now on is one day closer to complete recovery. The worst is over.

Kevin

Sunday afternoon Barbie left to return to Lincoln, the girls, and her schoolwork. She had arranged for Daren and Rachelle to stay with me, as I was not allowed to be alone in case I got sick and needed to return to the hospital. I sat alone in the guest house waiting for them to arrive. The story that had begun with a dream only a few days before kept weaving its way through my thoughts, constantly evolving like the ever shifting colors of oil on wet cement. I realized that to stop this, I had to fix the story in time, or in other words, I had to write it down. Actually, writing is very difficult for me. I can handle the idea part, but the application of fingers to keyboard intimidates me. Still, it seemed this story needed to be told. So I began.

Two weeks later I finished my first work of fiction. Initially it was my desire to include my writings here in this book, but it is a long short-story.

I wrote it without much thought as to any allegorical meaning that might reflect my own recent experience. However, upon reading it again years later, I recognized the clearly subconscious themes from that time that are pervasive throughout the story. I was interested to see that I included two characters that suffered drowning and the resultant consequences. Only now do I fully feel the impact of the prescient nature contained within the story since the complete parallel to my own experience did not at that time yet exist.

(For those readers that would like to read this story entitled *Solids*, the following link will allow you to download the file.)

www.arborniche.com

Part 6

INTERMISSION

CHAPTER 57

Protocol dictated that I remain near Stanford to assure that my health did not deteriorate. While Barbie was in school Monday through Wednesday I had a lot of time alone to consider all that had just happened. Two major hurdles were now behind me. I imagined a future where I would no longer need chemotherapy. I put my life on the line, betting that replacing my bone marrow would be genocide to the rogue clones of a mutant plasma cell that had brought me to the brink of destruction. Freed from this threat, I would return to life for some time. I hoped for at least four to eight years. Alone, and lost in thought, my internal dialogue worked overtime. Reflection and anticipation were integral ingredients to my ponderings.

Wednesday, April 1, 2009
Lesson Learned
Day+ 19 Health Score 81

"Dad, you always do that when it's going to be a teaching moment," Rebecca reminded me. I do not remember what the issue was. But she was a senior in High School at the time and just had told me of some experience she had had where the outcome was undesirable. I moved forward to the edge of the couch cushion and raised my left hand with my index finger pointed as if to indicate that I was now literally going to make a point. I was just about to expound wisdom on "what do we learn from this experience?" when

she caught me with the observation above. I realized that my children had seen this particular pose all of their lives, since I tended to turn every experience into a lesson in life learning. It's not that they resented this tendency of mine, but that it was so common in my approach to every problem.

So at this point in my journey I pause to reflect: "class, what have we learned thus far?"

First of all, it must be stated; life isn't fair. It was never meant to be. Bad things happen that are beyond our control. Unfortunately, because of this some people become discouraged or despondent; some will ask, "Why me?" and even, heaven forbid, try to blame others for their problems, even blaming God. This response only leads to wasted energy and wasted time. It would be like a man sitting in a taxi in mid-town Manhattan; the driver is off getting a knish and toffee peanuts. He sits alone, the meter running, while the world is passing him by.

My nature has always been different from this. I record very few failures in my life, mostly because of the way I define failure. Failure is when an outcome is bad and you do not learn anything from the experience. Generally, I can always learn something from my "failures" and not make the same mistake in the future. Simultaneously, I find that often, in failure, we learn the most. I believe that we gain confidence from our successes and learn from our failures. We need both..

Then one day, you learn you have a rare and fatal illness. How does that fit in to your life philosophy? Everyone who is faced with a diagnosis that is fatal goes through the same process. Mortality is no longer an abstract idea. It is as real as what you had for breakfast today.

People react very differently to this knowledge. For me, however, it is just another challenge that I must learn from. I have learned things about myself in the last nine months that I could not have learned in any other way. This is good. Additionally, I still expect things to go well, and they have; unbelievably well; miraculously well.

Faith is a critical part of this process. I have not only my faith to rely on, but have been blessed with the combined faith and prayers of countless numbers of people. I cannot comprehend the combined effect of the faith of so many on my behalf, but I feel it every single day. There is so much goodness out there; I wish that everyone could see it.

I have just come through the bone marrow transplant. It was not uneventful. I was really sick. But my doctors were swift and skilled in their care for me. And what they learned from my complications will give them the confidence in treating those who follow me.

But I never feared that I would not make it this far. I expected things to turn out well, and they did.

Fear of failure that paralyzes a person into inaction is the greatest curse that could inflict any individual life. Faith will always swallow that fear.

Kevin

On Thursday, April 2nd, we finally arrived home, I hoped for the last time. Life could now return to our "new normal," as Barbie called it. Caitlin was doing amazingly well in school and with her music, having become strong and independent in our absence. Rebecca was adjusting to life after her brief marriage and was now planning to return to BYU to finish her degree. As sad as it was for her to suffer through her own loss, we had been blessed to have her there for Caitlin during the past three months.

Spring was upon us and I was filled by the beauty all around me. When I got home, I went into the backyard and just stood there for the longest time taking in the majesty of God's creations. The crisp air in my nostrils, the breeze on my bald head, the warmth of the sun, the vision of clouds and sky through the new leaves of the oaks; everything added to an immense sense of being alive.

I went back inside to begin again my task of living.

CHAPTER 58

As I sorted through a pile of mail, I found a letter from my former Chief of Urology at Yale, Dr. Weiss. He informed me that there was to be a special celebration for the life and career of Dr. Lytton, my former senior partner. Dr. Bernie Lytton was himself an institution at Yale and in the field of urology. He had served as an intern in the streets of London, pulling the injured from the rubble during the Blitzkrieg in World War II, and eventually arrived at Yale in the early sixties. For nearly five decades he would define urology as he fearlessly advanced it in both science and art. During my eleven years as his partner, he took me under his wing and shared with me his wisdom and skill. As the master of the undergraduate residential college, Jonathan Edwards, he would often include Barbie and me with an invitation to "Master's teas" where we met and dined with dignitaries from around the world. He was one of the last true gentleman surgeons.

I was so delighted to be asked to speak in his honor. Barbie and I immediately planned on traveling back to Connecticut for the event.

Saturday, April 4, 2009
Looking forward
Day + 22 Health Score 82

I see a day in the not too distant future where people will ask how I am doing. I will answer, "I am fine." But the resulting conversations will not be about my health. We will discuss our mutual patients, our friendships, politics, the economy, movies etc. My illness will not take center stage. Every day now I continue to make progress toward that goal. I do have my work cut out for me. My doctors said I would be fatigued for some time and that is true. However, yesterday we went for a walk in the neighborhood and I had no problem walking 3/4 of a mile.

I am now on the "Hobbit" diet, but in smaller portions: Breakfast, Second Breakfast, Elevenses, Lunch, Dinner, Supper and Midnight Snack. I wake up hungry. Besides all of the water weight that I lost, I also dropped 10 lbs of body mass, mostly fat and muscle. I need to build back the muscle, (not the fat). Of course, this will be easier when I am finally off steroids completely in about two weeks. Notwithstanding, I have six months to prepare to cycle 100 km.

Now that the bone marrow transplant process is done, I may not write every day. I felt that a daily log of what the treatment process involved might help another who might be facing the same ordeal. I really feel that you get a more true account when writing in the present rather than retrospect. I hope that my experience will be of some value to others.

Last night we visited with our close friends, the Boatmans, whose son Tyler underwent surgery two weeks ago for cancer. He has a Wilm's Tumor. Tyler is seven. He completed radiation therapy and is now on chemotherapy. While there, Tyler and I compared our scars and catheters. I showed him where my Hickman catheter was removed and he was very curious to know if it hurt when they removed it. I reassured him that it did not. After he saw my heart transplant scar, over the next half hour he slowly removed his steri-strips, one by one. When he finished the last one he jumped up to show me his scar as well. We also talked about how life with one kidney would be normal and he could do whatever he wanted to. He asked what if the other kidney got sick. I assured him that that would be unlikely. It amazes me what insight a seven-year-old can have toward his condition. Kids often possess more strength in these matters than do adults.

Kevin

Tyler went on to have chemotherapy and radiation therapy to his chest. It was a very difficult year for him and his family. But in the end he was cured and continues to do well to this day.

Wednesday, April 8, 2009
Kappa
Day + 26 Health Score 83

It looks like NPR co-opted Barbie's phrase, "a new normal." Of course, they were describing the new economy, not our family life. Yesterday was a busy day. Since Santa Clara and Stanford are so far away, we try to pack in as much as we can. We left at 4:00 a.m. to be at Kaiser, Santa Clara at 6:15 a.m. for the heart biopsy. Then we made a visit to the cardiac transplant clinic. 20 miles north brought us to Stanford for a chest X-ray and one last visit to the ITA to make sure I was improving from the pneumonia. Everything looked well and I was discharged from the ITA to clinic. We then had an appointment with Dr. Schrier at 3:00 p.m. to address the amyloidosis. At this point we watch the light chain levels and my symptoms. As a urologist, I have watched some of my older male patients become obsessed with their PSA levels (marker for prostate cancer). The same can happen with light chain levels. However, measurements for both PSA and light chain levels can be vary spurious in their values, even in different tests from the same lab. So it is not a good idea to put too much weight on one number.

I asked when I should get my first lab test. They told me I should wait at least a month, but that it could take a few months to drop. Anticipating the clinic visit, I had a Kappa light chain level done on Sunday (probably a little too soon). To call the transplant a success, the value should drop by 50%. But which original value should I use? The Stanford pre-BMT value of 32 mg/dl or the Kaiser pre-BMT value of 16.5 mg/dl? The kappa light chains level from my test on Sunday was 9.3 mg/dl, which is certainly trending in the right direction. My heart biopsy was NER, No Evidence of Rejection. I have not had that result in over four months. (Then again, with no bone marrow for two weeks, there was nothing to cause rejection).

All in all, things are moving in the right direction. We bought an exercise bike today so that I can begin reconditioning and training. The bike may be stationary, but I am moving forward.

Kevin

As the days wore on I was anxious to see a palpable improvement in my health. Initially, the excitement of completing my therapy gave me a transient boost of energy, but this was soon spent. I tried to always be positive but found fatigue to be my fast friend. I could not go anywhere without him. I did the shopping, cleaned the pool, and took care of bills. I love to cook, but the effort of it tired me out. Barbie studied non-stop for her organic chemistry class and Caitlin continued in her ever-expanding social life with three non-intersecting circles of friends. However, occasionally there would be a day when I awoke and felt almost normal. I found that no matter how bad I felt, just walking outside would make me feel better. The healing power of nature is quite potent.

Monday, April 13, 2009
Weekend in Pacifica
Day + 31 Health Score 85

I never expected to be 85 this soon. That is what I was prior to the stem cell transplant on my better days. It is probably because I went into work today; mostly to take care of administrative items and prepare for my eventual resumption of duties. It felt so normal to be there. I am anxious for the day when I begin to see patients again. It will be here soon.

Since we had an appointment with Dr. Arai (BMT) on Friday and planned to attend the amyloidosis support group in Walnut Creek on Saturday, we decided to stay in a hotel Friday night. We stayed in the Best Western Lighthouse Inn in Pacifica. Our room was literally 10 feet from the beach. As you can see, we are continually drawn to the beach, hoping to become Pacific like the ocean. The support group is quite helpful, in that the fellow participants can often answer the questions that the doctors cannot. They also had a breakout session specifically for caregivers. Those who care for the chronically ill face very difficult challenges that are often overlooked by the rest of the world, which focuses on the person who is ill. I am glad that Barbie was able to attend.

We spent Easter with our friends, the Hinsons, and ate prime rib. Skip ham; I think prime rib should be the new tradition. We then spent the evening visiting and singing. Rebecca and Caitlin sang one of the songs that they have written together. I am surrounded by talented women.

Kevin

Sunday, April 19, 2009
Health Score 83
The Lonely Adrenal

The adrenal glands live just above each kidney. (Hence the name ad-renal) Even though they are small in size and well-hidden deep inside the body, they are very busy. Among the myriad of useful stuff they make to keep us alive and moving are glucocorticoids or steroids. However, when the "big guns" move into town, they cannot compete. Prednisone would be like the Wal-mart of steroids. Clearly the low cost leader and used for everything from arthritis to poison oak. (Poison ivy for those east of the Mississippi.) After a transplant, you live on prednisone for months. This would make Decadron the Costco of steroids; buy in bulk and save.

The poor adrenal gland grows locally (yes, it is the Farmer's Market, perhaps stretching the metaphor a little too far) and eventually goes out of business.

Then one day you move to a place where Costco and Wal-mart do not exist, and the adrenal is now your only source. That is a good thing, but now my adrenals have shrunken to the size of two raisins; it will take a few weeks to get production back to normal. What does that mean for me? I am about a half bushel low on energy.

As you can probably guess, I am off steroids now. Yeah!! But my body now has to readjust. Mostly it means I move pretty slowly in the mornings. But hey, who doesn't?

I saw Dr. Arai on Friday and everything is going well. My chest CT scan shows resolution of the pneumonia. I finally rode my bike yesterday. Not too far, but enough to really provide a good workout.

Tomorrow I will drive with Rebecca to Utah, as she returns to BYU for the Spring Term. We will miss her so much.

Kevin

I truly saw steroids as the enemy and had hoped that the bone marrow transplant would allow me to stop taking them. I had been on steroids for two different reasons. First, they were part of my anti-rejection regimen which began after my heart transplant. Steroids do many things including suppression of the immune system and inflammation. I had continued on low dose steroids (Prednisone 5 mg daily) up until the stem cell transplant. Chemotherapy to control my amyloidosis also included a massive dose of steroids using Decadron. Now I was at a point where I might be able to avoid both and thereby truly feel normal again.

Another function of steroids is to help the body deal with stress. Now that I was physiologically on my own, my buffer to deal with any untoward physical demand was greatly reduced. I knew that eventually the adrenal glands would kick in and produce what I needed. I only hoped that prior to that the withdrawals would exceed accounts receivable, and my adrenal account would balance out.

CHAPTER 59

Monday April 27, 2009
Dimmer Switch

The hardest thing about coming home is learning to pace yourself. The nurses and doctors warn you. I have given my patients the same advice for years. But once you walk through that door, all of those ignored priorities are there to greet you. Additionally, after becoming the emaciated man twice in one year, one has a desire to find that lost muscle mass to match the new baldness.

I feel like a light switch; either on or off. I need to install a dimmer switch.

Last week was quite busy. On Monday I drove with Rebecca to Utah, since she starts school again tomorrow at BYU. She will continue in her major, Marketing and Advertising, and should graduate in June. She did not tell me that her apartment was on the third floor. The altitude and the multiple trips up and down winded me. Alexandria and Jeremy are doing well. Alexandria got an intern position doing quality assurance at a meat processing company. Jeremy was supposed to take the MCAT last Friday, but a computer glitch shut down the testing center, delaying him by two months to take the test necessary to apply to medical school. He was, however, very calm about it; resolving to put that extra time to better use. Sam and Michelle are doing well and looking forward to the slower pace of summer. I was also able to visit family and old friends (a roommate from 32 years ago), making it an enjoyable trip.

I flew home Thursday to celebrate Caitlin's 16th birthday, but the real party was on Saturday. We had a barbecue/swim party for about 25 friends. She had a great time; but for me, Sunday was now a day to crash. My health score yesterday would have been 76. Today, however, I am back to 82.

I will now pace myself a little better.

Kevin

To save money, After leaving Rebecca in Provo, I booked a cheaper flight with a layover in Las Vegas. By the end of the flight I was completely spent. I remember this as the moment where everything really began to go downhill for me.

Monday, May 4, 2009
Still Waiting

It seems that I am always waiting for something. Last week I ordered through Amazon.com two gallons of energy and a half pound of motivation; it has not arrived yet. While I was visiting the Urology department today, one of our nurses asked what my health score was. Honestly, I had to report it at about 77. I think it still may be from all of the medication changes. My doctor put me back on the exotic anti fungal at the same time that I stopped my steroids. Sue, the heart transplant nurse warned me that it can take a month to recover adrenal function sufficient to supply the body's basic needs.

My medical assistant, Dina, told me in no uncertain terms that she would not let me come back to work until I had a note from my doctor. Dr. Sardar provided me with such a note and, "barring some unforeseen incident," I will return on June 15th. I will, however, start at part-time.

Kevin

May 31, 2009
On the right path

Sometimes the path to recovery feels like hiking on the Appalachian Trail. Trying to stay sure-footed, you spend most of your time looking down to avoid tripping over half-submerged roots and protruding rocks. Occasionally you have to stop and look up to see the pale green translucent light as the sunlight pours through the spring leaves above. Then you remember why you are on the trail in the first place.

The last month has been quite difficult. I have slowly been getting weaker, and subsequently more despondent. My appetite has diminished and I have to force myself to eat. My lab results do not show a positive response to the Stem Cell Transplant. Everyone says that it is still too early to tell, but I cannot always remain positive about the future. Essentially, I have no idea what is going on. Yes, this is from the guy who always has an explanation for everything. Not being able to write something positive left me without a desire to write; but that is disingenuous. I should not be afraid to reveal all sides of this journey. In desperation, I did something without getting my doctors' approval first. I started to take steroids again, ironically the very thing I had so been looking forward to stopping for so long. I will see my BMT and Oncology physicians at Stanford on Tuesday to discuss future treatments;

I feel that they are going to start me on steroids again anyway. However, in only 24 hours the improvement is more than coincidental or purely placebo. The foot neuropathy that was so uncomfortable is lessened and my energy has increased. We are flying to New York on Wednesday for a reunion at Yale University and I needed to be stronger for the trip. I just could not wait any longer.

I keep reminding myself to be patient. All this will improve with time. The more time the better. As I incline my gaze upward, the light is always there. I am reminded that I am progressing on the right path, one slow step at a time.

Kevin

I never really sleep well on planes. After the bone marrow transplant I was on very strict precautions to prevent infections. My diet was called antibacterial, and excluded anything that could not be cooked or well washed. Additionally, I was supposed to wear a HEPA filter mask in public. Airplanes are especially risky due to the recirculation of the air. I tend not to worry that much about these things. I take what precautions I can. The flight to New York was hard, though. Despite this, we made our way to the Air Train at JFK and to the rental cars. We made it to our friend's house in Hamden and felt as if we had never left. Lynnette and Scott Strobel were our "family" in Connecticut and it was wonderful to be reunited with them. Caitlin had been best friends with their daughter, Rebekah, since they were both two.

The following day I attended a special grand rounds where Dr. Weiss was recognized as the distinguished surgeon of the year by the Yale Surgical Society. I was just starting to have some thin brown hair growing back, so I did not look completely bald. As I entered the reception, I saw many of my former colleagues and former residents. Many kindly shared that they had also come to see me.

I was reminded of the great love I felt for all of my friends and former residents. Memories of long nights and difficult cases washed over me as I pressed hands with each new familiar face. So many had moved on and become successful in their respective practices.

Dr. Weiss had always been like a father to me. I used to say that he was the best boss I ever had, and that is still true today. I was so pleased to see him accept such a great honor.

I did my best to put on a good face. Everyone commented on how great I looked. Washed and shaved, wearing a suit and tie, I pulled off the façade of improved health. This event was not about me. I spent my batteries for them.

What no one saw were my frequent trips to the bathroom and the water fountain as I tried to compensate for losses.

The next day was the festschrift for Dr. Lytton. Dr. Lytton certainly had aged since I last saw him. I spoke with him and his daughter in the hallway after the morning session of the meeting. I asked about his wife, Norma, and how she was doing. His face became ashen as he feebly mouthed the words, his eyes wet and red with emotion, inquisitive as if asking, did not you know? "She passed away." I was speechless. I felt horrible as I had, in that instant, reopened a wound still fresh. I did not know….. His daughter, sensing both of our loss in the awkwardness of the moment spoke. She kindly described her passing from cancer. As she spoke I sensed the deep love from her and her father and the sense of mourning that remained. I, stumbling, apologized for my ignorance and shared my sadness at her loss.

After lunch, Barbie joined me since it would soon be my turn to speak. Traditionally, in a festschrift one is asked to speak on a topic relevant to one's expertise in a particular field. I was humbled to realize that I was surrounded by not only the most esteemed urologists in the country, but also some very prominent scientists, including one Nobel Prize winner. I sat there thinking, "my talk is not scientific at all, but it is about something upon which I am an expert: being a patient." Soon it was my turn. I believe that at least half of those attending knew that I was ill and so I hoped my remarks would be accepted in the spirit in which they were given.

As I stood, my knees felt weak, but the smiles I saw gave me strength to continue. I began to speak about what I had just learned.

The Doctor as a Patient
Kevin R. Anderson, M.D.
June 5, 2009
Yale University

It is a great honor for me to be able to return here to Yale to celebrate the life and career of Dr. Bernie Lytton. As a young faculty member here, Bernie was always a friend and a mentor. When one considers the process of becoming a doctor, it takes years to get where we are. Our education begins in college and medical school, followed by prolonged training in residency and fellowship in our chosen field. We continue to learn as we practice and study and research. This process never ends.

Contrarily, there is no such preparation to become a patient. It is abrupt, awkward and ultimately unsettling. All that defines us as physicians and surgeons is lost when we become ill. Namely, we lose control. Normally, in our ordered lives we call all of the shots. As a patient, we are completely dependent on others. This transition is not an easy one.

May I share two examples which illustrate this on my own journey. Last year I was diagnosed with restrictive cardiomyopathy and primary amyloidosis. To confirm the diagnosis I underwent a right heart catheterization and cardiac biopsy. Afterwards, as I was still lying on the fluoroscopy table, with a cordis in my neck, the cardiologist informed me that my cardiac index was 1.7, half of what I should normally be pumping. She suggested that I be admitted to the unit for a continuous dopamine infusion while I waited for the work-up to be done. My immediate thought was that dopamine is what we give really sick patients in the unit that are "circling the drain." I certainly wasn't that sick. My second thought was that of my work schedule. I had a full clinic the next day and many surgical cases the following week. She understood. I had not yet become the patient. I then asked, "Will I need a heart transplant?" Her unexpected answer hit me like a sledge hammer. "Only if you are healthy enough," she said.

She left me alone on the table to answer a page. As I lay there alone, I realized for the first time in my life the literality of my own mortality. It was as if someone had turned on a light and I could see the door at the end of the tunnel. Life now had an expiration date, and death was on the calendar. I silently wept.

The following week, I was sitting in my office. I had just done two cysto cases and was waiting to return to the OR to do a percutaneous stone case and, finally, the laparoscopic nephrectomy that I had had to cancel from the week before because of my biopsy. The phone rang and it was my cardiologist. She simply informed me that the biopsy was positive for primary amyloidosis, kappa light chain type, involving my heart and that I would need to stop working immediately. As I thanked her and hung up it was as if my heart had already been ripped out of my chest. This emotional pain was far worse than any physical pain that I would ultimately feel a month later when my heart was physically removed. I have always been defined by my responsibilities to others; I was lost not knowing who I was. But I still had work to do that day. I wondered if my fragile emotional state would affect my ability to operate. But as you all know, that is when the years of training kick in. Whatever you *are feeling, when you walk into the OR you leave your life outside as you focus on the task at hand. The case went beautifully. As I spoke to his wife after the case and explained that the tumor was contained, I realized that this man would now live longer than I would. But that was not a sad thought. It was oddly reassuring.*

As I walked away, I became a patient full-time. To be a patient is to wait, to wonder, to be poked and tested repeatedly, to be tired all the time, to silently be afraid, to feel alone in a crowd, to submit, to trust your doctor implicitly, to wait some more, to leave your family and friends behind, to be cut open, to be poisoned. To be a patient is to always hope even when no one knows the answer. To be a patient is to cherish the beauty of the moment.

The doctor as a patient has the special challenge of never second guessing your own doctor, to be completely compliant, even when you might do it differently. I avoided telling people I was a doctor so that they would not change their normal routine or protocol. To demand being treated as a V.I.P. is to risk sub-standard care.

Many people have asked me if I have learned anything from this experience and if I would be a different doctor to my patients. I have been changed profoundly. First of all I am extremely grateful, and the only way I can repay the gift I have been given is to give back. From the day I left, my goal has been to return to work. This I will finally do in two weeks.

All patients, regardless of the severity of their condition, need three things. First, they need to feel that they are being heard. This is difficult, as we often minimize or dismiss extraneous symptoms that to us seem irrelevant to the diagnosis at hand and explain them away as benign. We must train ourselves to accept their report with the weight that they assign it.

Second, a patient will never leave my office without hope. Not false hope, but hope in something that together we can do to extend either the quantity or quality of their lives; even if it is only to achieve a personal goal within the next two weeks. The quality of their life is directly proportional to the degree of their hope.

And lastly, I will remember that many patients feel very alone in their illness. I can help them by showing them examples, or introducing them to others who have overcome similar challenges.

I have been very fortunate to have outstanding doctors, caring nurses and friends and family who have supported me. But there are no words to describe the constant companionship that is the love of my life, my wife, Barbie. I owe her my life.

We surgeons are not usually a self-reflective group. We prove things by randomized double blind studies. Sometimes we are blind to the impact of our own life. Even though my life expectancy now falls below the mean, median and mode. I find a symbolic life extension as I reflect on the lives that through my efforts have been increased in years and those years filled with quality. Equally, I find the same fulfillment in having had the privilege to teach others, medical students and residents, this same art.

By this accounting, Dr. Lytton, the consummate physician, surgeon and professor, should be near immortal. To all of you I give my heartfelt thanks. I am truly a lucky man.

I was fearful that I would emotionally break down during my talk, because each time that I re-read it as I practiced, I would cry when I got to the part about Barbie. I determined not to look at her until I was done speaking. However, what happened afterward completely caught me by surprise. In all my years attending conferences and medical meetings, I had never seen this. As I finished, the entire audience stood and began to applaud. I knew that something that I had said must have touched a chord deep inside that we could all understand and relate too. To receive a standing ovation from so many that I admired was terribly humbling. I searched for Barbie and saw her in the back, tears in her eyes, smiling back at me. That one glance said it all.

Monday, June 8, 2009
Tale of two rooms

Occasionally I find myself without the proper language to reflect an experience. Mostly because the reaction that occurs lies deeper than words than might be floating in my shallow vernacular. We just returned from four days in Connecticut. The putative reason for the trip was to celebrate the recognition by the Yale Surgical Society of my former chief, Dr. Robert Weiss, for his years of service to Yale University. Additionally, the previous chief of urology, and my partner during my time there, Dr. Bernie Lytton, was celebrated in a festschrift the following day. (I had to look up that one) A festschrift is the celebration of an academic career through the writings of one's colleagues. I also was asked to speak. Saturday and Sunday was spent with dear friends from church.

The image of two rooms comes to mind as I contemplate the impact of these reunions upon me. The first room was Fitkin Auditorium in Yale University, where I sat every Monday morning for eleven years for Urology Grand Rounds. In addition to my esteemed colleagues with whom I served on the faculty, a significant majority of the residents whom I had trained were also present to honor Dr. Weiss. We rehashed our favorite embarrassing stories of our short time together.

However, Dr. John Phillips summarized that time very eloquently as he spoke of the "persistence of memory" and the "transformative" effect of those brief three years that each resident spent with us, dryly observing that he had things that had been in his refrigerator for longer than three years. The bond created between professor and resident is forever forged in the daily combined effort to cure disease and alleviate pain. Those were days never to be forgotten. Dr. Lytton and Dr. Weiss, my mentors, created both an inquiring and nurturing environment during a few years that remain the richest of my life. As the room filled to capacity, so equally did my memories of those days that we all spent together in one common pursuit: the care of patients, both today and in the future.

The second room was the chapel of the Woodbridge Ward, where our family worshiped for eleven years. I had spent thousands of hours of service in that chapel, for many years as bishop of the congregation. At work my role was to alleviate physical pain; however, at church I struggled to resolve spiritual pain. I always felt so much love in that room, and yesterday was no exception. Again, true and lasting friendships have their genesis in the sacrifices that we make together. It felt as if we had never left. Barbie, Caitlin and I were at home again; a different home, a different life.

Today, emotionally and physically spent, I spent the day recuperating. Tomorrow it is back to Santa Clara for my two month heart biopsy.

When the persistence of memory reflects so much joy, you realize that every room remains empty until we fill it with friendship.

Kevin
Monday, June 15, 2009

Back to Work

Tomorrow I go back to work. It has been eleven months since I stopped working. This is momentous for me. My first day is already hectic as I begin by doing lithotripsy (breaking stones) in Sacramento. It seems fitting, as stones have always been my forte. I am still fatigued; the severity of which varies from day to day. But I am invigorated by the prospect of seeing patients again.

Soon it will be one year since Barbie and I began this website. At the time, I had no idea the impact that this endeavor would have on me. The wonderful feedback that we have received has carried us through some tough times. I remain unaware of its total readership. Some have suggested putting a counter on the site to see how many hits we get. However, there is some bliss in ignorance as I assume there are only a small number of intimate friends reading this. Thus, I tend to write without self-censoring.

Kevin

When I began the blog I had no idea of the impact it would have on my life and the lives of others. I was contacted from people all over the world asking for advice on what to do for their newly diagnosed amyloidosis, or that of a loved one. I once spent an hour on Skype with a couple 6,000 miles away in Chile discussing, in Spanish, the treatment options for his mother. I learned that we also had in common our service as missionaries in Buenos Aires, Argentina. But one particular cyber-encounter truly impacted me.

After one amyloidosis support group, I was struck by the confusion surrounding a particular heart test called the ejection fraction. To provide a better picture of this test's limited usefulness in patients with restrictive cardiomyopathy, which we all had,

KEVIN R. ANDERSON, M.D.

I wrote the following blog.

Monday, March 1, 2010
Ejection fraction vs. cardiac index

*Occasionally I will hear someone with amyloido-
sis comment on their Ejection Fraction with the idea
that it correlates with the degree of heart involvement
from their disease. It seems prudent to discuss ejection
fraction versus cardiac index. Primary amyloidosis (or
familial), when it involves the heart, tends to cause
restrictive cardiomyopathy. As the name indicates,
restrictive refers to the stiffness of the heart and the
subsequent difficulty in achieving muscle relaxation.
However, contractility may still be preserved. In other
words, the heart can pump, it just cannot fill. Ejection
Fraction or E.F. measures the percentage of blood
volume expelled by the left ventricle with each beat.
As a percentage it does not tell you the actual volume
pumped per heartbeat. Therefore, if you start with a
cup of blood and push out 1/2 cup per beat, the ejection fraction is 50%. If you start with 1/2 cup in the
left ventricle and push out 1/4 cup with contraction,
the E.F. is still 50%. But your volume output is 1/2
of what it should be.*

*Cardiac index measures the actual volume of blood
pumped per minute (adjusted for body size). This is a
much more accurate measure of whether your heart is
working up to the capacity your body needs.*

*The ejection fraction can be measured non-inva-
sively with an echocardiogram. However, measurement
of the cardiac index generally requires cardiac catheterization. A heart stiffened by amyloid deposits does
not relax well, and the right ventricle has very little
time between beats to adequately fill. A fast heart rate*

further diminishes filling time and cardiac output drops (so do we). A slower heart rate cannot provide enough blood per minute to meet demand. The restricted heart therefore finds an optimum rate and stays there. For me it was 85 beats/min. If I took a beta-blocker and it slowed my heart rate, I felt horrible. If I ran, I fell down. When my cardiac index was finally measured it was 1.7 L/min/meter-squared. I copied the normal range from Wikipedia:

The normal range of cardiac index is 2.6 - 4.2 L/ min per square meter.

If the CI falls below 1.8 L/min, the patient may be in cardiogenic shock.

Now I know why my doctor told me to stop operating (eventually).

Bottom line: Just because your ejection fraction is normal does not mean your heart is.

Food for thought.

Kevin

After I wrote this blog, I was contacted by a woman from Oregon. Her husband, a dentist, had primary amyloidosis with all of the same symptoms that I had. His cardiologist was not offering anything because his ejection fraction was normal. Upon reading the blog, they made an appointment with his doctor, a copy of the blog in hand. Ultimately, they convinced him to do a heart catheterization and measure his cardiac index. He was in cardiogenic shock. His cardiologist sadly informed him that he would need a heart transplant to survive, but that he was not a candidate because of his diagnosis of amyloidosis.

At this point his wife simply stated that they knew of an amyloidosis patient that received a heart transplant from Stanford and that they would travel to Northern California to see if he could get a heart there. Upon hearing this the cardiologist reconsidered and promised to check with the local heart transplant program to see if he might be considered for a new heart.

A short time later he was the first amyloidosis patient to get a heart transplant at the University of Oregon. He has done well since and is now teaching at the dental school there.

Sunday, June 21, 2009
Happy Fathers day

Kevin is weak again. The weakest I have seen him since "recovering" from the bone marrow transplant. He has symptoms of a bad virus that strips him of fluids and causes him to run out of energy quickly. Each day since Friday he has gotten weaker and weaker and sleeps more during the day. It is hard now to know what to do. The docs have tried so many variations on his drugs I'm not sure what is left to try. He is supposed to go back to work on Tuesday so whatever is making him feel this awful needs to resolve by then.

I will be done with my summer Sociology class this Thursday. It will be a relief to have one more class complete. I remain optimistic about Kevin's health. I have come to a greater understanding that the things you have no control over, you must accept with grace and strength. It is what it is.

Happy Father's Day to all you dads.

Barbie

Part 7

SICK TO DEATH

CHAPTER 60

Mortality Awareness event # 7

During the bone marrow transplant, I was given countless variations of medications. One difficulty my doctors faced was how to manage my anti-rejection drugs. The bone marrow protocol and the heart transplant protocol were at odds with each other. Clearly, I did not need anti-rejection drugs if all of my immune system was annihilated. But, when and how would I restart my drugs? Dr. Arai did her best. However, one drug that was stopped was not restarted: Valcyte. Valcyte is an antiviral drug that has a specific indication for cytomegalovirus or CMV. This is a common virus that many of us have been exposed to, but is particularly dangerous in transplant patients. Even so, most patients can discontinue this drug within six months of their transplant. My case was a bit unique. One could only guess where my new immune system was at this point. I knew that one of the fatalities from the Mayo Clinic study was from a CMV infection after bone marrow transplant. I spoke with Dr. Arai one day and asked her about taking an antiviral medication. Her protocol generally used Acyclovir, so that was what I was prescribed. I hoped this would improve my symptoms, but I only got worse.

I had no appetite; the sight of food caused a sense of nausea. While driving, if I saw a billboard with a juicy, succulent steak I would have to turn my head away as if I were seasick. I bought a case of Ensure and forced myself to drink them. I began losing weight and within three weeks had lost 15 lbs. As I spent most of the day perched like "The Thinker" on the toilet, I thought of cholera patients, dying of dehydration even though they had plenty to drink. I was losing water faster than I could drink it.

A friend of mine with amyloidosis was on total parenteral nutrition (TPN) because his disease had destroyed the nerves to his gut such that his intestines no longer functioned to absorb food. To survive, he had to have an intravenous infusion of fluid and nutrients every day. I secretly feared that this was happening to me. I shared this fear with Barbie. Even though I did not want to worry her, I could not face this alone.

Thursday, June 25, 2009
A little Lost
Health Score 62

I am really sick and I do not know why. It is one thing to suffer the side-effects of treatments that you hope will make you better. However, I thought that I was done with that. I am so weak it is hard to move. It could be a virus, or the amyloidosis may now be affecting my gut. I have no appetite. I have very little motivation. I am using all of my energy to hold on to hope; since ultimately, that is the only thing we have.

This is not a result of me going back to work; I have been like this for almost two months. It is just getting worse. Returning to work was wonderful. At work, I must always remember that I am the doctor and not the patient. As I tried to explain to a patient yesterday that at age 77 he need not worry too much about the prospect of prostate cancer he interrupted, "Stop right there, Doc, I plan on living to 107, don't you?" I stopped myself from saying what I wanted to say, and instead said, "That's a great goal, don't ever give it up."

In the past, every time I felt really sick I would wonder, "will I get better?" I always did. I have to believe that I will.

Kevin

Dr. Robbie Pearl, the CEO and executive director of The Permanente Medical Group (TPMG) had scheduled a special meeting for all of the department chiefs in Northern California to be held in San Francisco. Given the economic devastation of the last six months, we were to convene to determine how Kaiser would weather an ever-shrinking membership caused by sudden and massive unemployment. I was excited to interact with other chiefs in the region, especially with Dr. Weisshaar, not as a patient, but as a colleague.

It became clear on Friday morning, however, that my drive to the bay area would not include a stop in San Francisco. Rather, I would head to Santa Clara to be admitted with severe dehydration for fluid resuscitation and evaluation to determine the cause of my unexpected regression. Frustration and fear enveloped me. Once again my desires to serve and support in my responsibilities were dashed. But it was clear that things had become too serious to ignore. I remained uncharacteristically quiet as we made the three-hour drive. Soon I was in a gown, in a bed, three doors down from where I had waited for my heart transplant nearly a year before. I was devastated.

Friday, June 26, 2009
In the hands of great docs again

This morning Kevin and I headed down to Santa Clara Kaiser for him to be admitted again. He spiked a fever last night and was weaker than ever. We knew he needed fluids and some good old fashion hospital care. Since we've been here he has been seen by the Cardiologist team, Infectious Disease, and Gastroenterologist team. His symptoms this time have made him extremely weak and fatigued. He said every day feels like the second day of a bad flu. These teams together are trying to figure out what is going on with him. They need to rule out heart rejection and amyloidosis in his G.I. tract. We hope this is a nasty virus, because viruses can get better. He has had all kinds of labs already and will have a colonoscopy in the morning. He joked that this is one procedure that he has never had. For dinner he gets to drink Go-lightly, but Kevin calls it run-quickly. This is to clean out his G.I. tract for the colonoscopy in the morning. He is relieved to be here. At home he tends to self-diagnose. Now he can relax and let everyone else take care of him. It is a good thing.

Barbie

Saturday morning brought one of the few tests or procedures that up to this point I had not experienced. A long black steerable snake would be maneuvered through my colon to ascertain the source of my misfortune. Charitably, I was to receive happy drugs to make this a pleasant process. Unfortunately, I picked the weekend where the hospital computer system for inpatients "went live." No longer could doctors' orders be written on mere paper. This meant that it would take an hour to get approval from the pharmacy to get the drugs released to the operating room. I sat on the cold table, half naked, while the gastroenterologist argued on the phone for some drugs. That was my last recollection. Drugs cause amnesia as well as pain relief; as such, my remaining memory of this was, a la *Men in Black*, expunged.

I was later told that my entire gut was sprinkled with fluffy white patches representing amyloidosis. Biopsies were taken to check for a viral infection as well. Now we waited.

The rest of the day was one of great discomfort, both physically and emotionally. I could not keep terrorizing thoughts from plaguing my consciousness. Was this the beginning of the end? I dared not share too much with Barbie. I had always been so positive through all of this. Even on my worst day during the bone marrow transplant, I never gave up hope. I always knew that I was going to make it. But that was not how I felt now. For the first time I was truly overcome with fear. So many times in my life I have been close to death, but never felt it sting like I did now.

Dr. Epstein came by. He is the psychologist for heart transplant patients. As we talked he sensed my despair. He finally spoke one prescription of advice: "try to visualize yourself better." I already knew that. He did not have to say it. I am the eternal optimist. And yet, in that moment, I could not see it. I felt blind to hope. This was so unfair. It was so not me. I felt ashamed that I could not be stronger, more positive. I tried so hard to see myself better, but it was so hard. I wanted to sink so deep into the mattress that Barbie could not see my failure. I was not strong. I was frail and human. I felt guilty that my faith in God was not stronger. I prayed for strength. I have seen so many miracles in my life. How was it possible that I could forget?

The evening wore on. I played with the cold dinner items on my plate. Food was horrible to me. I forced down a few bites. Darkness dressed the window as night fell. Darkness is life without hope. I cannot say that I lost all hope; I held on to a thread. I remembered Dr. Epstein's words.

I pulled out my computer to check my recent labs.

About a month after the bone marrow transplant I had checked to see if it had worked. My first blood test showed that the light chains were 90; half of what they had been prior to the treatment. I wondered what the half life of the protein was in my body. If the bad cell clone had been eradicated then there would be no elevation of kappa light chains anymore. It was all or none. Either the bad plasma cells were dead or they were not. Even if a small population of cells survived, they would continue to proliferate and I would be none the better for my sacrifice.

I waited a month and rechecked the level just before I was admitted. I saw the result was back in my chart. It was flagged abnormal. My finger hesitated to click open the result. One touch and there it was, simply a number, cold and cruel in its digits. ...364... My heart sank. The transplant had failed. This was twice as high as what I had started with. My brain raced to find an explanation. Cause and effect − *CAUSE AND EFFECT!!* No justification came. The disease, my disease, remained unchecked. All of the risk, all of the sufferings; the stem cell transplant had failed and I was none the better. I was undone.

I started to cry uncontrollably. Barbie came to see what was wrong. I told her and she climbed into bed next to me, her comforting head rested upon my shoulder. We spoke in hushed tones, each questioning what this meant. After so many miracles, I was confused. Had I been saved for this? She, in an effort to console me spoke of God's will. Then a thought entered my mind and, uncensored, partially escaped my lips.

"Maybe it is God's will that I...."

I could not finish. To say it might sever the thread of hope that remained.

All along I had said that I was not afraid of death. This was still true. I was ready for God's will, no matter what. My faith reassured me that this life was not all; that I would be with Barbie forever. But, I was not ready to leave her. The thought was unconscionable. I would not say the word. The thread would remain unbroken.

Sunday, June 28, 2009
A new day – A new life

I am on an emotional roller-coaster. Dr. Epstein, the psychologist, said I know too much and that I should try to focus on the realities of right now and to visualize improving. I do know too much about how I feel and what it might mean. Many of the pathways are not good. Balance is everything. You cannot lose more water from your gut than you take in. No matter how much you drink, you will become dehydrated. That is where I have been for the last two weeks. There are three possible causes. First, this could be a residual side effect of the bone marrow transplant and I will just have to hope it eventually improves. Second, it could be from progression of my amyloidosis; if so it is not likely to improve and would ultimately kill me. Third, it could be caused by a virus, specifically cytomegalovirus (CMV) which can possibly be treated. We are hoping for the latter. The biopsies from the colonoscopy should be back tomorrow or Tuesday. The I.V. fluids they have given me have helped, but mostly I sleep all day and remain very weak.

Last night I was quite despondent after seeing that my light chains had not improved, confirming to me that the BMT did not work. Barbie lay next to me in my hospital bed to console me. Through the shared tears she wondered if this too were part of God's plan. Speaking aloud, I responded, "maybe it is God's plan that I will....." I could not say the word; not in front of Barbie, but she knew. Just because I accept my eventual death, I will not hurry it through defeat and apathy. I have always accepted God's will and in so doing, have been blessed with the most fulfilled and happy life that a man could ever hope for. My faith in Him will not falter just because I am in temporary pain. Barbie and I agreed that we can deal with the intellectual preparations for the inevitable without opening that emotional scab just to reconfirm what we both already know. This is not denial; it is survival.

Today is better. Dr. Blum, the infectious disease specialist, came by and gave me hope. I am determined to eat all that I can. Bishop Merrill called to say we were missed and that our friends are praying for us. And then my brother-in-law, Daniel, called from North Carolina. He is in medical school at Wake Forest. His wife, Emma, today gave birth to their second child and first son. He said that they had chosen a name for him. When he spoke the name, I was speechless; overcome by a profound sense of humility and honor. What a wonderful day it has become. A new soul has arrived and his name is Kevin Ezequiel Dison

Kevin

In the end, I was not strong enough to lift myself out of the swirling darkness of despair. I had to rely on others to pull me out. Sunday, God answered my pleas through others. My home teacher, Frank Penney, came to visit me and give me a priesthood blessing. Bishop Merrill informed me that the following Sunday the members of my ward would have a special fast for me, and finally, in my life I had never expected the ultimate honor of having a new life named for me. Together, the combined love and hope of others filled my bucket until it was overflowing and patched the hole that was in the bottom.

Monday morning arrived as I opened my eyes. Reality returned and so did my memory. It was only 36 hours before when I despaired with hope strained. It was only 24 hours before when hope returned. Now it was time to act and look forward. The biopsy finally returned and a new plan was made as my fears faded.

CHAPTER 61

Thursday, July 2, 2009
Home again

Barbie and I returned home on Tuesday. The initial biopsy results showed cytomegalovirus (CMV) in the colon and some "fluffy" stuff that required further identification. This turned out to be plaques of amyloid protein in the stomach and intestines. I am now on high doses of an antiviral drug called Valcyte. Additionally, they temporarily stopped my Cellcept (an anti-rejection drug) to allow my immune system to fight the virus. Next week, when I am feeling better, I will start the chemotherapy to fight the amyloidosis; hence my new slogan, "chemicals for better living."

I am feeling a little better. Of course, just being home does that. I am still very weak, but I am eating better and getting plenty of fluids. Barbie is a wonderful nurse. Yesterday we were pleasantly surprised to have a visit from Samuel and Michelle, who are here for a family reunion for Michelle's family. The pool was 86 degrees and I went swimming with Caitlin and my niece, Sofia.

I face a difficult road; the next two weeks are critical. We will have to fight these invaders now on two fronts simultaneously. I cannot do this alone, nor do I have to. I will always have Barbie at my side.

Kevin

Tuesday, July 7, 2009

The past week has been very difficult. I have had little motivation to do anything. I have not been on my computer for four days. Every day I would wake up, eat a small breakfast, take my medications and go back to bed. I am completely wiped out all of the time. I have had to stay home and not work. Emotionally, Barbie and I are spent. If this is only caused by a virus, then I should improve. But if the bowel problems are from amyloidosis, I may never get better. You can imagine what that feels like when the proximity of death is so palpable.

Every day I eat and drink as much as I can tolerate; this means a constant consumption of very small amounts of food and liquid. I am maintaining my weight so far.

Today, I have had some good moments. I had to give a lunch lecture in Rancho Cordova to a group of primary care physicians. Mostly I answered questions about urologic issues and cases. However, at the end I presented a case which, in essence, were all of my symptoms and findings before I was diagnosed. Finally, from one corner of the room I heard, "amyloidosis." I was quite pleased that someone thought of it. The physician told me afterward that he once had cared for a patient with renal amyloidosis. At least the other doctors will think of it in the future.

I am hopeful. I will start Revlimid this weekend, which did seem to work last fall to treat my amyloidosis.

Kevin

Saturday, July 11, 2009
Rain in July

As soon as I get to 180 lbs, I'll post a picture of myself. That may require the consumption of quite a few Drumsticks, (Not chicken, rather the ice cream type) Finally, on Thursday, I began to feel better. This was just in time to begin chemotherapy on Friday and today I was down again. This is probably because I had an I.V. infusion of Cytoxan and began taking Revlimid. Notwithstanding, I feel like the antiviral treatment is working. However, I need to pace myself and not overdo things just because I wake up craving doughnuts.

Rebecca flies home tomorrow to visit for a week, which is exciting. She did well her last term at BYU and is now working until she begins school again in the Fall. Caitlin continues to be the most difficult teenager one could imagine, (I jest; she daily amazes us with her insight and compassion). As parents we somehow hit the jackpot to have such wonderful and responsible children. Clearly this is because I married way above myself. When the mother is a saint, you end up with angels. I must beware lest I become like my dad; the epitome of hyperbole.

It is hard to plan ahead when you cannot predict how you will feel tomorrow. I look for a string of three good days to indicate a pattern. However, this Wednesday I begin Decadron, which means that by Friday I should be a bipolar zombie. I think Barbie will be out of town that day. Somewhat like "Dr. Jekyll! everybody hide."

Everyone has been so incredibly supportive. I have fantastic doctors, wonderful colleagues and staff in our department and so many friends who encourage us. If

I feel down, I read the comments that people post on this site and I am lifted. Thank you. We must continue to find the beauty in every day. Yesterday I saw an elderly man completely bent over at the waist. He could barely walk, and yet he slowly moved through the farmers' market with his daughter, picking out fruit. What courage it must require of him just to leave the house. Today it rained. It rarely rains here in July and I just love that smell of fresh rain on hot pavement. What beauty did you experience today?

Kevin

Part 8

REFLECTIONS

CHAPTER 62

Essay on Balance

One crisp Saturday morning I travelled to Oakland from my home in Novato to take an intelligence test. I had just gotten my driver's license on my 16th birthday two months previously and enjoyed cruising across the Richmond Bay bridge, windows open, AM 610 blasting on the radio of my brother's cherry and white GTO. I rode toward the interview full of confidence. It seems that on the scale of my lifetime presumed level of "smartness," I peaked at sixteen.

I entered a room in a building next to the LDS Oakland temple. Soon a distinguished, well dressed man with close-cropped hair entered with a sheath of papers. He glanced at me, generated a cautious smile, and extended his hand. As his firm hand clenched mine he fixed his eyes upon me, sizing me up. The evaluation had begun.

I had applied for the most prestigious award offered to an incoming freshman at Brigham Young University, named for the current president and prophet of the church, the Kimball scholarship. It was his job to see if I was worthy of such an honor. I was not.

He began a litany of questions that had nothing to do with me. The randomness completely caught me off guard. I am pretty adept at seeing patterns and interpreting their meanings. I had met my match. I stumbled through some preliminary questions reasonably well. Then he asked what I thought that the implications of recent events in Beirut would have on future U.S. foreign policy. Honestly, I did not know, nor did I care. I tripped over my cockiness as I spewed incoherent nonsense in response. He made a silent mark on his hidden clipboard. And then, without even looking up he asked, "how do you feel about entropy?" As the verbal brick lobbed at my forehead finally felt to my lap, my neurons went into overtime. This word was new to me. I could have admitted my inadequacy and just said, "I don't know." But after my last failure I felt I had to pull this out. I began, "I am not familiar with that word, but based on its root derivations "trop" means to grow such that entropy might mean to grow out from within? I waited anxiously. A wry smile reached his lips. "Not bad," was all he offered.

I walked out of the interview feeling slightly less smart than when I walked in. I was not going to be a Kimball scholar. And I had no idea how that word would haunt me for the rest of my life. ENTROPY.

Ironically, a week later in chemistry, Mr. Hicks presented the first two laws of thermodynamics. First, that energy is conserved. And second, that all things in the universe progress toward a greater state of chaos or entropy. My heart sank when I heard that word. Why could we not have had this lesson two weeks ago? My fate was sealed.

The other life-changing concept I learned in that same classroom was the concept of homeostasis or BALANCE. These two words (are they only words? Their symbolic construction seems so inadequate to the magnitude of their meaning) are the yin and yang of order and chaos; always in balance.

In the past two years, my life had been out of balance. Health is life in balance; illness is life out of balance. As I slowly recovered from my third major health battle in less than one year, my body and mind struggled to find new balance. But then, that is the penultimate miracle of life; the body's capacity to heal itself.

The universe in which we exist is formed on a scaffolding of balance which is present at every level and sphere of our perceived existence. The Big Bang released a huge amount of energy. Initially chaos seemed to reign, but within seconds, as it all began to cool, order began to appear, time and space were created and everything began to fill and thereby create space. This new time, moved in only one perceived direction by the power of chaos or entropy, began the new notion of past, present and future.

Over time, forces gave way to particles, matter, energy and gravity. This led to the coalescence of "stuff." Protons and electrons became atoms, then molecules, elements, and ultimately stars. Somehow everything formed, despite chaos' ever-present bent on destruction. Energy can always reverse entropy. The stars ignited, forming a stable source of immense energy and gravity. The need for balance was essential at every level. The voltage of every single electron in our universe is identical. Even the slightest variation would cause the stars to collapse, and nothingness would ensue. Gravity, motion, and momentum keep us in orbit around our sun, which has been kept in balance for billions of years.

A question that has always occurred to the scientific part of my brain is, "how does life form in a universe where entropy ensures a great degree of chaos, since life itself is the exact opposite of chaos?"

The only way to reverse entropy is by adding energy. That is what all life does. It harnesses energy from the sun and builds things of greater complexity. Chaos is diminished and the second law of thermodynamics is reversed, for a time. To create life requires billions of individual higher ordered systems existing in balance for even the smallest single cell organism to exist. Water must be liquid. Water, unlike most other substance on earth, actually becomes less dense when it solidifies into ice. In most cases, solids are more dense than their liquid-phase counterpart. This anomaly of water means that ice floats, something we all take for granted. Consider what would happen if ice sank. Water would freeze on the ocean's surface and then proceed to sink to the sea floor. Before long, the entire ocean would be solid ice and this would be a lifeless planet.

This liquid water then sets up the perfect example of balance, which we call an ecosystem. The energy of the sun evaporates the water into clouds and the winds and tide, helped by the gravity of the moon, send that water to land where it falls as rain, giving us fresh water to maintain ever more complex forms of life. This cycle ultimately resulted in us: humankind. The smart ones. Sentient beings, self-aware almost to a fault. We exist with minds so advanced that we can observe and study the world around us and philosophize over our place within it. We daily employ our six senses to explore this universe of three long dimensions in which we move in time, ever trying to avoid the chaotic influence of entropy. Sight, hearing, touch, smell, taste and balance are the senses we have to make sense of our physical solid world. Sight allows us to capture electromagnetic wave/particles in little photon packages of light. Hearing and touch both measure changes in pressure waves, which we hear as sounds or feel as pain, cold, heat, pressure and changes in body position. Taste allows for gross chemical analysis of salt, sweet, sour, and bitter. Meanwhile, the nose gives us a symphony of odors, some quite pleasant, making a bland meal fantastic or causing us to avoid a skunk in the forest. And the sixth sense, often ignored, keeps us grounded. Our inner ear tells us where we stand in relation to the earth's core. It measures gravity and centripetal force. The sixth sense literally keeps us physically balanced.

We use these senses to "make sense" of everything. Originally, we had only our un-augmented faculties to do this. Then we cleverly built tools to make more accurate measurements of things we could not see, hear or directly touch. From the plumb bob to the large hadron collider, each new tool has allowed us to delve deeper into the world that surrounds us, from the far reaches of galaxies beyond ours to the inner mechanics of quantum particles. And at every new discovery we find an elegant balance that maintains order. We crave order just as we crave control. We are wired to see symmetry and hear symphony. We search for predictability so we can bury our fears.

In all ecosystems on earth, life adapts to maintain a protected place and survive. Nature is cruel and without sentiment. The balance of life is always changing; any new interloper can and may ultimately be the demise of another. Most species have found ways to protect themselves, assuring a secure supply of sunlight, water, food and protection. But ultimately, if they cannot adapt to change, it will be their undoing

Humans are quite different. We believe that we are smarter than nature and can indefinitely control the environment around us. Therein lays the hubris of humankind. We believe that we can know everything, and that everything can be proved or disproved. We believe that we can control everything *ad infinitum*. We create clans, tribes, societies, countries and empires to do just this. We assume that with enough money and power we can sustain a comfortable world that is out of balance with nature and keep the imbalance in our favor forever. This defies everything we know about homeostasis of large systems over time. Balance will always be returned; we just pray that it will not be in our lifetime.

First, we need to control our environment. This begins as our head emerges from the womb and we emit a scream disturbing a pre-set group of neurons in our parents' brains that is quite averse to cacophony at that pitch and frequency. The immediate result is that we are cleaned, clothed, fed and protected. As we age, we refine our methods of control over others to ever greater levels of subtly. Those who are more subtle are more successful at shifting the imbalance of power to their benefit. The unsubtle throw rocks. Through myriad personal interactions reflecting this need to control, we build societies, which afford us quicker access to things we want or need. We differentiate tasks, but then need a system of governance to demand protection of what we deem to be ours. "This is my stuff and you cannot have it." We never grow out of this sentiment. We appoint kings, elect parliaments and senates, and they make laws to control everyone as a group on a theoretically level playing field.

This system and way of life is complex. Now instead of crying we use words, those glorious abstract symbols that are a testament to our elevated status above all other life on earth. And once we start talking, we cannot stop. Despite our amazing ability to speak, effective communication too often eludes us. The cognitive dissidence between behavior and voiced intention leave us distrusting and fearful.

To maintain a society out of balance with natural resources, security, shelter, protection, education, and progress does not require money, although that is what political systems assume.

The currency of balance is energy, whether it be expressed in amperes or dollars.

In every human exchange, what we are buying or selling is energy. We use money as a surrogate for the energy from the sun that grows the trees, the energy put out by another human to cut and mill those trees, the meal that fed the architect to design the house and the craftsmen to build it and fill it with furniture. We get the money to buy this cumulative energy expending effort by using our energy to take out a kidney that has cancer. We fix our house to keep nature out. The windows block the wind, we burn fuel to keep us warm. We have created an unbalance in nature, albeit a good one, to make our lives comfortable. The question then arises: how long can we keep this going? It is simple, as long as we can harness the energy to do it. Energy is always required to keep entropy outside our door.

Politicians often do not seem to understand this principle. Any promise that leads to a law requiring an indefinite input of money/energy to sustain the societal benefit of the aforementioned promise will ultimately fail. We have created a society of entitlement without personal responsibility. When in truth, every individual is entitled to nothing such that everything one receives is either earned or it is a gift.

The savvy statesmen will inherently understand this and know that any program or enacted law will have to be self-perpetuating in its energy requirements. Essentially, whatever good it produces will pay for itself. This is not impossible. But it requires an understanding of what motivates people to act.

It is all about incentives. There are many types, but I will focus on three: fear, money and altruism. In a human interaction where we have a stake in convincing another person to part with something they value to help us, it is often one of these incentives that we offer. To get elected, to get our valuable vote, often a politician must employ all three. "My opponent is bad." "I will fix the economy and get you a job." "I love my country and am a true patriot." We all have made decisions based on these incentives. The question is: can we overcome incentives that by their nature create imbalance and inequality, specifically fear, and move past money alone to embrace altruism, patriotism, work ethic, loyalty, sacrifice, kindness, faith and love? These incentives, when employed, are self-perpetuating. A law that has altruism at its core has the energy source already built in.

Of course, in a disparate society of so many opposing voices; the *art* is in the *compromise*; in extremes there is only propaganda.

Is there a solution? Time will tell. I am totally at peace with the apparent current chaos in the world. It is not that I do not care about human suffering. I care very much. But two things keep me positive. First, I can make a difference on an individual level by helping others every day. The second is much more esoteric. I take a long view. Decades, centuries even. Balance will always be restored. It is inevitable.

In a society where avarice and fear abound, the power of balance is consumed by the imbalance of power. But this will not last. Altruism, or the goodness of women and men, will set the scales right.

Balance exists within the strata where it belongs.

Within the society of humankind, the next stratum is me. I hope for and daily work toward balance in my life. I exist in two worlds. The second world is that which is perceived by my six senses. We call this reality, the world, the universe, space and time. In it I move through a space that has three perceptible dimensions. Time passes. I interact with people, with nature; with everything that is not me. It is this physical world that continues to exist even in my absence. Even my own body is part of this external world. I look at my hands as I type; projections of me into space that allow interaction, communication, effort and work.

However, the first world is that which exists in my mind, my soul, my thoughts and dreams. I am alone here. No one else can coexist in this immaterial essence. Through communication I can share this world with others; however this sharing is limited by the inadequacies of a corrupt language of shared symbols upon which we inconveniently depend. Our system of language is often rife with misunderstanding. We use different words for the same thing and then fight over those words, while ignoring the thing that matters most. I am not alone in this essential loneliness. Each sentient being also exists in his or her own private mind. From the moment of first memory, the dialog never stops while I am awake; even in sleep I am interrupted by dreams. I cannot turn off my mind; I can only distract it. All decisions, ideas, memories and aspirations begin here. As do all actions.

The interface between mind and brain, soul and body, has always been a mystery. The neurobiologist must reduce this interface to the symphonic coordination of billions of neurons firing simultaneously, which somehow gives rise to the sense of awareness, of being. There is nothing beyond electrochemical depolarization to account for this, my first world. Then there are the poets and prophets, who remind us that we are more than the subtotal of our molecules. We have a spirit within us, a purpose given us by God to fulfill. The non-tangible connection between mind and brain is bridged by spirit. The doubt of the scientist who cannot discover this spiritual connection through application of physical world observation does not prove the lack of the existence of a spirit. We all feel something more. All societies and all peoples through all time have described this spiritual connection.

To achieve true balance in one's life is to accept both our power and our powerlessness in both of these worlds. Balance consists of letting go of oneself while reconnecting with all of God's creations. As I became ill, my physical self increasingly descended into a state of imbalance, which is, of course, the best definition of illness. All of the cells in our body work constantly to maintain homeostasis: fluid balance, electrolyte balance, energy balance, electrical balance and waste balance. If the acidity within our cells and blood varies by even a fraction of a percent, we die.

One particular cell that was supposed to make a single protein started making a bad copy. When it divided, each daughter cell continued to make the same bad protein. Soon these proteins overwhelmed my body's capacity to destroy them or dump them, and the imbalance expanded. To heal people as a doctor, I must first be able to discover the imbalance and then reverse it. This is not always possible.

One of the most important ways to maintain balance at all levels of existence is through buffers. Buffers are a cushion that counters catastrophe. They give us room to react and respond. All of my life people have told me that I am lucky, that things always work out for me. In reality, part of my solution to life's challenges has always been to utilize as many buffers as possible to stave off chaos or bad luck. Consider our own planet. The ionosphere buffers us from the buffeting of solar winds that would otherwise devastate the earth. In a brilliant, if ironic reversal, that same atmosphere captures the same sun's energy to purify our water and deliver it against gravity to all the lands, providing what is essential for life. This biosphere provides the necessary buffers to allow life to grow and flourish. Somehow, the percent of oxygen is always 20.7. And what we consume, the plants give back. It is no surprise that we are all naturally drawn to the beauties of earth. We leave our man-made homes and offices and plan excursions to see mountains, oceans, waterfalls, and trees. Might it be that we inherently understand that our very lives depend upon these and then we attribute aesthetic beauty to them?

We create buffers in society called laws because our collective "ego-system" can be more destructive than nature's ecosystem.

Interpersonal relationships are fragile, proportional to the level of emotional investment and intimacy. Societal norms dictate appropriate manners and behavior toward strangers, acquaintances and casual friends. However, the deeper the relationship, the more possibility there is for pain. In love and marriage exist the greatest need for buffers. All marriages will eventually feel the mounting pressures that occur from day to day related to how shared decisions regarding children, resources and time are handled. This, coupled with the intense sense of trust that is required to maintain such a deep emotional bond, can lead to strong feelings that erupt in negative ways. Three essential buffers in marriage are, first, effective communication manifest through active and respectful non-judgmental listening, second, a sense of humor, and third, sex. Each of these allows a release of built up emotional pressure to return the couple to a sense of oneness.

We build better buffers in our life to give us more room to make better decisions before disaster strikes. This may mean that we give more space to the driver in front of us on the freeway or that we forego an expensive desired item to build a financial cushion for a future unseen need.

In the end, however, all things in the universe will increase to a greater disorder or chaos. We will all die. The matter that makes up our bodies will disintegrate into lower ordered molecules. We inspire; we breathe in. We expire; we breathe out. Until our last breath, when we expire. But inspiration reminds us that with each breath, we maintain the balance that delays chaos, that light is constant and provides the energy that keeps us ordered at a higher level. Chaos is darkness, whereas light and order is of God. The greatest buffer of all is our faith in God. When my body failed beyond repair and could no longer sustain itself, the miraculous power of prayer, offered by many to God on my behalf, kept me alive. This I know in my mind, my soul, my body and my new heart.

All of my life my mind has searched to understand the connection of body and spirit, of the physical universe and the realms of God. I see myself as a scientist and a man of faith. These two philosophies are not mutually exclusive. I see all truth as a giant puzzle. Through science and the power of observation and intellect we discover new truth. As such, we piece together and build a large section of the puzzle and call it our fund of knowledge. Through faith we learn of God and record his revealed truths. We use those truths to build another section of the puzzle, and call it theology. The hubris of humankind sometimes tempts us to demand all of the intervening pieces. When we fail to find them, we choose to reject one section of the puzzle or the other. I accept both sections of the puzzle, as well as the fact that I cannot, during this life, ever know all truth. This realization is amazingly liberating. It allows me to take the long view, motivates me to lifelong learning, and teaches me patience.

The wise man understands that he cannot know everything, but the smart man will ever continue to look for truth.

This leads me to a personal and somewhat unconventional idea of how the universe works. I do not imply that the following has any validity either in science or in the accepted doctrines of my church. These are just observations that exist between my ears and behind my eyes. As we descend further to strata that exist below us, we enter into the subatomic realm. At this level order is somewhat less constant or predictable. Quantum mechanics is then a statistical model of what these particles might do, not necessarily an ironclad prediction of what they will do. We are made of molecules, which are made of atoms, which are made of protons, neutrons and electrons. These in turn are made of stuff called quarks. Recent theoretical physics suggests that all of this "stuff" that is matter, including things that are not matter such as light and gravity, are made of vibrating bits of energy called strings. The idea is that the nature or "color" of the vibrating string will determine the way it manifests itself in our universe: as matter, energy or gravity. What is unusual about these strings is that they are not limited to the three-dimensional universe that we daily observe. Rather, they reside in 10 physical dimensions. Their 11th dimension is time. Three of their dimensions are long dimensions, which we see as space, length, height and width, whereas their other seven dimensions are very small and curled up.

So my mind asks my mind the question: "what if the connection between the physical body and the soul occurs in these other seven dimensions?"

I have a good friend, a professor of chemistry at Yale University, who would often say that science teaches us when and how, while religion teaches us why. He would always shudder when I proposed a connection between the two, but I cannot help wondering.

In church I am taught that all light comes from God and that it is through Jesus Christ that the light of life exists. The general theory of relativity, put forth by Albert Einstein, defines both space and time as relative. Thus, there remains only one constant in the universe: light. As a child I assumed that God existed in this universe just as I did and that time moved for Him as it did for me. Now I wonder. If there are other dimensions, other spheres, might he reside there? Is his time different from our time?

In medical school, we had a class in neurobiology and the teacher gave an example of dimensions of existence. I will illustrate with the following example. Imagine that you are a three-dimensional creature moving in your fourth dimension (time). You have the ability to view a two-dimensional world where its inhabitants can also move, but their third dimension is time. What would you see? Let's imagine that a circle moves from point A to point B. The circle would see itself as a circle at A, where it began, and at B where it ended and at every point in-between. However, since for you the third dimension is a solid, you would see a cylinder. In other words, you would see the beginning, middle and end all at the same time, as a solid object. What if there were a being whose fourth dimension was a solid? How would that being see us? Our past, present and future would all be *present* for that being.

These musings afford me a great sense of peace and purpose. If God sees our past, present and future as His present or as a solid, then God's knowledge does not necessarily mean that I do not have free will.

Ultimately, my purpose is manifest through my balanced approach to life. I live, I learn, I love. I now find myself *re-balanced* through the miracles of modern medicine, the will of a loving God and the constancy of my eternal companion, Barbie.

Balance has returned to my life and I have slowly healed.

CHAPTER 63

I continued to improve and soon returned to work. And since that time, I have not missed a day of work due to illness. In the first few months after my return it became clear that my experience as a patient had changed me as a physician. I tended to run late because I felt the need to listen better to my patients and spent more time with them. Occasionally I used my own experience to help them, but I was careful to not make it about me. It was just that I truly empathized with what they were going through.

Barbie and I continued to document our experiences through our website in the years that followed. I have included a few more blog posts that reflect some additional lessons learned as I slowly became whole again.

Sunday, August 16, 2009
Attitude of Gratitude

I woke up this morning with a profound sense of gratitude. As I lay here listening to my favorite sound, waves crashing on the beach, I thought of the gift I have today of being with our children and Barbie here in San Diego as we celebrate our first anniversary. Today Samuel and Michelle celebrate their first wedding anniversary. Barbie and I celebrate one year with my new heart.

Memory then transported me to August 16, 2008. My initial recollection of that day one year ago was disjointed. Anesthesia has the unsettling side effect of time compression. Only when you are continuously awake and memory becomes contiguous do you fully realize where you are and the magnitude of what has just happened to you. In that moment, I felt it more than I have ever felt it before: an overwhelming attitude of gratitude. It is not that I was grateful to be alive; I never even entertained the thought that I might not make it through the transplant. Rather, I was grateful for life. My gratitude was not directed at anyone or anything. I was simply thankful.

I am thankful for the loving faith and prayers of so many friends

I am thankful for caring and capable doctors and nurses

I am thankful for drug companies, chemists, PharmD's and pharmacists for providing me with the "Chemicals for Better Living" that keep my heart inside my chest and invading organisms out.

I am thankful to all of my partners in the department of Urology at Kaiser for caring for my patients while I was gone.

I am thankful to my staff for helping while I was gone and helping me come back.

I am thankful to my patients for being patient.

I am thankful to be doing surgery again.

I am thankful to the wonderful men and women in our church for taking care of our family this year. We could not have done it without them.

I am thankful to all of you for sharing this journey with us.

I am thankful to God for having trust that I had the strength to learn the things that He needed to teach me. I am not the same man I was a year ago.

Above all, I am thankful for Barbie, my reason for living. She is the love of my life. When I am with her, there is no pain, there is no illness, there is no fear, there is no hurry. With her I am truly happy and I will always love her with my "whole new heart."

Kevin

Sunday, Aug 23, 2009
The Art of Boogie-Boarding

When we moved to California five years ago, I was excited to participate in three of my favorite outdoor activities. They all begin with the letter "B": bicycling, backpacking and boogie-boarding. As I fell ill, my ability to do these sports also fell by the wayside. My new heart gave me new hope. I now am able to bike ride for short distances, but I am not yet ready for back-packing. I have anticipated all year our family vacation to San Diego where I could once again ride the waves.

Boogie-boarding is not surfing. Surfing is more work and more addictive. But I still get that thrill when I catch the perfect wave. As a sport, boogie-boarding demands not so much strength or coordination as timing. You cannot catch a broken wave (well, you can try but it is not as much fun) and if you are too far out, the wave rolls underneath you. The idea is to swim into the wave just as it is breaking so that it lifts you to the crest and you ride down the face. At that point you are in control, not the wave.

Last Monday I grabbed my boogie board and waited for the perfect wave. They come in sets, and I usually wait for the second wave in the set. This one was big. I caught it just right and as often happens, when it breaks I dropped. Only this time when I dropped, I felt something snap, and experienced immediate pain in my left chest. The word "osteoporosis" flashed through my mind. I am the only person I know who can break a rib water-skiing. I did that ten years ago. Now I have done it again. The pain was bad, but not excruciating so I kept catching waves while trying to protect my left side. I was not going to give up this easily.

I was fine until Tuesday. I went and caught more waves and did fine, but when I went in the beach house, something happened and the fracture felt as if it moved into my lung cavity. I could not breathe without the sense of being repeatedly stabbed in the chest. I worried that I might have started bleeding, since my platelet count before we left for San Diego was 50,000, which is low. Every movement, every breath, every heartbeat hurt. I waited to see if it would improve. After a half hour it resolved a bit and I was able to enjoy a delicious grilled salmon dinner that Michelle had prepared.

The next day we went to Disneyland. Fortunately, Wednesday is my Decadron day. Steroids have a strong anti-inflammatory effect, which greatly reduced my pain so that I was not "California Screamin" on Space Mountain. It was a magnificent day. Unfortunately, steroids also give me the hiccups, which do not bode well for rib fractures. I guess you take the good with the bad; c'est la vie.

Otherwise, our week in San Diego was perfect, filled with bike riding, scooter riding, jogging, walks on the beach, s'mores over a campfire, good food and good company. It was a perfect way to celebrate the anniversary of Samuel and Michelle's wedding, my heart transplant, and my 50th birthday (I got into Disneyland for free on my birthday). I doubt that next year will be as eventful as the last, which is fine with me, but I plan on enjoying it even more.

I am still on the cusp of the wave, waiting to ride down and take control of it. That is always where the thrill is. I am in for the ride of my life.

Kevin

Wednesday, September 16, 2009
Old patients

I think that most men marry above themselves. Some men marry much higher and have wives who are angels. I am certainly one of those fortunate ones. Today I looked at my clinic schedule and saw the name of one of my old patients; old in that I have taken care of him for years and, also, he is old. I previously treated his superficial bladder cancer, which requires that every three months we look in the bladder to assure no recurrence. For the last year Dr. Chiu, my partner, has been performing the follow up cystoscopies. I was pleased that I would see him today because he is such a pleasant man and his wife is an angel. The news was good, as the bladder was clean; no cancer. They had been aware of the cause of my absence and were quite content to see me as well. Sometimes the beauty in my day is reconnecting with old friends and finding them well (especially when I get to tell them that they are well.)

I then walked over to the hospital to see a patient from whom I had removed the bladder a year and a half ago for cancer. Her disease is metastatic now and she has had a number of complications. She had to stop chemotherapy because she felt so poorly while on it. I asked about her, and her husband asked about me. We have had many shared experiences during the past year. I know how she feels. Yet she remains hopeful, and so do I for her. I silently mused on why these things happen to such nice people.

While I was conversing with her, my phone rang; the area code was 408, Santa Clara. It was my biopsy result. I always know the news immediately by the tone of the greeting. This was good news. The heart biopsy showed 1R/1A, minimal rejection. I tried hard not to be emotional in front of my patient, but I was so relieved. She sensed my reaction and smiled at me to show understanding. The lines of doctor and patient became blurred for a moment. I reassured her that a time would come in the near future when her daily activities would not include conversations about her health. She laughed and said that she had one of those days a few weeks ago and how nice that was.

I am feeling quite well, as the steroid crash on Monday is slowly resolving. I'll be back to the chain gang, breaking stones, tomorrow and Friday.

Kevin

Tuesday, September 22, 2009
On Death

How do you tell a wife that her husband has died? I truly do not know. You cannot "break it" easily. In that millisecond between when you believe your spouse is still alive and then suddenly learn that they are not, reality is suspended and rationality ceases. It is too much for the soul to accept.

I was "on call" for the first time in 15 months today and was covering for my partner who is out of town. I saw one of his patients this morning, who had had a procedure on Friday to control bleeding from his prostate. He was fine and we discussed possibly sending him home tomorrow. At noon I got a call that he was "coding," meaning that his heart had ceased to beat and he was receiving CPR. I arrived to find the code team fighting frantically to save him. They worked heroically, each nurse taking his or her turn giving chest compressions while the hospital physician directed the effort. He did not make it.

I knew that his wife and daughter were on their way, and found them in the hallway. My search for a private room to speak with them came up empty. They sensed the seriousness of the situation; I could no longer delay. Their emotions mounted as I explained the events as they had unfolded. It is a scenario with which I have experience, but I never get used to it. Ultimately, there is always that moment when I can no longer avoid the flat statement, "he did not make it" or "he is dead." Euphemisms do not soften the reality. If there were a better way to say it, I wish I knew. I felt horrible. They could not handle the immense gravity of receiving the worst combination of words that can be strung together in any language. I stood there silent,

*feeling completely impotent in any attempt I made
to try and comfort them. I did not know what to do.
Finally the nurse came and had found a private room
where I could take them where their uncontrolled grief
could be expressed.*

*In every crisis there is often someone to whom those
suffering can turn, who remains their link with reality.
Soon her son arrived and he became that rock for her.
I was grateful for his strength in that moment. It was
as if he became my translator for the rest of the family.*

*As I drove home today, I wondered if I could have
handled the situation better. Probably, but I still do
not know how. I remember a similar situation when
I was the trauma surgeon in the ER at UC Davis
many years ago. A 16-year-old boy was brought in
with a fractured spine from an automobile accident on
Interstate 5. He was the only survivor. His mother,
two brothers and grandfather had been killed instantly
when his grandfather fell asleep and drove into the
back of a semi-truck parked on the side of the freeway.
It was my task to call the father in L.A. to tell him
about his surviving son. He then asked about the others. My first response was to say that they were seriously injured. The nurses in the room with me were
saying under their breath, "You can't tell him they are
dead over the phone." But eventually he asked, "fatally
injured?" I could not lie. I only said, "yes." I heard
only sobbing for what seemed an eternity. Finally, I got
the number of his father and pleaded with him to stay
home until I could contact his dad to get to his house.
I could not imagine him alone with this burden that I
had laid before him.*

It does not get any easier 20 years later.

*I was once in a seminar on death and dying where
they asked, "how do you want to die?" The question*

was followed by an academic discussion on the subject. But today I learned that that is the wrong question. If someone were to ask, "how do you want your spouse to die?" I guarantee that the dialogue would not only not be academic, it would not exist. Who can fathom such a question? Yet it is the survivors who must live through that unanswerable query. It is not a question of age or being at the end of a fulfilled life; death is death. Ultimately, our faith will give us strength. But that moment of finality can be terrifying for many. Is it better to go quickly and unexpectedly or be prepared by a slow and painful demise? I thought I knew the answer to that. But previously I had only seen it from the perspective of the one dying, not the one letting go. I saw it differently today.

Kevin

Tuesday, October 6, 2009
Kent from New York

My life is a river. The river does not know that the ocean lies hundreds of miles ahead. It continues on. On my journey I have met and come to know thousands of individuals. Some flow with me as part of my life. Others I meet, share a moment and never see again. But their influence stays with me, changes me as I move on. But the world has changed. Previously, these encounters were face-to-face, person-to-person. Now I have come to know individuals through the world of the internet. They are no less real, nor do they impact me any less for never having grasped their hand in a physical greeting.

Some time ago, Kent from New York commented on his progress with amyloidosis. We conversed over time as he prepared for the possibility of a heart transplant. I was glad to share my experience and give him hope. He was still working, but could feel himself slowing down. His close friend, Elise, informed me last week that he has died. This is hard for me. I feel like amyloidosis is an enemy we fight every day. It is not like fighting a conventional army that you can see and plan for. Rather, it remains insidious like a terrorist, attacking unexpectedly.

I know that Kent from New York fought a good fight. He did not give up. But I cannot shake this sense that he was somehow blindsided by this nasty deposition of unconscionable warped proteins. How they move within us without regard to the damage they leave in their wake. They infiltrate not only the heart muscle, which can lead to slow death, but also attack the wiring at the center of the heart, leading to a sudden fatal arrhythmia. Is there no defense against this?

We who share this diagnosis, and even more so, those who care for us with this disease, keep this fear silent within us so as not to tempt fate. Amyloidosis is an orphan diagnosis relegated to a dark corner of medicine; it is mentioned perhaps once or twice in medical school and then promptly forgotten by most doctors. Where is the celebrity to champion our cause? Amyloidosis is not only rare, but affects each patient so differently that any attempt at discovering its modus operandi is hampered by varied responses in rare patients, allowing for little statistical power in planning a unified attack.

Sometimes people ask me about my prognosis. I honestly do not know. Does that somehow make me like everyone else, blindly living every day with sublime ignorance of their own mortality?

Sometimes I wish that I could respond, when asked, that I have cancer. At least with many cancers there is a cure; or it only affects one organ in your body. People understand cancer. They do not know where to catalogue amyloidosis; and describing it becomes cumbersome.

Just because I share these thoughts does not mean that I am ever without hope, nor that am I sad for myself. I still find incredible joy in every day. I am, however, sad for Kent from New York and for his friend Elise. Because I will move on toward the unseen ocean and leave him behind. And yet, it may be that my sadness for him only stems from the briefness of my encounter with him. He may not have shared my sadness, because, like me, he lived a full and happy life of no regrets. If we truly could know the complete essence of any one person, would we mark their absence differently?

My hope remains strong; if I gave Kent hope it was not in vain. But he will be missed, as are all of those whose battle against amyloidosis has ended. My heart goes out to all of them and to those who continue to remember and to love them.

Kevin

Sunday, October 25, 2009
Guilt

Recently I corresponded with a patient who was just diagnosed with amyloidosis. Her presentation was unusual (what amyloidosis patient's is not?) but it struck me that she only had one organ involved and was not predominately kappa or lambda. Generally, primary amyloidosis is of one clone or the other. It turned out that she likely has familial amyloidosis, which is fortunately a much better prognosis. However, I was not really prepared for her response to such news: she felt guilty. She felt guilty that she may have passed the gene for amyloidosis to her children. I wondered incredulously, how can you feel guilty for something that occurred 40 years ago over which you had no control and which may not even occur? To try to assuage her guilt, I reminded her of the millions of good genes that she also gave to her children. However, I also sympathized with her feeling, like that of any loving and responsible mother, of duty and concern toward her children.

The very next day I was seeing a patient of mine in the clinic who has an incredibly difficult decision to make. She has metastatic bladder cancer and has already failed one course of chemotherapy. The toxic drugs made her life a living hell and she could not complete the course of treatment. The cancer is now in her lungs and her oncologist has suggested some experimental treatments. The potential for success is unknown. The expected side-effects are definitely known.

As she shared with me the acknowledgement of her own limited lifespan, she expressed guilt. Flabbergasted, I asked how she could feel guilt about dying. Once again, her thoughts were not for herself, but rather for her children. They wanted her to do everything possible to continue her life, even if that life was, for her, miserable. She felt that to die without trying everything might let them down.

We spoke of a balance in the middle: doing just enough to prolong quality time without doing what will not work and stealing those good days that she had remaining. Unfortunately, it is impossible to know exactly where that balance lies.

I do not generally feel guilt, but I do have a strong sense of duty. Maybe it is the same feeling under a different name. When I commit to something or someone, I cannot neglect to fulfill my responsibility. Last June it was clear that the bone marrow transplant had failed to control my amyloidosis. I was disappointed for myself. However, even more I was somehow disappointed that I might let down those who had gambled on putting a heart transplant into an amyloidosis patient. I was the first primary amyloidosis patient to get a heart transplant at Stanford in many decades. I was fully aware of the reason that this practice had been abandoned. There were many, and still are, who question the prudence of giving a heart to someone who is incurable. This, of course, leads to the question, "how long must I live to make this great effort on my behalf worth it?" I felt this even more poignantly when soon after the failed transplant I became very ill with cytomegalovirus. At the time, I mistakenly thought that my disease had irreversibly progressed and that I was going to die soon. The thought that crossed my mind was that if I die, they might think twice before offering another heart to an amyloidosis patient. I felt it was my duty to live long enough, in the words of Tom Hanks in Saving Private Ryan, *to "earn this."*

How does one measure the worth of a life? Is it in the number of days or rather in what you fill those days with?

I have seen well meaning family members demand that everything be done to add more hours and days to a life that is ending. Who decides when any individual life has satisfied the purpose of its creation?

I guess this is why there are feelings of guilt surrounding the act of dying. It is because we do not know these answers and we wish that we did.

My father died well. He was surrounded by his children and my Mom and quietly passed at home. However, six weeks earlier, his oncologist had offered him one last course of chemotherapy. We all knew that it would not work and that he would be miserable if he took it. The offer was made mostly out of obligation. Initially, my dad wanted to proceed and seemed annoyed that we might question the value in the treatment. I suggested to him that since he was doing so poorly that day, the drug would certainly make him worse, but that if in a week he had improved, we could start the chemotherapy then. He understood and accepted that plan, because in it there was still hope. I certainly still had hope that he would improve. He never did. But that was OK, since his last weeks were at home with his family. I know that he had fulfilled the purpose of his creation. Filling more days would not have changed that.

So what do loved ones do who must watch with powerless guilt as a friend or family member begins down that final path? They must understand that the dying feel guilty too. They need to listen to the words too painful to utter, to be patient with decisions so irrational and difficult to comprehend, and then remove those shards buried along our final common pathway and allow the last goodbye to be sweet.

Kevin

Years have now passed since I returned to work. It still has been a rocky path, strewn with both good and bad days, but the days now are mostly good. My mantras remain: "No matter how bad I feel today, I will feel better" and "Find the beauty in every day."

Ironically, despite my efforts to avoid chemotherapy (especially the steroid Decadron) it appears that I may be on these drugs for quite some time. I truly had hoped that the stem cell transplant would give me a reprieve, but alas, it was not to be. However, I am at peace with that notion. I maintain hope that these continued treatments are giving me increased quantity of days, while unavoidably exacting some quality. Notwithstanding, we have developed an agreeable symbiosis. The good and bad days are somewhat predictable and I feel that I do again have control in my life. The chemo has been working quite well to keep my light chains low and my new heart free of these toxic proteins. We now plan for future events whose timelines range in years instead of weeks. I continue to work and live a magnificent life, and just learned that soon Barbie and I will be grandparents.

Our children are all doing well. Rebecca ultimately graduated from BYU with a B.A. in Advertising. While there she fell in love with and married Jason Hammond from Highlands Ranch, Colorado and they have since moved to that area. Just this past year Caitlin married Ben Solari from right here in Lincoln, CA.

Barbie persevered through all of this and eventually graduated from dental hygiene school. She thoroughly enjoys working with direct patient care as she improves the lives of so many.

Sometimes people ask Barbie how long I will remain on chemotherapy. She generally responds, "until it does not work anymore." To the same question I most often say, "for the rest of my life." I guess it will be whichever comes first.

In the end there is no end, only more of the ever changing middle.

Tuesday, August 4, 2009
Circle of Life

And so we have come full circle. The day that I have dreamed of and desired for so long has finally arrived. The only word that I have to describe how I feel today is "complete." Today I performed surgery in the operating room for the first time in over a year. One year ago when I became a full-time patient, I felt that a part of me had been ripped away and wondered if this day would ever come. However, I was carried and made whole by the love that I have received from the myriad of individuals whose compassion was extended toward me. How do I deserve this? I do not know. What I do know is that if anyone ever considers this world of ours a dark and fearful place, he or she has only to see what I have seen for five minutes to feel

the absolute and immense goodness of people, regular people; those whom we see every day as we hurry to our next task. These people are you. You have sent me encouraging words, worried about Barbie and me, prayed for us, helped us and made us feel whole again. I wish that I could adequately thank you, the words I would attempt fall far short of the gratitude that I feel in my heart.

I know that the only way to convey this feeling is through my service to others. Today is a new beginning as I return again to that old path.

It is altogether fitting that my first surgery with my new heart is the same one as my last surgery so long ago. I removed a cancerous kidney laparoscopically from a woman this morning. The tumor appeared to be contained within the specimen. This will likely give her a high chance of being cured. I was assisted by a very capable chief resident, Dr. Yap, and many of the outstanding nurses and OR staff with whom I have worked for years. I cannot describe the joy I felt at being back in the OR. I felt as if I had come home after a long journey.

Recently, Barbie reminded me that my life has been saved at least three times this past year. I participated in saving a life today. Sometimes we save a life that is in immediate danger of ending due to injury. Sometimes we extend a life through the appropriate application of diagnostic acumen and skillful delivery of medicine and surgery. A caring friend's compassion can prevent the emotional death or destruction of a despondent and tortured soul with an outstretched hand assuring the sufferer that he or she is not alone. We all, at times, have participated in life changing graces towards others, even if we remain unaware that our actions were so directed. These saved souls who are lifted out of adversity then begin to lift others in their turn as the cycle continues. I plan to be here lifting others as long as my feet remain on a firm foundation.

And so we come full circle and see ourselves as we never have before, renewed and ready to begin again.

Kevin

Epilogue

Mortality Awareness event # 8

Monday, March 29, 2010
Battered, Bloodied but still Breathing; Barely

At age twelve my mother sent me out onto the roof of our house to fix it. It was a flat roof over the family room that had a leak in the corner. It was my job to reapply tar to that area. At some point I must have made some terrible mistake because I remember my mom yelling out of the window commenting on my error. She then added, "how could someone who is supposed to be so smart do such a dumb thing?" Immediately, in my mind I retorted, "who said I was supposed to be so smart?" Two years earlier the school psychologist had administered an I.Q. test, the results of which were denied to my immature eyes, but rather given to my parents. I don't think that was fair.

Today I did a really dumb thing. Among the activities that I truly love is snorkeling. Floating above such a variety of sea creatures is so serene. It has been years since I have had such an opportunity. We anchored in Cabo San Lucas this morning and I was first in line to get off the boat. Once on shore we haggled a good price for a water taxi to ferry us to Lover's Beach. This secluded beach resides near the tip of Cabo's famous rock formations. Within minutes I was in the water while Barbie, Rebecca and Caitlin remained on shore to read and sunbathe. I had a mask and goggles, but no flippers, as they had been too big to fit in my suitcase. Soon I was gliding through a cornucopia of beautiful tropical fish. But then disaster hit; my curiosity replaced my better sense. From the shore it seemed that the rock formation where I was swimming might contain a passage back on the opposite side between the rocks and the cliffs of insanity. I decided to venture on and explore this diabolical chasm. As I swam into the narrow space I saw hundreds of fish, but soon I noticed that the force of the waves hitting the rocks ahead were pushing the fish back underneath me. I craned my neck up out of the water to see if I could see a passage through them back to shore. I could not. At the moment I was debating whether to turn back, the ocean took away all of my choices. A wave hit me, from behind or in front, I could not tell. I saw bubbles and blue and frantically swam to what I thought was up. It was no use. I could not fight the power of the waves. I was gasping now, but my submerged snorkel prevented me from inhaling water. For a brief time I saw sun, but only for a second. I quickly took a half a breath, but then was under again. I fought to regain the surface but failed. It became clear that I was not strong enough to overpower the churning whirlpool. As I struggled in vain, I was abruptly thrown against the rocks on the cliff side. I saw a small rock jutting from the face and grabbed it, only to have it break off in my hand as another wave pulled me again down into the abyss. I thought, "how stupid I am. Barbie can't even see me; no one can. This is it, I am out of breath, I can't last much longer." It is amazing how easy it is to drown. This was the second time in my life that I had nearly drowned. The first time I was seven and fell into the Eel River. Fate, luck, or divine providence had intervened then as it did now. Soon a wave threw me to the rock side and for a split second I saw a substantial vertical outcropping shaped like a handle and completely covered with razor sharp barnacles. I held on for dear life and the wave receded, exposing a rock shelf near my feet. I swung my leg up and pulled myself out with what strength remained. I stood there for a long while and breathed. My will was again my own.

To get back to shore I would have to climb over the rock. I could not return the way I came. Once the hyperventilation slowed I began the slow ascent. Facing the rock I noticed hundreds of barnacles per square foot. "Oh well," I thought, "Our pathways cannot always be without pain. And besides, pain means that I am still alive." I got to the top of the rock and saw a place free of malevolent crustaceans and sat down. I looked at the rock next to me and saw bright red blood dripping at an uncomfortably fast rate. I looked at my legs and they were also covered in wet blood. In that moment I wondered what was my platelet count. I have been off chemo for a while so I assumed that they were adequate to the task. "Go Platelets Go.....Goooo Platelets!!" I looked towards the shore for Barbie. I thought I saw my family where I had left them reading their books. I sat for a while considering my next move. Below me a dozen blue-shelled crabs scurried sideways over the rocks. The rock face was more gradual on this side as the shelf became submerged. This was my way out. As I looked up, a man on the shore was calling to me. Right behind him was a very concerned Barbie. I waved to indicate that I was alright. I knew that they could not come get me, though. I slowly descended like a crab with my hands behind me and was finally back

*in the water with mask and snorkel in place. I swam
and soon saw the man's feet indicating that I could
stand. Barbie then came and walked me back to our
towels where we waited for the water taxi. Everyone on
the beach was shocked to see this bloody mess of a man
limping and dripping as he passed them on the sand;
so much for Lover's Beach. We assessed my wounds.
I had cuts all over my body, mostly on my hands, feet
and lower legs, but nothing that needed stitches.*

*Barbie wanted me to see the ship's medic, but
you know me; I am a surgeon. I have taken care of
these types of wounds many times. Certainly I could
treat myself. After a shower, Barbie lathered me with
Neosporin and applied a multitude of Band-aids. I
gave myself a broad spectrum antibiotic and went to
lunch.*

*Sometimes the rocks in my head and the rocks
against my head meet and the result is not pretty.*

*I will survive to live another day so that tomorrow
I can strap on a harness, hook onto a steel cable and
glide a hundred feet over the jungle. At least that will
be safer.*

Kevin

I often hide my true emotion behind detail and wit, and this blog
entry was no exception. In truth, the experience terrified me, and
the memories haunted me for months afterward. I was so angry with
myself. I had risked so much. While I was underwater anticipating
death, visions of my life had not passed before me. Rather, I felt horribly guilty for wasting a perfectly good transplanted heart, while simultaneously imagining a frantic Barbie never finding me again. As I had
first made the decision to approach the rocks, I had felt a very strong
impression warning me to turn back. I ignored it out of pride and
stupidity. How could I have forgotten the fragility of life so quickly?

On the drive home after our cruise, the monotony of I-5 provided too little mental distraction as I replayed the scenario over and over in my mind, feeling comfortless.

I walked slowly toward her, my arms and hands bloodied with scores of blessedly painful reminders that the lights were still blazing. My tears were washing away the saltiness as she became more clear to my view. My legs were red-streaked with drops drawn by gravity to my feet, my soles incised, the deep gashes filling with sand in each step closer to her, my soul still intact.

The line of time had split. Only 13 minutes earlier I had succumbed to the abyss. Gray became blackness; warmth was supplanted by the coldness of slowing molecules. Starved of oxygen, the cells slowly died and fell apart. Principles of uncertainty had carried me to the precipice of excess dimensions; in this one, life was vanquished by chaos as I floated away, bereft of all control and fairness. Soon I was beyond the rocks, then I passed the arches that stood as sentinels marking the end of Baja California. Open ocean became my grave. My final thoughts were of her. Frantically searching the beach for a glimpse of me. Crying out to foreign strangers in a foreign tongue. This final vision tortured me in both universes.

How could one moment, one decision, one thoughtless blunder send me to such a division of fortune? For months afterward the thoughts of her in that moment of realization that I was lost, with no explanation and no goodbyes, would harangue me to despair. The thought of her pain, her tears and the agony of her loneliness was unbearable to me. I did not share this nightmare with her. Because the current reality was the one where my soul was still intact. It was not her burden.

Was I just lucky? Was I protected? Or did both events actually occur? Certainly, in my mind I experienced both. I remember both. But my Father, my God, was there with me as He has been from the beginning. This I felt. Those other questions remain academic, as they should.

Yet in this moment, in this reality, I felt the wondrous warmth of the sun as it beat down upon Lover's Beach. Each step bought me back to her, that same light illuminating her concerned, yet relieved face. Light, I was always taught, is the one true constant in the universe. Its speed never varies; its energy is felt everywhere. Time and space are relative, but light is always constant. It is the source of all life.

A new constant now stood before me, a second solid equal to the power of light and just as essential: love.

Love filled my senses as we embraced. I held her and she held me up. In the power of love are encompassed the ideas of "infinite" and "eternal" and "sacrifice." There is patience and humor and forgiveness. There is passion and joy and tears. There is beauty and faith and hope.

There is Barbie.

The Middle of Infinity

ACKNOWLEDGEMENTS

First and foremost I thank Barbie. She is an author of this book just as I am. Her blog posts tell the story in a way that I could not. Additionally, she contributed immensely both in the editing and proofreading of the book. Both John Phillips, M.D. and Stephen Lamb, M.D. provided early reviews and encouraged me to proceed with publishing. I am so fortunate to have found Sarah Bringhurst Familia as my editor. She is magnificent and brought coherency and correctness to my words. I recognize 99Designs.com for assisting me to find Giovanni Auriemma who created a work of art in the cover design. I thank my doctors, family and friends for all of their support.

Finally, this book would not exist without the decision of Shane's parents to donate his heart so that I might live.